# The
# Scientific
# Image
## From Cave to Computer

Harry N. Abrams, Inc., Publishers
New York

# The
# Scientific
# Image
## From Cave to Computer

By Harry Robin

Historical Foreword by Daniel J. Kevles

ACKNOWLEDGMENTS

IT IS KEENLY PLEASURABLE to recite the names of those who provided information and advice in the course of making this book. I especially thank William Clark and Daniel Kevles, whose passion for the history of science stoked my own, and Katharine Donahue and her assistant Cynthia Becht, who responded so graciously and effectively to my numerous inquiries. I also thank Valerie Anderson, William Bickel, Irwin Braun, Hung Hsiang Chou, Erica Clark, William Dailey, Jeanne D'Andrea, Elizabeth J. Foster, Marvin Freilich, Kimball Garrett, Walter Goldschmidt, Brian Harris, Elaine R. S. Hodges, Paula Hurwitz, David Keightley, Rocky Koga, Allan Kreiger, James Northern, Irving Jack Pincus, Michael Posner, Rose Rosenstock, Herman Rubin, Philip Rubin, Eric Schulzinger, Judith Smith, J. D. Stewart, and Richard Wingell.

And finally, my gratitude to Phyllis Freeman, my editor, to Barbara Lyons, picture researcher extraordinaire, to the designer, Elissa Ichiyasu, and to Rebecca Tucker and María Teresa Vicens, who so patiently abetted this book.

EDITOR: PHYLLIS FREEMAN

DESIGNER: ELISSA ICHIYASU

PHOTO EDITOR: BARBARA LYONS

Library of Congress Cataloging-in-Publication Data
Robin, Harry.
The scientific image : from cave to computer / Harry Robin ;
historical foreword by Daniel J. Kevles.
p.   cm.
Includes bibliographical references and index.
ISBN 0-8109-3823-5
1. Scientific illustration.
2. Science—Graphic methods.
3. Visualization.
4. Imagination.
I. Title.
Q222.R63   1992   91-48053
502'.22—dc20   CIP

IN MEMORIAM
WILLY HARTNER
1905 – 1981

# Contents

# Introduction

ONE AIM OF THIS VOLUME is to encourage the appreciation of scientific endeavor by examining the abundance of scientific images we have inherited from preliterate and succeeding cultures. The scientific mind may be characterized as the bearer of two torches: one of insatiable curiosity and the other of a will to impart understanding. Nevertheless, scientific studies are usually published in a language seemingly impenetrable by the nonscientist. Images—even complex ones—can, however, impart the scientist's objectives in startlingly direct ways. Aristotle, who was an acute observer, proposed that we cannot think without images. Images trigger an internal motion: the deliberate perusal of the elements in a picture. By seeing into the picture, the viewer transforms the static image into an active intellectual experience. In some instances such scrutiny may generate an aesthetic response, or at least pleasure in the curiosity and ingenuity displayed by the scientist/illustrator (scientific observers do not themselves always generate the images they use, but often employ skilled artists to illustrate their findings).

Understanding the content of a scientific illustration requires some description of the phenomenon to be studied, as well as an understanding of its labels and terms. Unlocking the meaning can bring about the exhilaration of a shared intellectual passion, a passion that has animated the scientific community throughout the history of mankind. It may lead to new ways of understanding some aspect of ourselves and the world in which we live.

In each of the six sections of this book there are examples of the scientist's—and our own—connections to Nature: from phenomena in the universe, to our earthly environment, to the complex structures within us. Scientists use images in specific ways to communicate what they have learned, and these dictate the organization of this book.

*Observation* includes the simplest use of illustration as a device to record observations, with no particular analysis of the thing observed: "I looked, and this is what I saw."

In *Induction*, there is a slightly more refined form of imagery, one that incorporates an element of interpretation. The scientist is saying, in effect, "I looked, and this is what I thought."

*Methodology* shows the aspect of science that sets it apart from other human endeavors—the manipulation of Nature in order to understand its workings. Communication of this understanding through images is an act of both joy and satisfaction; it allows the scientist to say, "This is how I think it works."

Some images already exist in Nature or are generated automatically as the result of experimental procedures. Examples of such images are presented in *Self-Illustrating Phenomena*.

Illustration has also been used to represent the uniquely human endeavor of categorizing things around us and giving them names. Grouping things forces us to think about why they are the same or different. We can hand someone a chart and say, "Think of it this way," as with the images in *Classification*.

The most abstract thing in Nature, of course, is the human mind itself, which still eludes scientific explanation. There are many "realities" that exist only in the mind—three-headed horses, black holes, the structure of subatomic particles are all things that cannot be directly perceived but that we have no trouble imagining. And it is here, perhaps, that illustration is most critical—giving concrete expression to purely "thought experiments." We see these in *Conceptualization*, the final section of the book.

The perusal of scientific illustrations offers an incomparable view of mankind's intellectual evolution. Yet another, quite different, experience may be evoked from the contemplation of such images. It is eloquently described in the following statement by Albert Einstein:

*The most beautiful and most profound emotion we can experience is the sensation of the mystical. It is the sower of all true science. He to whom this emotion is a stranger, who can no longer stand rapt in awe, is as good as dead. To know that what is impenetrable to us really exists, manifesting itself as the highest wisdom and the most radiant beauty which our dull faculties can comprehend only in the most primitive form—this knowledge, this feeling is at the center of all true religiousness.[1]*

# Historical Foreword

DANIEL J. KEVLES

ALTHOUGH WIDELY SEPARATED IN TIME, the cave drawing and the computer image are both artifacts of the human effort to record nature or render it intelligible. Human beings seem to have always used visual representation to comprehend the natural world and their place in it. The plates in this book demonstrate how illustration has assisted in describing, classifying, ordering, analyzing, and finally mastering the world. Yet they also indicate that the modes of assistance have changed in response to transformations in the subjects and conceptions of science, as well as the modes and possibilities of graphic protocols. As a result, like verbal or mathematical texts, these illustrations reveal the evolution of discourse about nature and of the conventions—cultural and artistic as well as scientific—in which the discourse was conducted. They open windows into the historical interplay of science, art, and culture.

In early and medieval times, drawings of plants—for example, Pedanius Dioscorides's ninth-century "Thistle" (see page 26)—identified the organisms and specified their pharmaceutical uses; depictions of alchemists and their processes illuminated the transformations of base metals—if not into gold then at least into something useful. Perhaps the most compelling subject for illustration has always been ourselves, our anatomies, and the ministrations that might alleviate our sufferings. Here artistic imagination could exercise considerable latitude, since in Europe and the Orient alike, law and custom prohibited direct examination of the human body. European understanding of human anatomy was based on the descriptions of Galen, in the second century (see page 168), which had drawn on extrapolations from the anatomy of animals. Chinese renderings of the human interior sometimes resorted, perhaps in the interest of economy, to hermaphroditic drawings (see page 167). Equally prime as subject matter were the heavens, which from ancient times and across cultures were tied up with ideas of the creation of the world and about the gods responsible for it. The imagery, like the ideas, was usually anthropomorphic, projecting sovereigns, servants, and animals onto the constellations as though to reduce the stars to terms of human familiarity.

By the late medieval period, the thirteenth and fourteenth centuries, philosophers had developed an anthropocentric system, one that placed the Earth at the center of the universe, fixed each of the other planets on its own sphere and the stars on another, and had each sphere eternally rotating, its motions powered by its love for God. Authority for this cosmology came from the works of Aristotle and Ptolemy, whose treatises, along with those of other Greek philosophers, had been introduced into Christian Europe, often from Arab translations, in the twelfth and early thirteenth centuries. These texts were studied and taught in the new universities at Paris, Bologna, and Oxford as well as in similar centers of learning that were subsequently established elsewhere and that, together, formed an institutional setting for the pursuit of scholastic philosophy.

Aristotle held the Earth to be a sphere, and, contrary to what twentieth-century schoolchildren are normally taught, so did most scholars before Columbus. That belief was clearly evident in the thirteenth-century illustration by Johannes de Sacrobosco (John of Holywood), the author of a famous medieval textbook entitled *On the Sphere*, which explains why a sailor in a crow's nest can see farther than one on deck (see page 185). Like Aristotle, medieval philosophers explained the fall of heavy bodies towards the Earth's center as natural and projected motions as violent or unnatural, in contrast to the motion of fire, which naturally rises.

Medieval scholars did raise questions about Aristotle's physics and about his cosmology, including, for example, his claim that ordinary space and the basic terrestrial substances—earth, fire, air, and water—extended only to the Moon and that the translunar region was composed of some kind of ether, the substance of all celestial bodies. The skeptics wondered whether an arm would be etherealized if it were poked into the region beyond the Moon. Logic led some scholars to propose that God, being all powerful, might have created other worlds beyond the Earth and established an infinite space for His residence. In the thirteenth century, Sacrobosco assumed that the region between the Earth and the Sun was sufficiently ordinary to permit an explanation of solar eclipses in terms of the Moon's blocking the rays of the Sun as they traveled through a common space (see page 184).

Yet despite the questioning treatises, the criticisms of Aristotle's physics and cosmology were hypotheses that were generally not tested against nature. In the late Middle Ages, for Roman Catholic and scholastic authorities, the center of the universe remained the Earth, as it did in the fifteenth century, when in a drawing Nicholas de Cusa suggested that someone piercing the shell of the heavens would discover that the spheres were driven by a mechanical assemblage (see page 186).

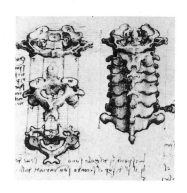

In the middle of the sixteenth century, Nicholas Copernicus advanced a heliocentric cosmology in his grand treatise, *On the Revolutions of the Heavenly Spheres*, and in retrospect, his representation of the planets as rotating in circles around the sun may be conceptually the most revolutionary set of concentric circles ever drawn (see page 187). However, at the time his theory met stiff resistance from astronomers. His planetary orbits did not fit known astronomical data any better than Ptolemy's as they had been intricately adjusted in the Middle Ages to fit planetary observations. A "Chart of Comparative Cosmologies" from the early seventeenth century indicates that Copernicus's system was understood to be merely one of several rival theories (see pages 154–55). The Copernican system was debated for decades by astronomers and philosophers before it triumphed and came to figure mightily in the cluster of developments called the Scientific Revolution. It was then that it became theologically controversial because it dethroned human beings from the center of the universe, a universe that by implication extended in real space beyond the Moon, perhaps to the remote distances of the stars.

The Scientific Revolution fed in part on a transformation in the comprehension of space that had originated in the fifteenth century with the invention of linear perspective, the theory and methods of representing three dimensions on a two-dimensional surface. The painter enthusiasts of perspective, some of them accomplished theorists themselves, were often conversant with works of mathematics, geometry, and proportion, and were acquainted with the engineers, architects, artisans, and instrument makers who put these findings to practical use. They expressed a cast of mind increasingly characteristic of the period—an eagerness to discover the world as it exists to common sense and, if possible, to master it. That cast of mind helped foster the innovation of exploring the natural world through controlled experimentation. It also stimulated the invention of instruments and tools for investigation—notably, in the seventeenth century, the telescope and the microscope, the air pump, the barometer, and the thermometer. And it brought the conventions of perspective into the illustration of the natural world and the human effort to use and understand it.

The new spirit was found in practical renderings ranging from engineering and manufacturing to anatomy and medicine. Graphics figured in the illumination of such subjects as mine ventilation, ore processing, or speculative technologies. Leonardo da Vinci's "Wing for a Flying Machine" (see page 201) is arresting for its artistry, while Athanasius Kircher's "Secret Listening Posts" (see page 206) reveals that a fascination with technological snooping is not new to the twentieth century. Raw metaphors suffused the treatment of anatomical and medical subjects specific to women, notably pregnancy and childbirth. However, da Vinci and Andreas Vesalius directly examined and realistically portrayed human anatomy to produce exquisitely detailed drawings of the human musculature and skeletal structure (see pages 36–37 and 40–41). Hans von Gersdorff did not flinch in his "A 'Wound Man'" (see page 171) from providing a graphic specification of the types of broken flesh that physicians might have to deal with as a result of the slashings of swords, spears, and arrows. Recognizably real human figures illustrated medical procedures such as the removal of a skull fragment, the setting of bones, the straightening of the spine, or the correction of crossed eyes.

Florence was a flourishing center of perspectival practice and theorizing, and so was Nuremberg, where Albrecht Dürer, an accomplished geometer, brought considerations of perspective to the representation of human and animal bodies (see pages 202 and 69), visualizing their parts as inscribed in three-dimensional solids. The Nuremberg school of perspective, which exercised itself on rendering the Platonic solids among other difficult challenges, was influential throughout northern Europe and perhaps derived from cultural roots similar to those that led Johannes Kepler at one point to model the solar system as an array of planetary orbits determined by a set of nested polyhedrons (see pages 188–89). While Kepler had a mystical attachment to geometrical harmonies, his geometrizing was tempered by the details of data. By the early seventeenth century, drawing heavily on the data that Tycho Brahe had painstakingly gathered about astronomical positions and motions, he had concluded that real space extended beyond the Moon, that Copernicus's heliocentric system was essentially right, but that the planets moved in elliptical orbits around the sun, sweeping out equal areas in equal time.

In Florence, Galileo Galilei took an active interest in artists' debates over spatial representation and drew on their theories to conclude that variations in the patterns of light and shade on the Moon seen through his telescope meant that its surface was at least as rough and irregular as the Earth's. Galileo's embrace of this idea, which he supported with a brilliant rendering of the Moon's phases in his *Siderius Nuncius* (see page 22), first published in 1610, earned him the suspicion of some Aristotelian cosmologists. His clear tilt in favor of the Copernican system, which he made manifest in 1632 in his *Dialogue Concerning the Two Chief World Systems*, brought upon him the condemnation of the Church, even though the treatise retained the Aristotelian circular orbits while rejecting Ptolemy's geocentric universe.

Galileo ignored Kepler's elliptical orbits because he considered the circle to be the obvious perfect figure of cosmic order, the geometrically natural form for the motions of heavenly bodies. Such reasoning nevertheless helped lead him to formulate the very anti-Aristotelian idea that came to be termed the principle of inertia—that even terrestrial bodies in a uniform state of motion around the Earth would continue that way unless some external cause operates to change their velocity. Galileo distinguished such motion from that of a body falling toward the Earth; he demonstrated that such a body fell with a constantly increasing rate of speed. The principle of inertia and the law of falling bodies were the terrestrial counterparts of Galileo's Copernican cosmology and they constituted fundamental building blocks of the science of mechanics.

In the seventeenth century, a mechanical conception of nature, adumbrated in the work of Kepler and Galileo, took increasing hold among investigators and was developed into an overarching philosophy by René Descartes. Descartes proceeded from the postulate that the physical world comprises extension—that is, matter. In his system, all extended space was filled with matter, fine particles that formed vortices (see page 192), and all phenomena, terrestrial as well as celestial, were the products of matter in motion, or more specifically, of the direct interactions of matter in motion.

Descartes rejected absolutely Aristotle's contention that matter had any inherent relation with other matter—for example, a tendency to a natural motion toward the Earth. He therefore eliminated Galileo's vestigial Aristotelian distinction between motions around and toward the Earth, declaring that all motions were the same and that they all obeyed the principle of inertia. He argued that light was a pressure transmitted through a medium consisting of tiny spheres and accounted for color in terms of differential rotations of the spheres, holding that greater rotation produced red and lesser, blue. Making use of the newly discovered law of refraction, he managed to calculate the angular height and other features of the rainbow (see page 56). For Descartes, human beings obtained knowledge of the external world through the motions of matter that we perceive as characteristic of light, heat, and other phenomena, all of which produced sensations, via movements in a pertinent nerve leading to the pineal gland (see pages 70 and 71).

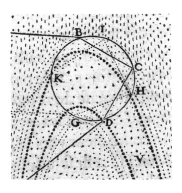

Descartes was by no means alone in seeking to interpret biological phenomena in terms of matter, motions, and mechanisms. Following in the footsteps of da Vinci and Vesalius, some natural philosophers analyzed how the body works as an integrated mechanical system of muscles and skeletal levers (see pages 72–73). William Harvey, who investigated the flow of blood in the body experimentally, observing the consequences of halting the flow at different arterial and venal points, interpreted the circulatory system as though it were a waterworks, a mechanism involving a pump, pipes, and valves (see pages 110–11). The detection of sperm through the microscope was appropriated to a model of fetal development that took the baby to be a tiny animal in the spermal head, fully formed at least in its parts, that mechanically unfolded during the period of gestation. Some philosophers supposed that mental functions must be seated in different layers of the brain or that mental illness must be expressed in the physiognomy of the patient (see pages 38 and 172).

However, the mechanical philosophy scored its greatest triumphs in explorations of the inanimate world—the world of light rays, falling bodies, and planetary motions. It achieved them in all these areas most brilliantly and successfully through the work of Isaac Newton, its greatest practitioner. Newton, who devised his own telescope, was a consummate experimentalist. Like Descartes, whose works he studied while he was an undergraduate at Cambridge University, he was a mechanist, but the evidence of the world compelled him to forge his own mechanical philosophy. He deployed prisms to demonstrate conclusively that white light comprises a spectrum of different colors (see pages 84–85). Reasoning that colors must be a feature of light and not of its medium of passage, he modeled light as a stream of tiny corpuscles moving at enormous speed, and associated colors with their sizes or masses.

In the *Principia Mathematica*, the great work of 1687 in which he advanced what came to be called the system of Newtonian mechanics, he adopted Descartes's universal principle of inertia, but he departed from the Cartesian rejection of the idea that bodies at a distance from each other in space might possess some inherent mutual relationship. The relationship that Newton insisted upon was gravitational force— that two bodies attract each other with a force that is directly proportional to the product of their masses and inversely proportional to the square of the distance between them. Newton's force was conceptually puzzling—how did two bodies act on each other across space?—but it was operationally precise, being exactly defined in terms of the motion it caused. Coupled with the rest of his mechanics, it could account equally for the fall of an apple on the Earth or the motions of the Moon and the planets.

The Scientific Revolution culminated with the publication of Newton's *Principia* and, in 1704, the first edition of his *Opticks*. It was an irreversible revolution, not only because its achievements were so stunning but because they established and sanctioned a new and powerful intellectual program. The program declared that nature was governed by laws, that the laws could be discovered through the application of reason and empiricism, and that they could be turned to human use. As the English philosopher Francis Bacon had put it in his influential *New Atlantis*, "The End of our Foundation is the knowledge of Causes, and secret motions of things; and the enlarging of the bounds of Human Empire, to the effecting of all things possible." The program also raised up a new paragon, the natural philosopher— the astronomer in the observatory (see pages 80–81) and the experimenter in the laboratory or the field (see page 93). This natural philosopher was a human presence; illustrations of the era show his hands pressing on the body or his figure overseeing a barometric experiment (see page 89). The comprehension and the effecting of all things might indeed come from the refraction of nature through his mechanical philosophy and his instruments.

DURING THE EIGHTEENTH CENTURY, natural philosophers, extending the ideas of Newtonian mechanics to physical phenomena other than falling bodies, worked to bring heat, light, electricity, and magnetism within the explanatory domain of mutually interacting matter. "Electricity" in this period meant static electricity, the type that a person could generate by shuffling across a wool carpet and might release as a spark from finger to metal doorknob. Such electricity fascinated the philosophers and the public alike. Contemporary engravings (see page 113) reveal that it was frequently a subject of public demonstration, suitable for the participation of women and children. All the same, electrical discharges could provide rude shocks, and lightning, which Benjamin Franklin demonstrated was a violently powerful form of a spark from the finger, could of course be lethal. The demonstration is dangerous, as the hapless Professor Richmann would have discovered, had he not been electrocuted instantly in making it (see page 116). Demonstrations that celestial lightning and terrestrial sparks expressed the same physical processes ratified the expectation that reason and experiment might lead to further comprehension of the natural world. In the mid-1780s, the universal applicability of the fundamental ideas of Newtonian mechanics appeared to receive quantitative affirmation from Charles A. Coulomb, who inferred from investigations of the interaction of similarly charged electrical bodies that droplets of electrical fluid repelled each other with a force inversely proportional to the square of the distance between them; and from observations of the interactions of magnetically polarized bodies that they contained magnetic fluids with the same form of mutual repulsion.

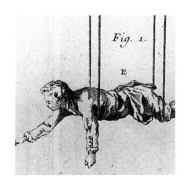

Yet electricity was not always static or, as in sparks and lightning, only briefly on the move. It could be made to flow continuously, as the combined studies of Galvani and Volta revealed by the opening of the nineteenth century. And when it did so, it produced phenomena—chemical changes, heat, even light—transformations that matter in Newtonian motion did not seem able to account for. Nor did it seem up to explaining the dynamic interrelationships of electricity and magnetism, which Michael Faraday brilliantly explored with ingeniously devised apparatus and quantitative mappings of magnetic lines of force (see page 121). Mechanical imagery like lines of force played a major role in studies of electricity and magnetism during the nineteenth century. James Clerk Maxwell exploited it in the early 1870s to forge his grand synthesis of electricity and magnetism—the four equations known as Maxwell's Laws. Yet while the imagery assisted Maxwell as he developed the theory, mechanisms were not integral to the finished structure of his laws. And according to the laws, a highly unmechanical electromagnetic wave could be made to propagate through space—a prediction that Heinrich Hertz decisively confirmed, in 1887 (see page 215).

Early in the nineteenth century, a challenge to the particle interpretation of light was raised by Thomas Young with his demonstration that light exhibited the interference effects characteristic of wave motion (see page 207). Wave phenomena could be seen in fluids like a circular dish of mercury (see page 135), and they could be interpreted in such media as the products of matter in motion. Nineteenth-century physicists, as natural philosophers came to be called, presumed that light traveled in a fluid-like medium, an ether, and with a finite velocity. In 1849, Armand Fizeau measured that velocity, and in 1882, Albert A. Michelson determined it with exacting accuracy, at 299,853 kilometers per second. But light waves appeared to be unlike the waves that propagated in mechanical media. Their speed equaled that of the electromagnetic waves predicted by Maxwell's Laws, strong evidence that light is itself an electromagnetic wave. They also interacted with matter in mechanically incomprehensible ways. Particularly perplexing, under certain conditions a chemical element would radiate or absorb light comprising a distinctive mixture of colors—that is, it would generate or soak up a spectrum of discrete colors characteristic of the element itself (see page 88).

On the whole, the nineteenth century was a period of glorious achievement for the physical sciences. Building on the work of John Dalton at the opening of the period, chemists managed to identify and specify the characteristics of the chemical elements sufficiently to permit the ordering of most of them in the periodic table. They determined that organic substances were composed of the same elements as inorganic ones. They made considerable progress in piecing out the fundamentals of chemical structure, particularly of the hydrocarbons once August Kekulé imagined the model of the benzene ring (see page

213). Their work established the foundation of an increasingly flourishing chemical industry. The prospering electric light and power industry owed its origins not only to Thomas Alva Edison but also to physicists like Faraday, whose notebooks Edison studied closely, and Faraday's successors in the investigation of electricity and magnetism.

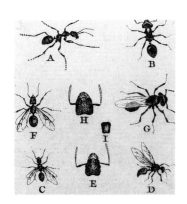

The Scientific Revolution had not bequeathed studies of the living world any agenda that resembled the Newtonian intellectual program. During the eighteenth and nineteenth centuries, explorations of animate nature followed disparate lines, including the classification and comparison of plant and animal varieties. Such work necessarily involved producing careful descriptions of organisms, usually in detailed graphic form. Naturalist portraiture placed a premium on rendering subjects with the kind of fineness manifest in Pierre-André Latreille's remarkably exact drawings of ants (see page 158). Observers depicted patterns of growth, fastening on geometrical organizing principles such as the spiral (see page 63). Unlike earlier representations, which showed plants and animals in contexts suggesting their uses, the representations of this era focused on the organisms themselves or, echoing romantic convention, portrayed them in their natural habitats. Biological portraiture often reached a high level of artistry, the degree of quality typified by the anatomist Richard Owen's "Chambered Nautilus" (see page 62), with its exquisite draftsmanship, or the "Xanthornus Flaviceps" (see page 35) by the British ornithologist John Gould, whose watercolors of birds ranked with those of his American counterpart, John James Audubon.

The classification and comparison of fossils constituted the backbone of paleontology, a science that spoke to the absorption of nineteenth-century geologists in the issue of how the crust of the Earth had taken shape. They knew that the Earth had a long history: it contained fossil remains of animals that were extinct, and different fossil groups tended to be concentrated in particular geological strata, which succeeded one another in time. In the 1830s, Charles Lyell advanced what became the dominant interpretation of the planet's crustal development: it had changed gradually through a continuing accumulation of local disturbances — volcanic eruptions, earthquakes, erosion, and deposition, all of them processes uniform in the geologically distant past with those observable in the present. Debates over the details of the evolution of the Earth were ably assisted by drawings such as W. H. Holmes's "Geological Study of Amethyst Mountain," which, by depicting the exposed cross section of the mountain's strata in space, provided a picture of how the Earth in the region had evolved through time (see page 33).

During the voyage of HMS *Beagle*, Charles Darwin read Lyell's work and was converted to his evolutionary way of thinking. In London after the voyage, Darwin learned from John Gould that the finches he had collected in the Galápagos Islands represented thirteen different species of the bird. Such post-voyage analyses — not, one might note, Darwin's observations while in the Galápagos — crystallized the doubts that he had developed about the fixity of species and led him to begin to work on what became his theory of evolution by natural selection. The basic outline of the theory was already clear in his mind by 1839, when he published an account of the voyage that noted and illustrated the differences among the finches but that refrained from discussion of their deeper significance (see page 32). As an aid in forging his ideas, Darwin employed the figure of a branching tree (see page 160) — the "tree of life," he said in his notebooks, echoing the biblical image — eventually interpreting it to represent successive speciation. The only diagram in *On the Origin of Species*, that graphic metaphor would become a standard device among biologists for depicting evolutionary change and — as the frequently reprinted version of it by Ernst Haeckel indicated (see page 161) — for proclaiming that Man stands at the apex of the evolutionary process.

The theory of evolution eventually touched virtually every field in nineteenth-century biology, including several that flourished in the laboratory. Prominent among them was research in the generation and development of individual organisms. During the first third of the century, the microscope provided the means to demonstrate that the cell is the common structural and functional unit of living matter.

Embryological studies led to rejection of the doctrine that organisms are contained preformed in the sperm or egg and to embrace of the doctrine of epigenesis—that they developed from the fertilized egg via processes of cellular multiplication, differentiation, and organization. Precisely what occurred in fertilization to set off this remarkable process was a question of intense interest. In the mid-1870s, Herman Fol showed that just one sperm entered the egg (see page 48) and he collaborated in the determination that the sperm carried a nucleus that joined with the egg's to form a single entity. By the mid-1880s, cellular biologists had learned both that the nucleus contained a set of string-like bodies that they called chromosomes, because, if they were stained, they could be seen when the cell divided, and also that these chromosomes were duplicated in the intricate process of cellular division, with one set going to the nucleus of each daughter cell (see page 49).

What these facts meant was murky. They suggested to some biologists that the nucleus, a product of contributions from each parent, must figure fundamentally in the transmission of characteristics from one generation to the next and also in the process of cellular differentiation that yielded the mature organism. However, these microbiological processes posed deep problems for the theory of evolution by natural selection. Natural selection had to have some favorable, inheritable change to select. What did it act upon if the cell nucleus faithfully transmitted the basic characteristics of an organism from one generation to the next? Like the physical sciences, the biological ones ended the nineteenth century on a problematic intellectual note despite—in a sense, because of—the splendid achievement of the theory of evolution.

I N 1895, WILHELM ROENTGEN discovered an extraordinary type of invisible radiation—he called them X rays—which excited the attention of the world because they could pass through matter and even render a photograph of the bones encased in human flesh. During the next several years, physicists in France detected another mysterious radiation, the type that Pierre and Marie Curie dubbed radioactivity. In the same few years, in England, J. J. Thomson identified charged particles in a cathode ray tube, declared that they appeared to be matter from which all the chemical elements were constructed, and called them electrons. At the opening of the twentieth century, physics was suddenly alive with new and revolutionary questions concerning the nature of X rays, the role of the electron in electricity and magnetism, and the structure of the electronic atom.

The questions got answered, as did the conundrums manifest in the physics of matter and radiation, by the invention of quantum mechanics and Albert Einstein's special theory of relativity. Quantum mechanics proved adequate to the task of accounting for the structure of the atomic nucleus, including its radioactive transformation, and the behavior of elementary particles. Together with the theory of relativity, quantum mechanics overthrew the Newtonian system as the foundation of the physical universe, particularly the Newtonian assumptions of absolute space and time. As a result of Einstein's theory of general relativity, the formulation of which he completed in 1915, the three-dimensional space of the Renaissance was replaced by a space that curved in proportion to the magnitude of mass in the vicinity. Einstein calculated that it curved enough in the region of our Sun to bend a light ray from a distant star and sketched the deflection in a letter suggesting that astronomers might test his theory by looking for the bending during an eclipse (see pages 194–95). An astronomical expedition detected the expected deflection during the eclipse of 1919, and Einstein found himself suddenly world famous, proclaimed as the Newton of the century.

Not long afterwards, it was pointed out that the equations of general relativity implied that the universe had an expansionist history. Since the mid-1920s, evolutionary cosmology—eventually dubbed the Big Bang—has gathered increasing empirical support, particularly from observations that other galaxies are moving outward from ours in all directions in ways implying that the universe is expanding

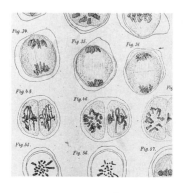

from what had been a highly compressed state some ten to twenty billion years ago. In recent decades, the paradigm of evolution has scored major advances concerning our own tiny region of the universe, too, with confirmation of Alfred Wegener's theory of continental drift (see pages 210–11) and with the advent of empirically well-supported theories of the evolution of our solar system (see page 193).

In 1900, investigations into what natural selection might act upon helped lead to the rediscovery of Mendel's long-neglected laws of heredity and gave rise to the science of genetics. By the interwar period, experiment had amply demonstrated that the stuff of heredity consisted of genes. Theoretical analyses had shown that changes in genes—mutations—or new combinations of them could produce the modifications in organic characters necessary for evolution, thus boosting Darwinian theory by suggesting how natural selection worked. Darwinian theory was further bolstered by the increasing sophistication of evolutionary biologists, particularly by their breakaway from the teleological bias of some of their late-nineteenth-century predecessors. The change was expressed by the modifications evident in drawings of the evolutionary tree. No longer a single trunk leading to Man at the top, the tree was transformed into an array of many independent forks and branchings. A late-1970s version shows a set of vertical lines of organic development, thus implicitly declaring that all other species are biologically coequal with *homo sapiens* before the bar of nature (see pages 162 and 163).

During the first half of the twentieth century, geneticists learned that genes are situated on chromosomes and they hypothesized that, like chromosomes, genes must be material entities. That hypothesis was, of course, confirmed, in 1953, in the discovery by James Watson and Francis Crick that genes are double-helical strands of deoxyribonucleic acid (DNA). The two strands of the helix, each running antiparallel to the other, are joined by chemical bonding between two pairs of bases—adenine to thymine and cytosine to guanine—which form rungs along the helix. Together, the four bases comprise the alphabet of the genetic code, with each base being one of the letters in it. Variations in the linear ordering of the letters spell out units of genetic information—the sequences of code that are called genes (see pages 222 and 223).

No genetics is of greater interest to human beings than their own. In 1956, biologists in Sweden determined that we possess forty-six chromosomes (see page 173)—that is, twenty-two pairs of autosomes and one pair of sex chromosomes termed "X" and "Y," after their shapes. Compacted into these chromosomes, a set of which is contained in each human cell and is smaller than the dot of a pencil, are about six feet of DNA, collectively called the human genome. The human genome has three billion base pairs, enough information to fill 500 encyclopedia volumes, each with 1,000 pages containing 6,000 letters of the DNA alphabet.

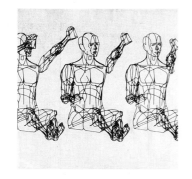

In the late nineteenth century, scientists had organized themselves into professional societies and called for greater institutional and financial support of research. In the twentieth century, they increasingly received both as basic science became tied ever more closely to the national interests of economic growth, defense, and health. Great industrial and governmental laboratories exploited the physics of electrons, crystals, and nuclei to forge technologies ranging from televisions to missile warheads. Otto Lilienthal's ingenious attempt to infer methods of achieving aeronautical lift from the geometry of the stork's wing (see page 68) gave way to the systematic use of fluid mechanics to design supersonic aircraft (see page 141). Long-standing medical practices like inoculation came to be understood and engineered in terms of the general biology of the immune system, the basic principles of which Paul Ehrlich had grasped at the turn of the century (see pages 216–17).

The scientific and technological advances of the twentieth century depended heavily upon improvements and innovations in scientific instrumentation that enabled human beings to see Nature more distantly, more comprehensively, more finely, more deeply. High-speed photography caught matter in remarkable instants of motion (see page 140). Powerful telescopes gathered light from distant galaxies, providing the initial empirical basis for the Big Bang theory. Satellites displayed temperature and weather patterns on a global scale, while space probes revealed the intimate features of the planets. Particle accelerators and electron microscopes permitted examination of minuscule structures such as atoms and viruses. Computers calculated and simulated a seemingly infinite variety of intricate phenomena, including breaking down human movements into schematized representations—in a sense, animating da Vinci's rendering of the human torso at successive rotational angles (see page 225).

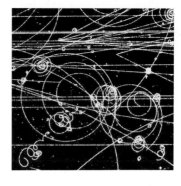

The powers of instrumentation have assisted in driving much of twentieth-century scientific illustration into the realm of abstraction. The professionalization of science helped establish an ethic of impersonality that imposed the passive voice on the texts of scientific research and removed human agency from graphic descriptions of it. In contrast to the typical eighteenth-century drawing, the experimenter is absent from twentieth-century depictions of experiments. Perhaps more important, the experiment, the data, the theory—all are embedded in the conceptual framework, usually complex, of the field of investigation. To comprehend the meaning of the portrait—to understand the diffraction pattern of a crystal, the tracings of an encephalogram, the shadows in a brain scan, the configurations of nerve synapses—the audience needs to be acculturated to the framework, including the techniques by which the portrait was produced. Nevertheless, particle traces in a bubble chamber etch out a chaos of lines and curves that resemble a black-and-white Jackson Pollock (see page 143), and computer-generated fractal patterns integrate shards of color into gorgeous figures (see page 226).

Twentieth-century scientific illustration is capable of a compelling purity of color, texture, and form. Like certain branches of modern art, it needs no conceptual acculturation to touch our sensibilities. Whether accessibly representational or not, scientific illustration merits what this book modestly yet imaginatively urges upon us—attentiveness as a graphic object of aesthetic appeal as well as intellectual illumination.

# I
# Observation

The genesis of visual representation
is that fashioning by Nature of a
picture of herself, in the mind of man,
which we call the progress of science.
—THOMAS HUXLEY, 1869[1]

D RAWINGS OF DIRECT OBSERVATIONS are the simplest and oldest form of scientific illustration: the scientist reports, "I looked, and this is what I saw." The motivating force for the making of such pictures originates in the direct interplay of the object or phenomenon and the observer. The picture freezes the experience so that, for example, a particular condition of a plant or an animal or an astronomical spectacle can be studied some time after the organism's decay or the passing of the event.

The sole purpose of the images in this section is to describe. The examples here are pictures made by all types of scientists—priests, shamans, scribes, astrologers, and astronomers—as well as by artists who have illustrated scientific reports. They were drawn on animal bones, rock surfaces, clay tablets, papyrus, parchment, and paper; some were drawn in margins to further elucidate an accompanying text.

Before the advent of printing, manuscripts were copied by hand, and these precious herbals, bestiaries, and records of astronomical observations were treasured by scientists and their students. In fact, from antiquity through the Middle Ages the study of manuscripts constituted one of the main activities of science. From the fifteenth century onward, with the dissemination of printed books, information was more widespread and curious minds were impelled even further to investigate and report more sophisticated observations. But in all cases, even in our own time, illustrations of direct observations are often the first actions leading to the understanding of natural phenomena.

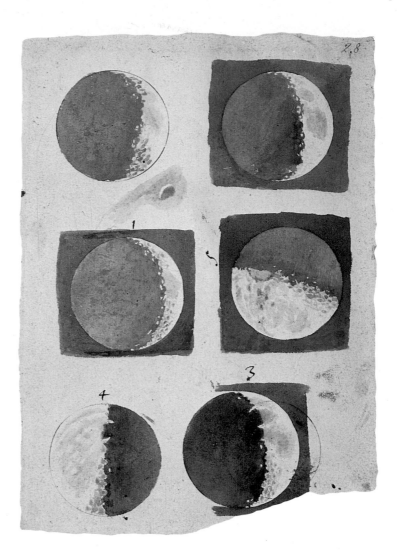

## Six Phases of the Moon

1616

IN 1609 GALILEO LEARNED that a new optical instrument—a telescope—had been invented by Hans Lippershey in Holland. Galileo, a scientist gifted with considerable practical ability, immediately proceeded to construct a telescope of his own and with it began to record his observations of heavenly bodies. A year later, he published and distributed his observations in a series of newsletters entitled *Sidereus Nuncius* (The Starry Messenger). These newsletters promised to reveal "great, unusual, and remarkable spectacles, opening these to the consideration of every man, and especially of philosophers and astronomers."

Galileo, who had some training in drawing and watercolor, made his own illustrations for the series. These drawings showed that the Moon was not a smooth sphere, as had been thought previously; its surface was marked by mountains, valleys, and craters, just like those found on Earth. By measuring the shadows of the Moon's mountains cast by the Sun's light, Galileo was able to calculate the heights of the mountains, which he showed to be comparable with those of Earth.

At this time, Galileo was relatively unknown outside the University of Padua, where he was a professor of mathematics, but he also dealt with "natural philosophy" (the natural sciences). His personality—often skeptical and derisive toward other scientists—had earned him the dislike of his colleagues. Despite this, he was very popular with his students, and his lecture hall was the largest in the university.

# Map of the Moon

H EVELIUS HAD CONSTRUCTED the finest observatory in Europe in his own house at Danzig, where he built a 150-foot-long telescope with large-diameter lenses that had been ground and shaped on a lathe. *Selenographia*, his atlas of the Moon's surface, published thirty-one years after Galileo's Moon sketches, was illustrated with his own copperplate engravings.

The superiority of Hevelius's telescope can be appreciated by comparing Galileo's fourth drawing (page 22, bottom left) with Hevelius's map. The map correctly displays features of the Moon that are recognizable in our own time. The half-disk cut by the shadow line of Galileo's drawing at the left of the center corresponds to Hevelius's "Sicilia," at the same position. Such assigning of names to specific details or sites on maps serves to make communication between scientists more efficient—"Sicilia" may have received the name because of its island-like appearance in the "Mare Mediter[raneum]" and the unique volcano and crater formation at the center of the island, which would correspond to Sicily's Mount Etna.

The two dashed circumference lines surrounding Hevelius's Moon map indicate the limits of the sightings caused by the "wobble" in the relative positions of Earth and the Moon in the course of Earth's orbital motion with respect to the Sun's light as it illuminates the Moon.

Alíí porno. Alíí Polypleron.
Nascitur in paludibus plurimum & pratis.
AD CAPITIS DOLOREM.
Herbae Plãtagis radix collo suspêsa dolorê mire
tollit.        AD VENTRIS DOLOREM.j
Herbae Plantaginis sucus tepefactus fometãdo
uentris dolorê tollit mire: & si tumor fuerit: tu
sa & imposita tollet tumorem.

APULEIUS BARBARUS
C. FIFTH
CENTURY A.D.

Plantain

PUBLISHED C. 1484

ALTHOUGH THE *Herbarium* in which this illustration appears was first printed about 1484, copies of its drawings and texts had been circulated for almost a thousand years before they were collected and printed as a book.

Since the plantain was prescribed as an antidote in the treatment of snakebite or scorpion sting, the two animals included in the illustration served as an indicator or mnemonic device for the physician. These visual clues helped promote swift and reliable identification of plants for use as specific medicines.

Barbarus's *Herbarium* was later incorporated into a highly esteemed medical text, the *Hortus Sanitatis*, published in Germany in 1491.

# Vallisneria spiralis

THIS DRAWING IS FROM DARWIN'S two-volume *The Botanic Garden*, which was published in 1789–91. Erasmus, the grandfather of Charles, was a physician and an enthusiastic botanist. He, like other English gentlemen of his time, had great regard for science, which they believed could guide mankind to perfection.

The significant element in Darwin's drawing of *Vallisneria spiralis* is the spiral form of the flower stems. Many botanists in the late eighteenth and early nineteenth centuries believed that this "spiral tendency" was the generative force operating in the growth of plants, shaping even blossoms and fruits.

*Vallisneria spiralis* is found in ponds and streams. Its female flowers (at the top) rest on the water surface until they are fertilized by airborne or waterborne pollen released by male flowers. The coils of the spiral stems then contract and pull the female flowers below the water surface: the fertilized seeds develop underwater. Both stages are shown in this drawing.

Darwin delighted in expressing his observations in poetical form. In the section entitled *The Loves of the Plants*, he writes about *Vallisneria spiralis*:

*Vallisner sits, upturns her tearful eyes,*
*Calls her soft lover, and upbraids the skies.*

He goes on to attribute to the airborne pollen the desire to search out the female flower, comparing the "behavior" of the male and female flowers to the behavior of insects in courtship.

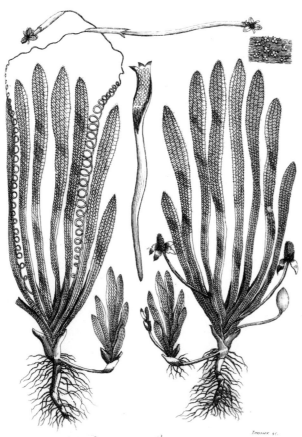

*Vallisneria Spiralis.*

# Thistle

NINTH CENTURY

*Observation*
26

D IOSCORIDES WAS A GREEK PHYSICIAN who served in the Roman army under the emperor Nero. Like many early physicians, he depended on herbs and other substances for medicinal treatments. The thistle is one of approximately 600 plants and 1,000 minerals and animal derivatives for therapeutic use described by Dioscorides in his *De Materia Medica*, the first extensive pharmacopeia. The manuscripts contained no illustrations, and later authors used Dioscorides's texts as a basis for illustrated copies of his work, which became the most important resource for botanical information in antiquity.

Dioscorides's manuscripts were preserved and copied by Arabian physicians in the ninth century. However, it was not until 1478 that the *De Materia Medica* was published in book form, translated from the original Greek into Latin.

Shown here in full bloom and afterbloom in a ninth-century Arabic version of the book, the thistle, which could be used for medicinal purposes only in its afterbloom stage, was recommended for infusion and application as an eyewash, or to be drunk as a digestive tonic, a muscle relaxant, a lactation stimulant for nursing mothers, and a cure for jaundice.

Mark Catesby, an American colonist who had emigrated from England, was a self-taught painter and etcher. Catesby made 220 hand-colored etchings of animals and plants for his two-volume *Natural History of Carolina*, published in England in 1743 and now acknowledged as the first major contribution to American natural history.

This drawing of the *Caffena* identifies a plant used by the Indians for brewing a drink made from its berries and leaves. They drank this "in large quantities as well as for their health and with great gusto and pleasure," Catesby observed.

In the European plant compendiums published before Catesby's, the inclusion of a harmful animal in the drawing served as a note for specific treatment by the physician and herbalist (see page 24). However, in the comment that accompanies this drawing, Catesby states that this snake is harmless, that it feeds on flies and other insects, and that it can be easily domesticated.

## Caffena vera Floridanorum

1743

*Observation*

27

Pelargos en Grec, Ciconia en Latin, Cigogne en Francoys.

Ο' πελαργὸς ἀφεῖ τε τὰς λίμνας ᾗ τοὺς ποταμοὺς βίφε() φωλεῖ ᾗ τ̔ χειμόνος οἱ ᾗ πελαργοὶ ᾗ οἱ ἄλλοι τῶν ὀρνίθ
ὅταν ἑλκωθῇ τι μαρναμένοις ὀπιπτέασι τὴν ὀσίγανον. ἀφεῖ μὲν οὖν τῶν πελαργῶν ὅτι ἀντεκβίφονται ᢧὸ τῶν ἐ
γόνων θρυλλεῖται παρὰ πελλοῖς. Arist. lib. 8. c. 3. & lib. 9. c. 6. & 13.

PIERRE BELON
1517–1564

# Stork and Snake

1555

Belon's *Natural History of Birds*, PUBLISHED IN 1555, became a reference and textbook treasured by sixteenth- and seventeenth-century European naturalists, and is now considered a classic in the history of zoology. It was of special importance to zoologists not only for Belon's precise illustrations of the birds but also for his meticulous accounts of their habits: their cries, their feeding, their locomotion on land, water, and in the air, and their migrations.

Belon received a degree in medicine from the University of Paris, and several years later his reputation brought him to the attention of King Francis I, who appointed him physician to numerous diplomatic missions. It was during these sojourns in countries bordering on the Mediterranean that Belon developed an interest in what was later to become a new discipline in medical studies—comparative anatomy.

Although in the biological sciences, perhaps the most important primary activity is the observation of living organisms, when that is not possible, the study of drawings of those subjects is necessary. For *Natural History of Birds*, Belon probably employed Pierre Gourdelle, an eminent painter, to make the drawings, most likely from stuffed specimens.

In this drawing, a stork stands at the bank of a stream holding in its beak a captured snake, natural food for the stork. The vegetation emerging from the water resembles papyrus, also native to the stork's habitats along the Mediterranean.

Ruini, a bolognese nobleman, was an eminent lawyer with a great interest in horses. In the book from which this precisely observed illustration is taken, Ruini reminds his readers that *cavaliere*, an honorary Italian title, was derived from the Italian word for horse, *cavallo*.

Ruini's book provides careful explanations of each element of the horse's anatomy, describing characteristic diseases of the animal along with suggested remedies. His book, too, is the first to have been devoted to the anatomy of an animal other than man and constitutes one of the foundations of comparative anatomy.

To make anatomical studies of animals in lifelike positions, anatomists and artists hung the carcasses in quasi-normal postures by ropes attached to scaffolds. Then by setting the flayed, dead animal in a landscape, the illustrator attempted to give the carcass a pleasant appearance.

# Musculature of a Horse

c. 1598

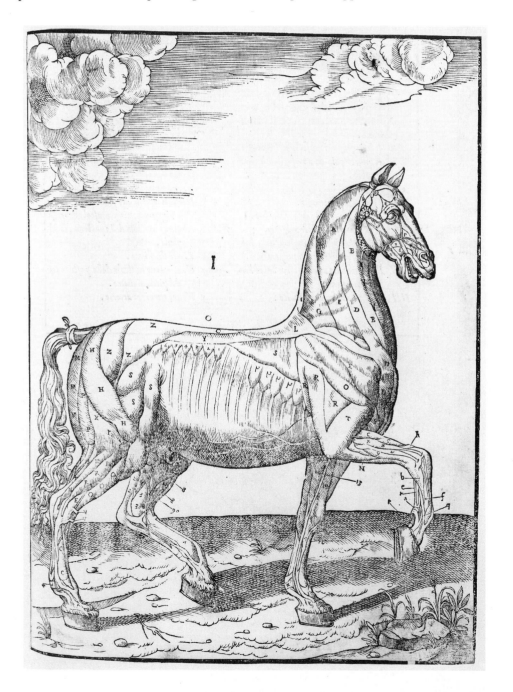

## Metamorphosis of a Butterfly

1705

M ERIAN HAD THE GOOD FORTUNE to grow up in a Swiss-German family of illustrators, painters, engravers, and printers, and her own talent as a painter and illustrator is evident in her extraordinary botanical and entomological studies. These works were reproduced in several publications during her lifetime, including her *New Flower Book*, which may have been a teaching manual for young upper-class women who were sent to her studio for training in drawing and painting.

During a two-year stay in Surinam (once known as Dutch Guiana) with her husband, Merian executed many studies of indigenous animals and vegetation, among them *Metamorphosis of a Butterfly*. In addition to the accuracy of its representation, the drawing is notable for the grace and refinement of its composition, which carries the viewer through the process of the insect's growth and transformation, combining different periods of time in a single picture as in a medieval narrative painting.

ABAD, AN ENTOMOLOGIST and scientific illustrator, made this watercolor and gouache painting of a butterfly while on the staff of the Institute of Entomology in Madrid, Spain. It is a prime example of his outstanding craftsmanship.

The butterfly is drawn with closed wings rising vertically above its body. It has a wingspan of approximately 3 inches, and is unique in the display of bristle-like hairs over its body. This very rare species is found only in one mountain pass, called Puerto Pozazal, near Santander in north-central Spain. Its name was originally *Parnassius* ("high-flying") *apollo* ("beautiful") *pozazalensis* ("in the Pozazal Pass"), but this last term was later changed to *pardoi* ("dark-colored").

RICARDO ABAD
RODRÍGUEZ
B. 1913

# Parnassius apollo pardoi

1978

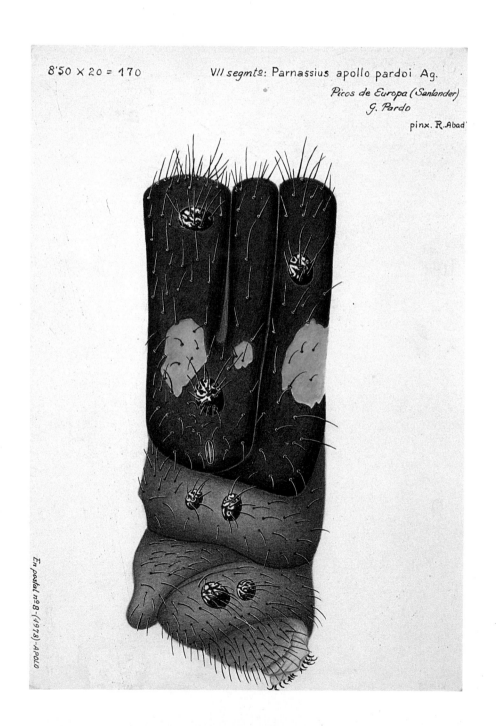

8'50 × 20 = 170

VII segmt<sup>a</sup>: Parnassius apollo pardoi Ag.

Picos de Europa (Santander)
G. Pardo

pinx. R. Abad

En postal nº 8-(1978)-APOLO

# Finches from the Galápagos Islands

1839

THIS ILLUSTRATION APPEARS in the published edition of the diary Darwin kept during the voyage of HMS *Beagle*—a five-year British Admiralty expedition that traveled the coasts of Brazil, Uruguay, Argentina, Patagonia, Chile, the Galápagos Islands, and some islands in the Pacific Ocean from 1831 to 1836. The arrangement of the four birds' heads compares the shapes of their beaks—an observation that became extremely important in Darwin's speculations on evolution. The drawing was made by John Gould (see page 35).

According to prevailing nineteenth-century theories, each separate species would have been *created* to exist on a separate island. Darwin gradually recognized that this was an untenable assumption. Instead, he suggested that the Galápagos finches were descendants of finches that had strayed from the South American mainland and, in the course of successive generations, had developed beaks better accommodated to the varieties of foods available in the different islands' meadows, bushes, trees, and grasses. Heavier, larger beaks could more easily break the husks of larger seeds, and pointed beaks could more easily pierce the softer seeds and berries. Darwin concluded that variations among species must occur to meet the conditions necessary for survival.

During the voyage, Darwin classified at least 14 different species of finches in the Galápagos Islands—all different from the finches found on the South American coast, some 600 miles away. The distinctive differences among the island finches were visible especially in the sizes and shapes of their beaks. These birds are now called "Darwin's finches," in tribute to their contribution to the development of Darwin's theory of the evolution of species.

The records and speculations in the journal Darwin kept during his voyage reveal his considerable bewilderment about the scientific implications of the collected data. In 1836, writing home from Australia, Darwin expressed his inability to comprehend the mysteries of creation: "Surely two distinct Creators must have been at work."

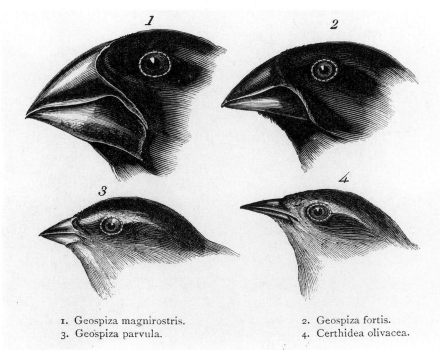

1. Geospiza magnirostris.
2. Geospiza fortis.
3. Geospiza parvula.
4. Certhidea olivacea.

FINCHES FROM GALAPAGOS ARCHIPELAGO.

*East Fork.*

YELLOWSTONE PARK, declared the first U.S. National Park in 1872, encompasses sections of Wyoming, Montana, and Idaho — areas of extraordinary interest to geologists. Holmes, a specialist in geological illustration, was sent by the U.S. Geological and Geographical Survey to Yellowstone to study the geology of Amethyst Mountain.

Like several others in the region, Amethyst Mountain was formed by a series of volcanic eruptions, the last one estimated to have occurred about 600,000 years ago. Amethyst is unique, however, because one of its sides was virtually sliced away like a piece of cake by glacial erosion, which exposed a multilayered rock structure with numerous strata of fossil forests.

In order to make this sketch, Holmes positioned his easel some distance from the exposed side of Amethyst and used a telescope to view the mountain as a whole. He delineated the layers of rock, fossil trees — standing upright and fallen — and fossil bushes. Extrapolating from his observations of its surface, Holmes even suggested what might lie behind the great vertical cut.

WILLIAM H. HOLMES
1846–1933

Geological
Study of
Amethyst
Mountain

1879

*Observation*

33

ELAINE R. S. HODGES
B. 1937

# Pine-Bark Beetle

1988

*Observation*
*34*

Tʜɪs ᴅʀᴀᴡɪɴɢ ɪʟʟᴜsᴛʀᴀᴛᴇᴅ an article in the *Journal of Forestry* on the infestation of Chilean pine forests by pine-bark beetles, insects discovered in 1985. Hodges, a scientific illustrator on the staff of the Smithsonian Institution, wrote the following account of the process of making a 9-by-12-inch drawing of a beetle approximately ¹/₅ inch in length:

*I used as my reference for the beetle a dry, pinned specimen of the insect, which I drew with the aid of a microscope. For the eggs and the bark I used 35mm slides, black/white photos and photocopies, text diagrams, actual wood, and my own experience with insect eggs and knowledge of plant anatomy. Rough but proportionately accurate sketches of the beetle were prepared using the microscope's camera lucida, a tool to trace outlines of what is seen under the microscope. These sketches of the beetle's parts were combined to make the animal look as though it was crawling. Then details were drawn by eye from the microscope. The detailed preliminary drawing was traced and rendered on film in a composition that included characteristic "galleries" dug by the beetle as it eats under the bark and lays its eggs. Different species of beetles bore galleries in different patterns.*

THE BRITISH ADMIRALTY commissioned Gould to record observations of animal life encountered during the five-year scientific expedition of HMS *Beagle*. One of the five volumes of Charles Darwin's report on the voyage is devoted entirely to Gould's paintings of birds.

Gould, aged twenty-seven at the time of his Admiralty commission, an ornithologist himself, was already highly esteemed among naturalists for his mastery of watercolor and lithography as well as taxidermy. Because specimens changed in appearance so radically and quickly after death, scientists welcomed Gould's meticulous renderings of animals that were precise and lifelike.

*Xanthornus flaviceps*, members of the oriole family, were observed by the *Beagle* expedition along the coastlines of Brazil, Argentina, and Uruguay. Their Latin name refers to their characteristic golden plumage.

# Xanthornus flaviceps

1840

*Birds Pl. 45.*

*Xanthornus flaviceps*

*Observation*

# The Human Spinal Column

1489

IN ONE OF HIS NOTEBOOKS, da Vinci spelled out what he believed to be the obligation and highest function of a painter: "The mind of the painter must resemble a mirror which permanently transforms itself into the color of its object and fills itself with as many images as there are things placed in front of it."

For more than a thousand years before Leonardo and for almost a hundred years after his death, general knowledge of human anatomy was based on the teachings of the Greek physician Galen (c. A.D. 130–200). Galen had dissected apes and swine and claimed that his observations applied equally to humans. For almost fourteen centuries, all questions relating to human anatomy and physiology were referred to the teachings of Galen, whose medical texts were considered authoritative (see page 168).

Da Vinci devoted a great deal of time to the quiet pursuit of a precise knowledge of human anatomy. It was not until the middle of the sixteenth century that ecclesiastical authorities throughout Europe relaxed the prohibition against the dissection of human cadavers, a ban based on the belief that the human body was a creation of God and therefore inviolable. Therefore, Leonardo, like others of his time, performed his dissections in secrecy. From these dissections, da Vinci made more than 750 separate sketches of muscles, hearts, lungs, blood vessels, bones, nerves, and brains. His dispassionate, usually accurate anatomical drawings are one of his legacies to our understanding of Nature.

Leonardo's drawings of the human spine are the first to show its natural curvature, with the vertebrae correctly observed and recorded in their interlocking arrangement (upper left).

At the upper right, da Vinci presents the spine in a frontal view. His facile use of shading enables us to see how the chain of vertebrae curves toward and then away from the viewer.

At the lower right, the spinal column is shown horizontally as seen from the back, with the upper vertebrae at the right and the lower vertebrae at the left.

To the left of this drawing, da Vinci delineates those vertebrae that lie directly under the skull and continue downward through the neck. At the extreme left, the first three cervical vertebrae (extending downward from the skull) are separated to show their individual structures. In his notes on this page, executed in his customary mirror writing, da Vinci urges the student to examine these bones both separately and joined together, the better to understand their structures and functions.

Da Vinci's drawings were discovered by William Hunter in 1784, almost three hundred years after they were made. All the known drawings were eventually published between 1898 and 1916.

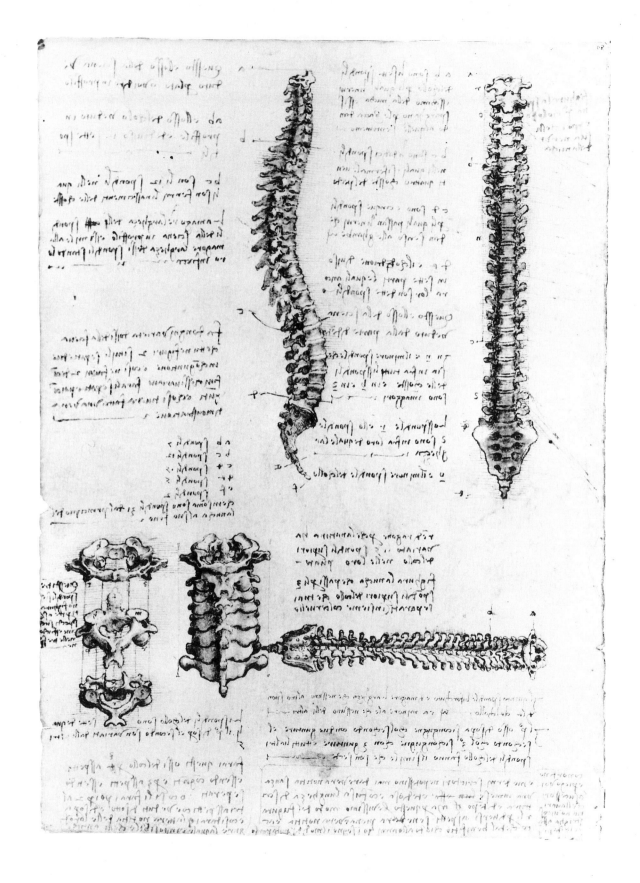

# The Layers of
the Brain

U NTIL VESALIUS'S BOOK on human anatomy appeared in 1543 (see pages 40–41), it was common for authors of anatomy texts to copy illustrations from previously published works, a practice that perpetuated many errors.

Dryander's illustration of the exfoliated layers of the brain was copied from an earlier work by Lorenz Fries, whose *Spiegel der Artzny* (Mirror of Medicine) was published in 1517. To that illustration Dryander added his own notations—incorrect, as we now know—of the sensory faculties controlled by each "layer" of the brain. The letters denote the functions in the various layers—for example, vision, taste, and smell.

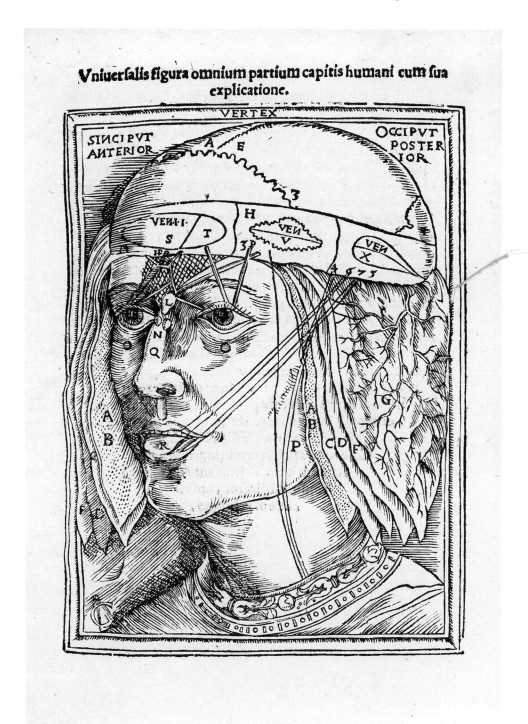

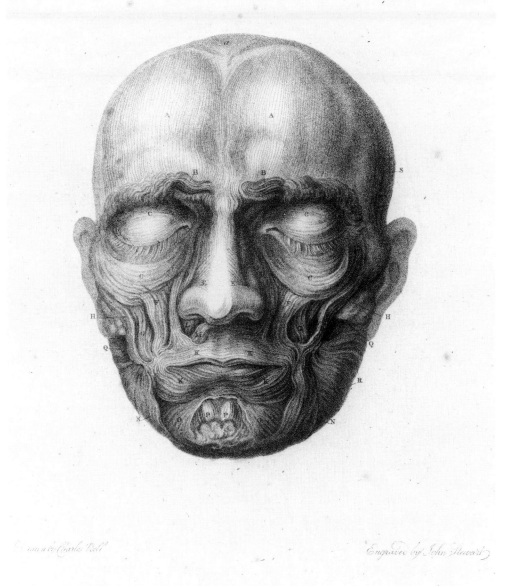

Drawn by Charles Bell.

Engraved by John Stewart.

London Published by Longman & Co. June 2d 1806.

B ELL, A BRITISH PHYSIOLOGIST, surgeon, and neurologist, was also a skillful illustrator. Careful, dispassionate observation and drawing of dissected specimens characterize the many illustrations he produced during his career.

Here Bell delineates the muscles that produce facial expression (the symmetrically placed letters on the various muscles are keys to their nomenclature). This is one of several drawings he made for a series of lectures given regularly at his home in London especially for a group of British painters who wished to improve their understanding of human anatomy, gesture, and expression.

Charles Bell's intellectual honesty was recognized and respected by a wide circle of colleagues. His *System of Dissections* (1789) and *Engravings of the Brain and the Nervous System* (1802) were illustrated with his own drawings, and the sketches he made while attending soldiers wounded in achieving the British victory at Waterloo (1815) are a testament to his dedication.

SIR CHARLES BELL
1774 – 1842

# The Anatomy of Expression

1806

*Observation*

## Musculature of the Human Male

1543

VESALIUS, THE SON OF AN APOTHECARY in the service of the Holy Roman emperor Charles V, displayed an extraordinary talent for medicine, and especially for anatomy, while attending medical school at Louvain in Flanders. In 1534, upon graduation, Vesalius, then aged twenty, enrolled in the famous medical college at Padua. After several days of examinations, the faculty recognized his unusual ability by offering him the post of lecturer on surgery and anatomy.

Several carefully detailed anatomical studies had been published during the fourteenth and fifteenth centuries. The explanations and interpretations, however, were still those of Galen (see pages 36 and 168), and also sometimes based on astrology, numerology, the doctrine of the "four temperaments," the "four humors" (blood, phlegm, yellow bile, and black bile), and other mystical concepts.

Vesalius performed all dissections himself, guiding his pupils with the help of four large anatomical diagrams he had prepared. By 1539 Vesalius was able to challenge Galen's authority publicly, in Padua and then in Bologna, by showing that Galen's anatomy might be accurate for apes and swine but did not correspond to that of human beings.

In Vesalius's masterpiece, *De Humani Corporis Fabrica* (1543), many of the illustrations were drawn by Stephen van Calcar, a student in Titian's studio. The finely printed text, which runs to about 600 pages, is divided into seven books: (1) the bones, joints, and skull; (2) the muscles (from which this illustration is reproduced); (3) the heart and blood vessels; (4) the nervous system; (5) the abdominal organs: (6) the organs of the thorax; and (7) the brain.

*De Humani Corporis Fabrica* is one of the major scientific treatises of Western civilization. The illustrations are often precisely accurate and display both Vesalius's and the artist's skill in counteracting the gruesomeness of flayed, dissected corpses by setting the figures in quasi-normal postures against pleasant landscapes (as did Ruini, page 29). Letters and numerals on the figure serve as keys to the names of the muscles. The drawings set the fashion for more than a century and were copied by many illustrators.

SECVNDA
MVSCVLO.
RVM TA.
BVLA.

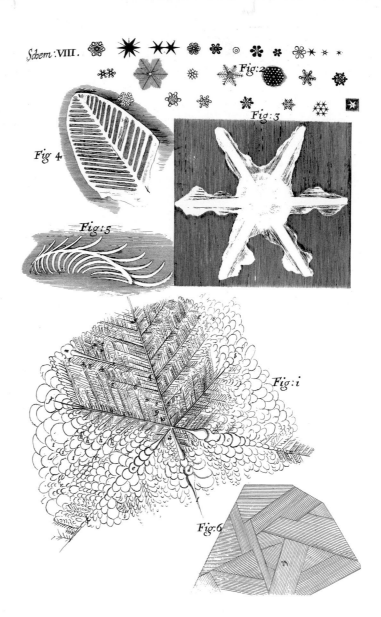

Schem : VIII . Fig : 2

Fig : 3

Fig 4

Fig : 5

Fig : i

Fig : 6

ROBERT HOOKE
1635–1703

# Micrographic Studies of Frost Crystals and Ice Patterns

1665

*Observation*
*42*

AT THE TOP OF THIS ILLUSTRATION, Fig. 2 is a series of drawings Hooke made while studying freshly fallen snowflakes under his microscope. Figures 3, 4, 5, i, and 6 are his drawings of ice patterns formed on various surfaces, also observed under the microscope. Hooke comments on the similarity of the crystal formations to the leaf organization of ferns, and expresses his wish that he could see a snow crystal as it formed in the clouds overhead, before its shape was "vitiated by external accident."

Hooke's reports to the Royal Society of London, collected under the title *Micrographia, or Some Physiological Descriptions of Minute Bodies Made by Magnifying Glasses with Observations and Inquiries Thereupon* (1665), are regarded by historians of science as fundamental in the development of botany and zoology. Hooke's insatiable curiosity and intellectual acuity are delightfully evident in the exquisite details of both his drawings and his commentaries.

In his preface, Hooke presents an eloquent argument for the adoption of a code of ethical procedure for scientists: honest observation, faithful illustration, repeated experimental verification of data, and careful speculation regarding cause and effect without resorting to magical or superstitious bias. These principles had been enunciated in 1605 by Francis Bacon (1561–1626) in his *Advancement of Learning*, and they were eventually to guide scientific investigators under the rubric "the scientific method."

# The Secret of the Gall

EVEN AFTER THE EXTRAORDINARY accomplishments of biochemists in the late nineteenth century, herbs and other plants remained a significant part of the physician's armamentarium. The cultivation of healthy medicinal plants was an important concern for physicians and horticulturists alike.

Malpighi, a physician and botanist who worked at the universities of Pisa and Bologna during the seventeenth century, recognized early on the value of the microscope as a tool for scientific investigation, and he devoted much of his professional life to the microscopy of plants and small invertebrate animals.

Plant diseases were, of course, common, and Malpighi approached their study in an objective manner, indifferent to the claim that they were caused by witchcraft. Some plants were destroyed or otherwise damaged by "galls," a term that describes swellings of the plant tissues. By meticulous dissection and microscopic study, Malpighi learned that the gall was actually the feeding chamber of a developing parasitical insect larva. In this drawing of a Mediterranean oak acorn, the larva (E) can be seen in the center chamber (D).

# Cell Types in the Mammalian Cerebellum

1894

I N THE LATTER PART of the nineteenth century, cell specimens were usually stained for microscopy with organic dyes which the cells absorbed, making them easier to see. Although many internal structures could then be observed, certain cells—especially nerve cells—resisted visibility despite the continuing improvement of dyes and microscopic optics. Because the endings of nerve cells could not be observed clearly, investigators accepted the conclusion that they were somehow connected in a "network" within the protoplasm, the basic material of living organisms.

Ramón y Cajal, a Spanish physician, retired from the practice of medicine because of chronic bouts with malaria and devoted the rest of his life to research in neurology. He was fascinated by the exquisite patterns of visible nerve cells; his experiments were attempts to see them more completely and clearly, as integral forms.

Sometime in the mid-1880s, Ramón y Cajal learned of a cell-staining substance—silver salts—which had been discovered and used by an Italian physician, Camillo Golgi (1843–1926). Adapting Golgi's technique, Ramón y Cajal was able by 1890 to observe and draw the complex interrelations of nerve cells in the brain and spinal cord. He could demonstrate that the nerve endings did not disappear into a vague protoplasm, and that they were discrete, although sometimes attached to each other. Ramón y Cajal concluded that the very small spaces between nerve endings—the synapses, first observed by German anatomist Wilhelm von Waldeyer-Hartz (1836–1921)—provided the means for intercommunication between nerve cells.

This drawing—the first illustration to present an accurate picture of the cerebellum's nerve cells—shows the variety of nerve cells Ramón y Cajal observed in one convolution of a mammalian cerebellum, the part of the brain that controls muscular activity; the arched outline around the drawing was used to suggest a cross section of one convolution. By subsequent microscopic observations, Ramón y Cajal firmly defined the neuron as the basic structural unit in the nervous system.

Ramón y Cajal and Camillo Golgi shared the Nobel Prize in medicine and physiology in 1906.

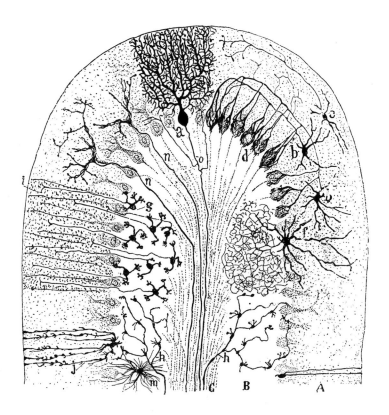

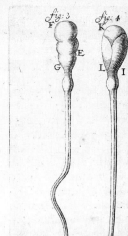

Wanneer nu een ofte meer dierkens uit het mannelijk-zaad van een dier, foo ver-re in de Baar-moeder is ofte zijn gekomen, dat defelve dat deel in de Baar-moeder hebben aangetroffen, dat be-quaam is om het felve te voe-den, ende tot foodanigen foort van 'fchepfel te bren-gen, als wat het lighaam daar het zaad van afgeko-men is; foo kan het fonder eenig nadenken feer ligt, en-de in Weinig tijdts gefchie-den, dat de ftaart of ftaarten van de gefeide dierkens ko-men af te vallen, of dat zy het gantfche vel en ftaart te gelijk verwiffelen, ende dit dus gefchied fijnde, foo heeft ofte behoud het fchepfel als dan een ey-ronde figuur; als Fig. 3. FGH. ofte Fig. 4. IKL. Ten anderen weeten wy dat de lighamen van al-le dieren, nog in de Baar-moeder fijnde, foo digt in een gebogen leggen, dat die meeft na een ronde figuur hellen. Is dit nu in de dieren die tot foodanigen groo-te gekomen zijn omme gebaart te werden, foo is zulks ook fonder twijfel in foodanige kleine fchepfels, die wy met het oog niet konnen bekennen, die ik dan oordee-le

ANTONY VAN LEEUWENHOEK, a Dutch amateur biologist, was the first to describe spermatozoa, based on his observation of them with a simple single-lens microscope he had invented, which had a magnification factor of about 200. His drawings of organisms, usually isolated, incorporated simple outlines with minimum detail. The scale is never given.

This drawing shows Leeuwenhoek's observation of a live and a dead spermatozoon. The distinctive change may be observed in the shape of the live spermatozoon's head (left) and that of the dead one (right).

Leeuwenhoek sent almost 400 reports and drawings to the British Royal Society, which elected him to membership in 1680, the same year in which he was elected to membership in the French Royal Academy of Sciences. Because he could read only Dutch, he was essentially unaware of the work of other contemporary microscopists such as Marcello Malpighi. Leeuwenhoek continued his studies for almost fifty years, until his death at the age of ninety-one, and along with Malpighi, is considered a founding father of microscopic biology.

ANTONY VAN
LEEUWENHOEK
1632 – 1723

# Spermatozoa of a Dog

c. 1673

*Observation*

45

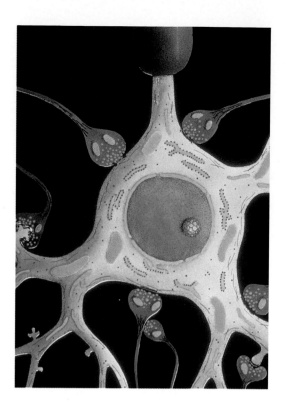

FRANCIS LEROY

# The Neuron and the Synapse

1988

S IR MICHAEL FOSTER (1836–1907), director of the Cambridge School of Physiologists, was the first to suggest that the space between adjacent neurons (nerve cells) might be the region in which these cells completed the transmission of electrical nerve impulses to activate muscular responses. Charles Scott Sherrington (1857–1952), one of Foster's students, verified and elaborated on Foster's hypothesis to provide—for the first time in the history of medicine—a cogent explanation of the physical and chemical substructures of the brain. Sherrington published a compendium of his research work, *The Integrative Action of the Nervous System*, in 1906. It must be remembered that at the turn of the twentieth century, microscopy was limited to optical systems, and could not provide views of the nerve-cell endings and the gaps—"synapses"—between them. Sherrington's book contains only one illustration of a gross neuronal matrix. It was not until the invention of the electron microscope in 1932 in Germany that phenomena as minuscule as neurons and synapses could be seen.

This illustration presents a diagrammatic view, based on electron microscopic observation, of the neuron-synapse relationship. Identifying colors were synthesized by computer graphics. The large orange structure is a neuron; its nucleus is the inner, tan-colored cytoplasm, the semifluid material that sustains the life activity of the cell. The branching extensions of the cell body are the dendrites (receivers), represented as small trefoil protuberances. At the right center, the nerve cell extends to its blue and brown axon (transmitter), which sends nerve signals to adjacent dendrites.

The critical part of this drawing—by Francis LeRoy—is at the left of center, near the top. Here the axon of an adjacent, stimulated cell surrounds the dendrite. The illustrator was careful to show that no physical contact is made at the surfaces of the dendrite and axon terminals; the intervening white space represents the synapse across which the electrochemical signal from the axon must flow to the dendrite. Information in the form of electrical signals proceeds through the axon of one nerve cell across the synapse to the dendrite of the second one. The electrical signal causes a chemical—a neurotransmitter—to be discharged into the synapse to make it electrically conductive in a specific fashion. Some 50 different kinds of neurotransmitter chemicals are now known to neurologists.

I N THIS PHOTOMICROGRAPH (from *The Mind*, by Richard M. Restak) the axon, at the left, has just transmitted an electrical signal to the dendrite, at the right. The separating cleft between the two neurons—the synapse—has begun to transport a chemical substance (the red vertical smear) from the axon to the dendrite. The chemical substance, the neurotransmitter, causes an electrochemical change in the dendrite. (The colors in this photomicrograph result from the specimen-staining laboratory procedure, which highlights the significant chemical substance produced by the transmission of the electrical signals in the neurons and synapses. The color system used here differs from that in the previous illustration.)

Researchers have firmly established the thesis that all animal behavior is the manifestation of the electrochemical activity of specialized neurons, connected into networks that are responsible for all the functions of the brain.

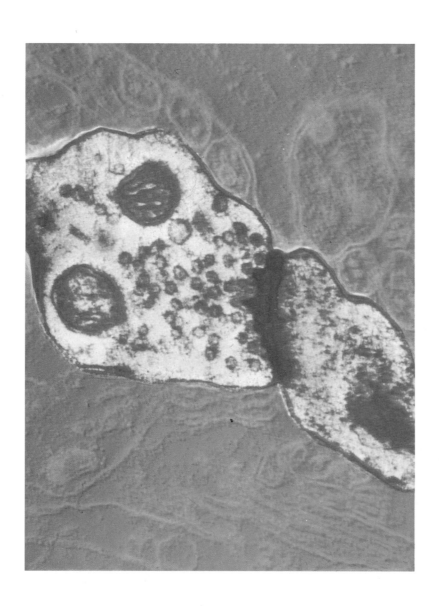

HERMANN FOL
1845–1892

# Fertilization of an Ovum

1879

D URING THE TWO CENTURIES that intervened between Leeuwenhoek's studies and those of Hermann Fol, the microscope as well as the processing of samples for study underwent phenomenal development. Optical technology provided finer glass for lenses, which could be ground with greater precision, and specimen-staining techniques came into use. In medicine, the microscope had become an important tool for identifying cell structures and bacteria, and biologists could now observe some cellular processes.

Fol was a Swiss biologist, one of several then studying the dynamics of the maturation, fertilization, and division of the ovum. In this illustration, three stages of an imminent fertilization of a starfish egg are represented. The magnification factor is approximately 600.

In Fig. 3a, four spermatozoa approach the ovum, propelled by their slender tails (marked Zq in Fig. 3b). On the soft membrane covering the ovum a small "cone of attraction" (Sa in Fig. 3c) forms opposite the entering spermatozoon. Immediately upon entry, the membrane covers the head of the spermatozoon (Figs. 4c and 4d), and fertilization of the ovum proceeds.

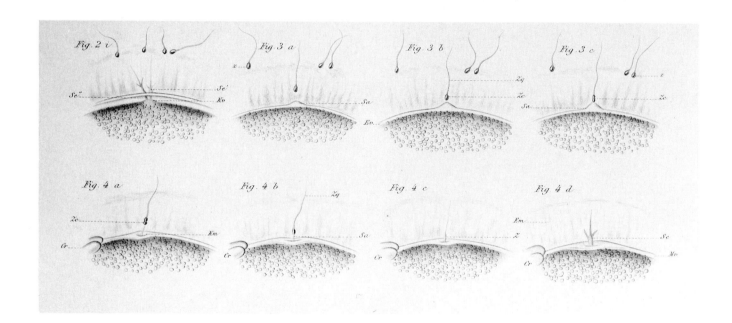

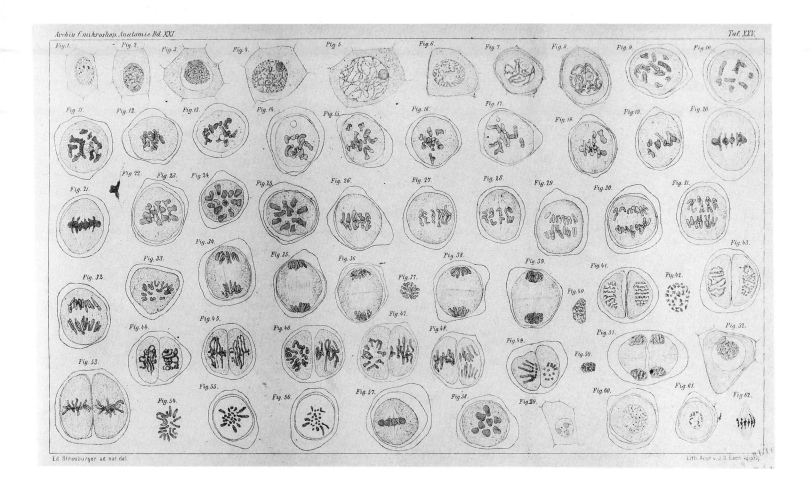

Strasburger received his doctorate in botany in 1866 at the University of Jena, where he taught from 1869 to 1880, before accepting a professorship at the University of Bonn. His skill as a microscopist, including his use of the recently developed aniline dyes for staining specimens, enabled him to observe for the first time how plant cells divide after fertilization.

Strasburger's discovery was reported with great precision. Ten stages are described here from the 62 drawings he made. The plant used was the *Fritillaria persica, Liliaceae*, a spring-flowering perennial herb bulb. From left to right, top to bottom, as pairs Figs. 12 and 16, 19 and 27, etc.:

12, 16: The nucleus of the fertilized ovum unravels into chromosomes. (The word "chromosome" was coined by the anatomist Wilhelm von Waldeyer-Hartz in 1888; it means "colored bodies," a reference to the cells' selective absorption of staining dyes.)

19, 27: The folded chromosomes move to the "equatorial plane" of the cell. Filaments develop from opposite poles of the cell.

30, 34: The chromosomes divide, move to opposite poles, and are bent into U shapes, apparently by being drawn away from each other by the filaments.

38, 41: The chromosomes now cluster and separate into two distinct groups. Note that a new, dividing membrane has been formed, making two new cells.

48, 51: The filaments appear again, the process is repeated, and four cells have been formed from the two earlier cells.

Strasburger's many observations and illustrations confirmed the validity of what had been a vague, intuited idea: that every living thing grows by cell division.

EDUARD
STRASBURGER
1844–1912

# Division of the Cell Nucleus

1882

*Observation*

*49*

# II
# Induction

Line mediates a silent conversation
between the draftsman and the
currents of his experience.
The draftsman attempts to
maintain a condition where the
senses meet directly with reality. . . .
He seeks the structure of appearances,
relatedness, and order.
—EDWARD HILL[1]

THE QUESTIONS "WHY?" AND "HOW?" are fundamental motivating forces in scientific endeavor. In contrast to the illustrations of direct observations in chapter I, this chapter presents examples from a variety of scientific disciplines that demonstrate how illustrations can suggest answers to these questions. They include an anthropologist's ingenious effort to understand the meaning of a primeval human's incisions on an animal bone (page 53); Charles Darwin's explanation of the self-fertilization of a common wildflower, a cowslip (page 61); the puzzling evidence of a "spiral force" operating in the growth of certain fauna and flora (pages 62–64); and the exquisite cellular and neuronal activity in humans (pages 70–73).

By bringing order and clarity to an illustration, particulars may suggest generalizations. Scientists must revise their explanations when they uncover a previously hidden aspect of a phenomenon. And since Nature does not "know" either clarity and order or vagueness and disorder, the dialectic is continuous.

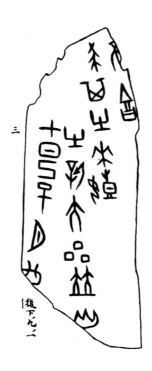

## The Sighting of a New Star

C. 1300 B.C.

T HE OLDEST KNOWN RECORD of the observation of a new star is marked in this inscription on a fragment of a bovine scapula. (The illustration here is a line drawing of the bone fragment and its ideograms; a photograph, with its tendency to flatten the shallow incisions, would have been difficult to decipher.)

Since astronomers in ancient China were also astrologers, they were expected to reveal the influences of heavenly bodies on earthly affairs. Their divinations guided kings and members of the nobility in their decisions on governing, waging war, the distribution of food, and other matters of state.

The inscription here records a unique coincidence: the appearance of a huge new star, a "nova," divined from reading cracks in the bone. The three steps standard in divination—the charge, the prognostication, the verification—are followed here. The columns read from top to bottom, beginning at the left:

*[An unknown astrologer/astronomer] divined: In the next ten days there will be no disasters.*
*The king read the cracks and said: "There will be harm; there will be the coming of alarming news. [If it be such and such a cyclical day], it will be inauspicious."*
*On the seventh day in the period dividing the night of* chi-ssu *[day six] and* kung-wu *[day seven], there was a new great star standing together with the fire star [Antares].*

Modern astronomers know that some distant, barely visible stars occasionally appear brighter; others may disappear; and the brightness or magnitude of some stars may suddenly increase. Such stellar explosions produce "novas"; extraordinarily powerful explosions produce "supernovas." Ancient records of the appearances of novas and supernovas are significant sources of information for the study of the ages and positional variations of stars, comets, meteors, and planets.

In addition to the scientific information it contains, this illustration is also noteworthy as an example of the transition from early Chinese pictograms to the ideograms in current usage. The individual glyphs on this bone fragment suggest references to real objects or phenomena, such as human figures, a bird in flight, a crisscrossing path, and fire.

P RIMEVAL MAN LEARNED to recognize cyclical events by following changes in the positions of celestial bodies in the night sky. Since the varying phases of the Moon could be observed night after night, notations of such observations developed into a method for marking the passage of time. Eventually, records of lunar phases and star positions enabled prehistoric humans to expect, or predict, the recurrence of events on Earth, such as tides and seasons.

The oldest records of the passage of time—in effect, calendars—may have been marks incised on bones by people living during the Upper Paleolithic period, 20,000 to 30,000 years ago. Paleontologists had long considered such markings to be decorations or records of successful hunts, but in 1965 this notion was challenged by the work of Alexander Marshack, a researcher at the Peabody Museum of Archaeology and Ethnology in Cambridge, Massachusetts.

This photograph is of a piece of animal bone found by French paleontologists in Le Blanchard rock shelter, in the Dordogne district of France, early in this century. The bone displays a series of incisions and shallow pits, cut in a curving, linear pattern with five turns. After examining the bone under a microscope, Marshack photographed it for further study, and concluded that the incisions mark the Moon's phases, invisible, waxing, full, and waning.

Marshack explains his diagram derived from the bone markings as follows:

*The sequence originates at the center left; the two marks represent the night of the last visible crescent and the first night of the invisible new moon (the black circle). Moving up to the right and curling back to the left, the full moon was recorded after it waxed, then faded and waned. Following the line around the curve and up to the right, four black dots represent the following new moon. The line curves downward and moves to the left, recording the moon's waxing and waning to another series of black dots, at the lower left (indicating another invisible moon phase); the line of the waxing phases continues to the right and curves to the waning and final invisible phase.*

The width of the entire group of incisions is approximately 1 3/4 inch (4.4 centimeters). Marshack was convinced that the pattern had been made purposefully, and that it could not be an ornament or decoration, but was indeed notational. The sequence must have recorded an early man's observations of three lunar months. Although his interpretations are disputed by some archaeo-astronomers, Marshack's work stands as a unique example of scientific iconology.

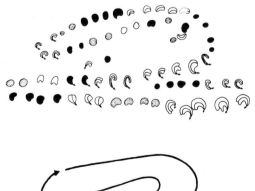

BEGIN

END

# Incised Bone Record

# Boar Hunt

**T**HIS VIGOROUS DRAWING representing the killing of a wild boar was found on the wall of the Remigia Cave, at La Gasulla in Spain. It may have been made by the boar hunters themselves or by a shaman to invoke Nature's continued benevolence.

The drawing is especially noteworthy because, by delineating the hunters' legs in extreme—almost impossible—extension (seen at left), the artist communicated both the sense of urgency and the extraordinary swiftness of the chase. The relative sizes of the hunters may indicate the importance of the leader, who set an example for the younger members of the hunting party. The largest figure's ankles and calves are decorated with tassels or fringes, possibly a sign of his leadership.

Just as illustrations of celestial phenomena serve astronomy, illustrations of human activity and behavior in preliterate antiquity serve the science of anthropology. The sites of drawings; the methods used (incision or painting on rock walls); the vitality of the figures; and often the compositions are all indicators for the reconstruction of the daily life and customs of a group, as well as its spiritual tenets.

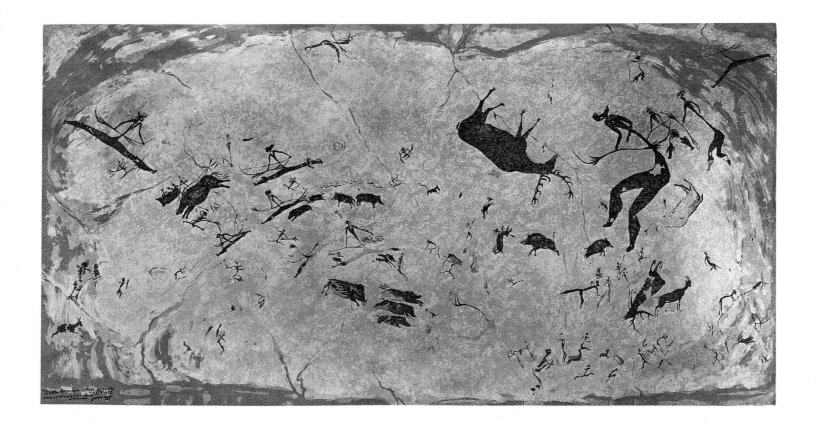

THIS IS ONE OF SEVERAL American Indian sandstone petroglyphs photographed at Nine Mile Canyon in Utah. Although the age and tribal origin of its shallow incisions have not been determined, anthropologists have found the welter of images a source of information about Native American customs.

Since Spanish explorers reintroduced the horse to the New World thousands of years after the extinction of a once-plentiful North American breed, the fact that some hunters are depicted on horseback suggests that the drawing was made after the arrival of the Spaniards. The purpose of the wheel-like objects has not been determined, but they also suggest a date after the Spanish arrival, since Native Americans did not use wheeled vehicles before then.

Several flayed, stretched skins, to be used for clothing or shelter, appear near the upper right. The incised curlicue border at the bottom of the drawing may signify water—a stream or river—near the hunting site. Throughout the image, the profusion of closely placed symbols contributes to the expression of a celebration of Nature's bounty.

American
Indian Deer
Hunt

C. SIXTEENTH CENTURY

*Induction*

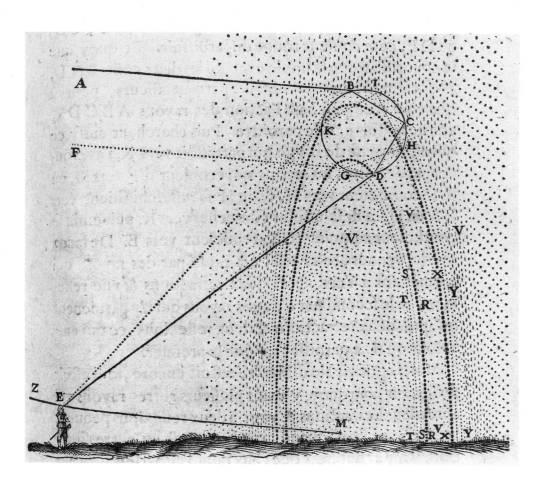

## Study of the Formation of a Rainbow

1637

DESCARTES, A SKILLED MATHEMATICIAN and scientific investigator, ingeniously combined two separate observations in this illustration to explain the formation of the rainbow's color spectrum.

The circle represents a glass sphere that Descartes had filled with water and that for his analysis represented the gross magnification of a single raindrop. Standing at position E, with his back to the Sun, Descartes could see the color spectrum by holding the sphere at an elevation of 42° above the horizon line, ZEM. This sighting occurred along the solid line ED. The Sun's rays entered the sphere along the line AB; they were refracted internally along the lines BC and CD, and moved out of the sphere to become visible along the line DE.

When Descartes raised the water-filled sphere higher, the spectrum disappeared and then reappeared when the angle reached 51° above the horizontal. However, he noted that the order of spectral colors was reversed. At the 51° angle, represented by the dotted line EK, Descartes's geometrical analysis revealed that three internal refractions would have occurred within the sphere: the Sun's rays would have entered along the line FG then and would have been refracted along the lines GH, HI, and IK.

Descartes concluded that the third refraction within the sphere—or raindrop—was responsible for the reversal (as in a mirror image) of the order of the colors in the spectrum. This reversed rainbow, called a "subsidiary" rainbow, is occasionally visible above the primary rainbow. Because of the third refraction within the waterdrops, and the consequent additional absorption of light energy, the subsidiary rainbow always appears as a weaker or fainter spectrum.

Descartes's explanatory illustration is particularly impressive because of his skill in combining the observation of the natural phenomenon with the geometry of a "magnified" raindrop—the water-filled glass sphere.

SWITZER, AN ENGLISH PHYSICIST, proposed this drawing as an explanation of the water cycle. The process begins when, induced by the Sun's heat, water vapor rises from the ocean to arrive at a layer of cooler air, where it condenses into steam and clouds (GI, F). The clouds (F) send down rainwater (G).

Wind blowing on the warm sides of mountains carries water vapor upward, while cool air on the shadowed sides condenses water vapor into rain (E, Q, X). Some rain seeps into the ground, where it collects (R).

Underground water empties into springs (at e) that flow back into the sea (V, T), where the cycle begins again.

# The Water Cycle

1729

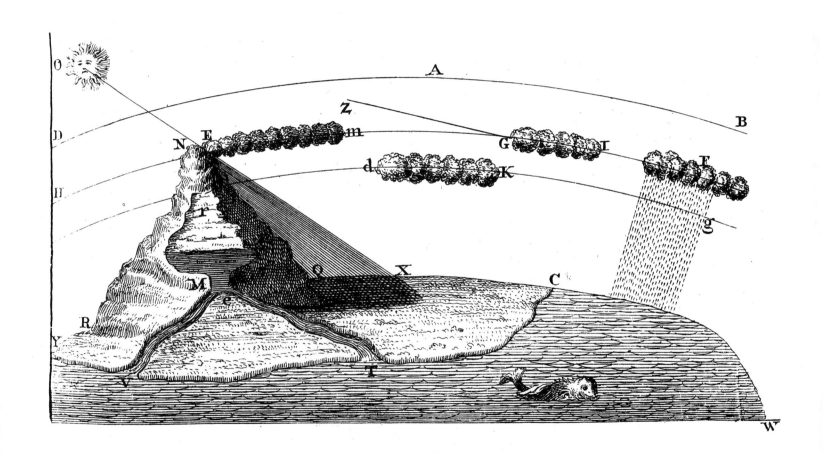

# The Mandrake Root

1438

BEGINNING WITH THE MOST primitive of peoples, the flowers, leaves, and roots of plants were the mainstay of medicinal treatment on every continent for several thousand years. In the first century A.D. the Greek physician Dioscorides gathered the information he had acquired on herbal medicine into the first extensive pharmacopeia, *De Materia Medica* (see page 26).

Physicians learned to use the mandrake root (*Atropa mandragora*) as an antiseptic, a narcotic, and a tonic. In the Middle Ages it was considered a soporific par excellence. Mandrake-root wine was recommended for insomnia, pain, and surgical antisepsis.

The root itself has the crude shape of a human form, with two separate lower extensions that suggest legs, a wide crown of foliage resembling the head, and armlike protuberances that extend from the root's "torso." This humanoid appearance led to the superstition that the mandrake root should never be dug up by a person, because its horrendous screams would kill the offender. Therefore, dogs were trained to uproot the plant, as this fanciful drawing illustrates. The herbalist kneels at the right, holding his hands to his ears to avoid hearing the mandrake's screams.

Lonicerus, a prominent physician in Frankfurt, included this woodcut in his *Herbal*, published in 1578. The illustration, which explains the scientific organization of a pharmaceutical process, is clearly the work of a highly skilled artist, who compresses the sequence of events that take place over a long period of time into a single elegant composition for teaching systematic herb cultivation and processing in a manner reminiscent of medieval art.

At the top center, a woman gathers herbs in the forest; the gardener prepares a place for a forest plant at upper right. At the lower right, a group of herbalists and physicians discuss the plant's utility.

In the lower center, the apothecary pulverizes the plant—which will be subjected to distillation— while a woman prepares herbs for the apothecary's mortar and pestle.

Finally, at the top left, we see a physician at a patient's bedside examining the dose of the herbal infusion before administering it.

Lonicerus's *Herbal* was highly respected by physicians. One and one-half centuries later, the great botanist Linnaeus (1707–1778) paid tribute to Lonicerus by naming a genus of plants *Lonicera*.

ADAM LONICERUS
(LONITZER)
1528–1586

# From the Plant to the Drug

1578

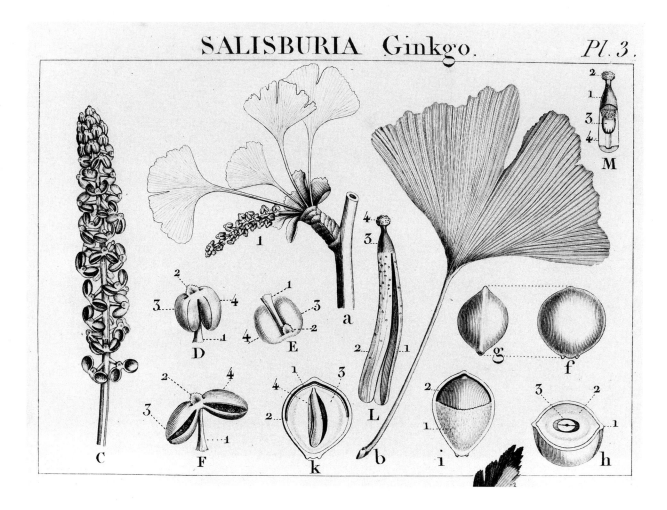

SALISBURIA Ginkgo. *Pl. 3.*

LOUIS CLAUDE
RICHARD
1754–1821

## The Ginkgo Tree

1800

RICHARD, A FRENCH BOTANIST, drew this chart of the parts of the exotic ginkgo tree in 1800. The tree, considered a sacred plant in China and Japan, was introduced to Europe from the Orient in the middle of the eighteenth century, and is still cultivated in the temperate zones of Asia and Europe, as well as America.

The ginkgo is a "living fossil," the only remaining species of the class *Ginkgoales*, which flourished during the Triassic period approximately 200 million years ago. Each of its leaves displays joined, twin "fans" (b). At an early stage of the ginkgo's reproductive cycle (C), a large number of stamens on a single stalk carry pairs of pollen sacs. The female bud (L) carries two seed structures (1 and 2), which evolve out of the twinned stem; details of the seed structure are revealed at M.

The seeds have the appearance of stone fruit; they are shown in four specific views (D, E, F, K) to enable positive identification. In the Orient, ginkgo seeds are a table delicacy.

Ginkgo trees are often used to line avenues because of their elegant appearance. When the ginkgo is in full leaf, it radiates a quivering aura of soft green light, which changes to soft gold before the leaves fall. They are exceptionally resistant to smoke, can withstand low temperatures, and require only minimal watering.

# Fertilization of Flowers

D ARWIN'S EARLY INTEREST in biology was encouraged by John Henslow, a professor of botany at Cambridge University who sensed his curiosity, intellectual power, and great aptitude for scientific analysis. It was Henslow who recommended Darwin (aged twenty-two) to the British Admiralty to serve as the naturalist on HMS *Beagle* for a scientific exploration of the Southern Hemisphere.

The five-year voyage (1831–36) enabled Darwin to study the flora and fauna of the coastal regions of Brazil, Tierra del Fuego, Chile, the Galápagos Islands, and the islands off the west coast of Africa. The speculations the trip engendered were to make it one of the most important in the history of biology.

Unfortunately, Darwin—vigorous and intrepid as a young man—suffered several insect bites on the journey, especially during a collecting expedition in the Chilean mountains. The resulting infection— diagnosed some thirty years after his death as due to the trypanosome parasite—caused an irreversible decline in Darwin's health (a recent biography suggests instead that Darwin may have suffered from a chronic psychosomatic malaise).

Darwin's mental powers were not affected by his illness, but his daily, semi-invalid routine was limited to a four-hour period devoted to specimen studies, followed by an occasional walk. He gathered flowers on walks, then studied and sometimes replanted them in his greenhouse.

Fig. 1—from *The Different Forms of Flowers*, the third book of Darwin's collected papers reporting his studies—shows two forms of the common cowslip, *Primula veris*, which grew in profusion near Darwin's Down house: the "long-styled" and the "short-styled." The "style" is the tube in the flower's reproductive system which connects the stigma, where the pollen is received, and the ovule, where the seed is fertilized. For his illustration Darwin cut away the calyx of each specimen to reveal the cowslip's reproductive organs.

At first, Darwin thought that the long-styled plants were female and produced seeds, while the short-styled specimens were male and produced only pollen. However, he quickly learned that both types produce seeds.

Fig. 2: In a series of experiments Darwin found that the short-styled flowers could be fertilized only by long-styled flowers, through *cross*-fertilization ("legitimate union"). *Self*-fertilization ("illegitimate union," in which the ovule was fertilized by pollen from the same plant) resulted in fewer and smaller flowers. Based on this observation, Darwin concluded that cross-fertilization must be advantageous for the species. He wrote that "No little discovery ever gave me so much pleasure as the making out of the meaning of heterostyled flowers."

Both drawings were prepared by the publisher of *The Different Forms of Flowers*, after Darwin's sketches.

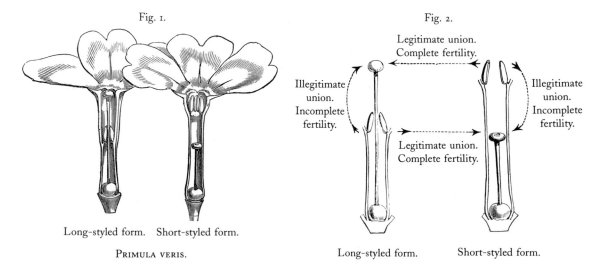

Fig. 1.

Long-styled form.   Short-styled form.

PRIMULA VERIS.

Fig. 2.

Legitimate union.
Complete fertility.

Illegitimate union. Incomplete fertility.

Illegitimate union. Incomplete fertility.

Legitimate union.
Complete fertility.

Long-styled form.     Short-styled form.

# Nautilus Pompilius (Chambered nautilus)

1832

Tʜɪs ʀᴇᴍᴀʀᴋᴀʙʟᴇ sᴇᴀ ᴄʀᴇᴀᴛᴜʀᴇ, a source of wonder to all who encounter it, is found in the southern Pacific and Indian oceans. Owen was the first to describe it scientifically.

Each of the nautilus's chambers is joined to the next by a thin siphon, which permits air to enter the chambers evacuated by the creature as it grows. The nautilus feeds as it traverses the ocean floor, its buoyant shell floating vertically above it. The interior of the shell is usually pink and opalescent.

Mid-nineteenth-century *Naturphilosophen* found in the chambered nautilus proof for their theory of Nature's aim—the perfection of form, demonstrated by the nautilus's spiral growth and its admittedly exquisite structure. This etching, executed after a drawing by Owen, was prepared for the publication of Owen's memoirs.

R.ᵈ Owen, del.

Zeitter, sc.

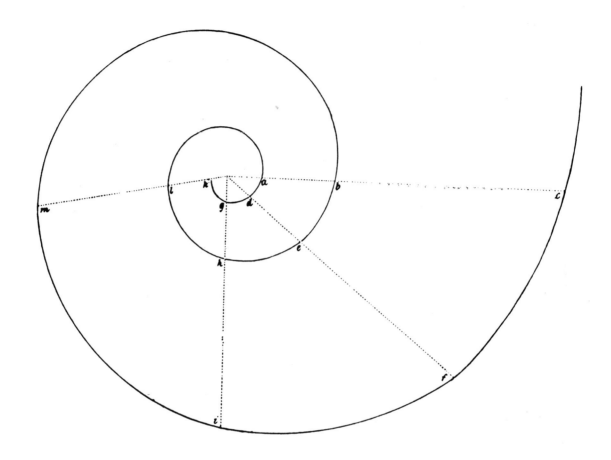

HENRY MOSELEY
1801–1872

MOSELEY, A PROFESSOR OF NATURAL PHILOSOPHY and astronomy at Cambridge University, applied his skill as a mathematician to the study of physical processes and natural forms. The pearly nautilus shell's sections, volumes, and spiral geometry were the subject of one of the studies he submitted to the Royal Society's *Philosophical Transactions*, which published it in 1838.

Through careful measurements and an illustration of a section of nautilus shell, Moseley showed that the sea creature's characteristic form develops as an "equiangular spiral." The dimension *ab* is one-third of the dimension *bc*, as are the ratios of *de* to *ef*, *gh* to *hi*, and *kl* to *lm*. This spiral, now known as a logarithmic spiral, is unique in that the figure grows larger without changing its shape.

Moseley's study verified the conjecture that the nautilus grows by the addition of shell and tissue to its terminal regions; the animal occupies only its shell's outermost chamber, and is thus able to exercise sensory, feeding, and other vital functions as its size increases.

Moseley's resulting generalization—that the growth energy required by living organisms is proportional to their mass—has since been applied to the study of plants as well.

## The Geometry of the Nautilus Shell

1838

*Induction*

## Spiral Form in
## a Pinecone

A PROFESSOR OF BOTANY at Oxford University, Church studied Scottish physicist James Clerk Maxwell's papers on electromagnetic force fields and concluded that analogous but opposing internal generative forces might be responsible for the spiral forms found in so many varieties of plants.

In this illustration of a transverse section of the apex of a pinecone, Church identified its overlapping spirals: five radiating counterclockwise and eight radiating clockwise. He numbered the individual seed pods in order to track their spiral succession as they appeared along the vertical edge of the pinecone.

S CHAEFFER, AN AMERICAN ZOOLOGIST, observed that an amoeba placed on a cylindrical surface always moved in a spiral path around the cylinder. To further study spiral movement, Schaeffer blindfolded a right-handed friend and instructed him to walk a straight line across a country field. Schaeffer plotted his friend's track, which described a clockwise spiral form until the blindfolded man happened to stumble on a tree stump.

## Spiral Path of a Blindfolded Man

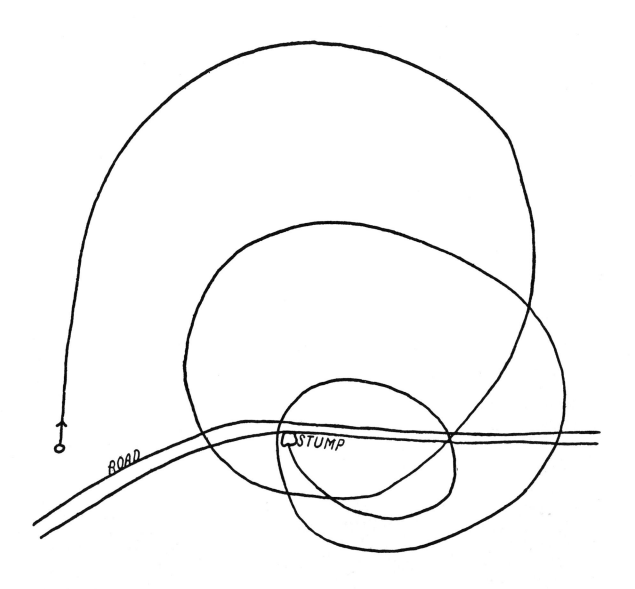

# Spiral Cloud System

1985

THIS ILLUSTRATION DISPLAYS Typhoon Pat in the western Pacific Ocean. The photograph was taken by the crew of the space shuttle *Discovery* on August 20, 1985.

Counterclockwise rotation is typical of storms that develop in the Northern Hemisphere; in Southern Hemisphere storms, the rotation is clockwise. A similar phenomenon of opposites generally occurs in human hair-growth patterns: men's hair forms a clockwise spiral; women's, the opposite.

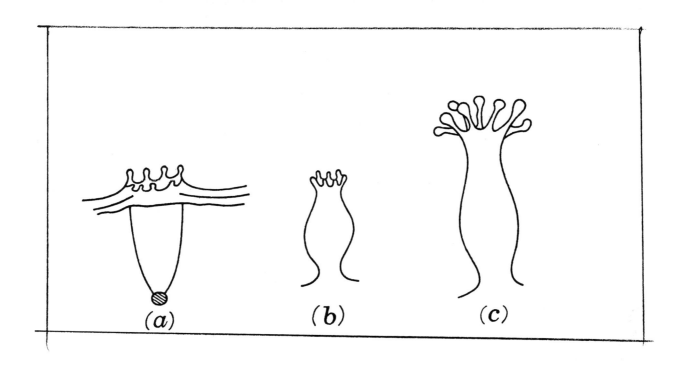

(a)  (b)  (c)

SIR D'ARCY
WENTWORTH
THOMPSON
1860–1948

## Liquid Splashes

1917

THOMPSON STUDIED ZOOLOGY at Cambridge University and became a professor of natural history at the University of Saint Andrews in Scotland, where he remained for sixty-odd years. During that time, he published a number of anatomical and descriptive studies of marine life, including a widely admired translation of Aristotle's *Historia Animalium* (The History of Animals) and a book on the forms of living organisms, *On Growth and Form* (1917), now considered a classic in biology.

Thompson used his mathematical talents to measure and speculate upon the shapes of horns, teeth, and tusks, jumping fleas and fish, buds and seeds, bee honeycombs and raindrops, soap films and oil bubbles, and the splashes formed by pebbles falling into water. All his studies display an underlying fascination with the search for order in natural phenomena.

These illustrations were chosen by Thompson to demonstrate graphically how a liquid splash (*a, b*) assumes the shape of a polyp (*c*), a small sea creature.

Thompson combined his meticulous observations and graphic demonstrations with eloquent commentaries. Even though subsequent biologists severely challenged Thompson's geometrical-morphological approach, the contemporary reader continues to be intrigued with the ideas of *On Growth and Form*.

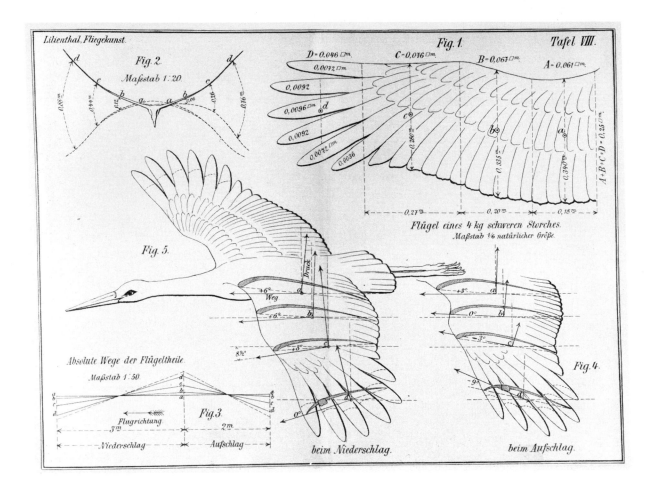

# Geometry of a Stork's Wing

1889

LILIENTHAL'S FASCINATION with the possibility of designing and constructing an aircraft for a human being began in his adolescent years and continued throughout his life. After serving in the German army during the Franco-Prussian War, he devoted himself to aeronautical studies and experimentation. In 1889 Lilienthal published his observations, calculations, and reports of his experimental flights in his book *The Science of Flight*.

Lilienthal studied the anatomy and flight of large birds and applied his observations to the design of gliders. In Fig. 1, Lilienthal measures the dimensions of a stork's feather layerings. Figs. 2 and 3 diagram the limits of the upstrokes and downstrokes of the wings. Fig. 5 reveals the cross-section contours of the massed feather layers, at successive distances from the body of the stork.

The shaded contours superimposed on the wings in Figs. 4 and 5 are especially significant. They reveal that Lilienthal had discovered that, in cross section, the top surface of an aircraft's wing should be longer than the bottom surface. If such a contour were supported by a strong internal structure, air would move more swiftly over the top surface and therefore be less dense than the air flowing below the wing's lower surface. The differential in air velocity and density between the upper and lower surfaces of the wing is the means by which "lift" is achieved. This requirement is recognized as a basic design factor in aeronautics.

Lilienthal is credited with having founded the science of aeronautics. In *The Science of Flight* he commented that "it is not given to man to fly easily in the air like birds. But the desire to do so gives us no peace." In 1891 Lilienthal made the first of his more than 2,000 glider flights. He was killed in 1896, when a glider he had fitted with a newly designed rudder crashed.

# Rhinoceros

DÜRER AND HIS OLDER CONTEMPORARY Leonardo da Vinci deliberately made the observation of nature a fundament of their work as painters. (Dürer stated in one of his notes: "Nature is the original measure of art.") Until the late eighteenth century, the word "art" had the simple meaning "craftsmanship" and did not carry the additional connotations it has today of "autonomous self-expression," or "the exploration of the *act* of 'making' art." Historians of science unanimously acknowledge da Vinci and Dürer as exemplars of the highest achievement in the craft of scientific illustration.

Dürer's *Rhinoceros*, however, was not drawn from direct observation. In this period, travelers and explorers in Africa and Asia brought back accounts of their observations eagerly read in Europe. Live animals and the heads and hides of hunted ones were often transported to European royal courts for the education and entertainment of the nobility, and for eventual study by naturalists.

Dürer's rhinoceros, which had been sent to King Emmanuel of Portugal as a gift from King Muzafar of Cambodia, arrived at Lisbon on May 20, 1515. King Emmanuel then shipped the rhinoceros to Pope Leo X, but the vessel sank en route to Rome. Fortunately, a Portuguese printer, Valentin Ferdinand, had made a sketch of the rhinoceros and sent it to Nuremberg, where Dürer had his studio and access to a printing shop. Dürer capitalized on the appeal of such an exotic animal by making and selling woodcut prints of it from his own sketch, based on Ferdinand's.

*Rhinoceros* was copied by many subsequent artist-illustrators and was considered an accurate description of the animal for a long time. Today, zoologists note that Dürer engaged in some whimsical conceits in his rendition.

Dürer's inscription in the top panel of the woodcut reads, in part:

*Its color is that of a freckled toad and it is covered by a hard, thick shell. It is of the same size as an elephant but has shorter legs and is well capable of defending itself. On the tip of its nose is a sharp, strong horn which it hones wherever it finds a stone. This animal is the deadly enemy of the elephant. The elephant is afraid of it because upon meeting, it charges with its head between the elephant's legs, tears apart his belly, and chokes him while he cannot defend himself. It is also so well armored that the elephant cannot harm it. They say that the Rhinoceros is fast, cunning, and daring.*

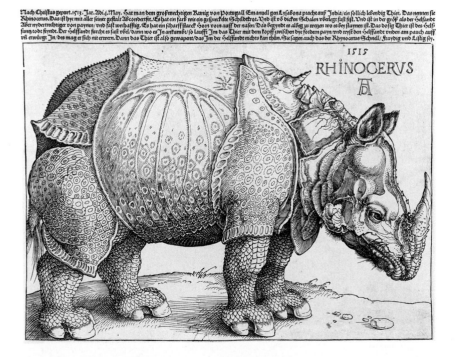

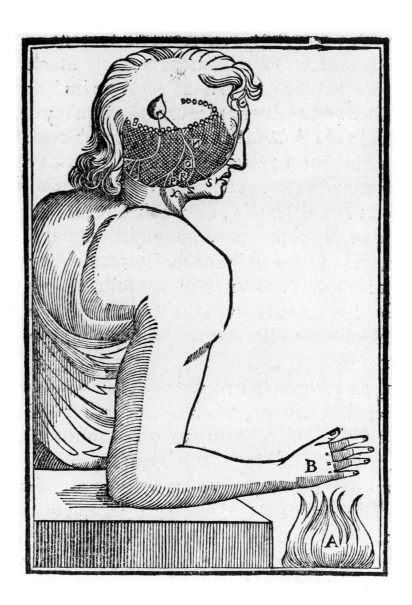

## Mechanical Response to the Heat of Fire

1664

Descartes, a mathematician and philosopher, approached the study of human physiology with a strong mechanistic bias: he believed that except for one, all processes in human life could be explained by the application of physical laws and an understanding of the structure of matter. The exception was an activity of the brain: thinking. In Descartes's view, the intellect was God's special gift to mankind. He thought that the mind existed outside the body and was independent of it, although mind and body could interact through the medium of the pineal gland.

Descartes proposed that this gland—a small structure situated deep in the brain—was unique to man, and that it permitted him to be aware of his connection to God, that is, to his soul. (The notion of the pineal gland's uniqueness to mankind was disproved several years later by the Danish anatomist Nicolaas Steno [1638–1686], who dissected and exposed pineal glands in lower animals.)

Descartes's explanation of the heat sensed by the hand is that it produces a motion of the "spirits in the hand's nerve tubes." This motion then produces a mechanical stimulation of the nerve tubes in the brain, which in turn affects the pineal gland (seen as a small pear-shaped area in the center of the skull). The pineal gland then activates a fluid that causes the muscles of the arm and hand to move the hand away from the flame.

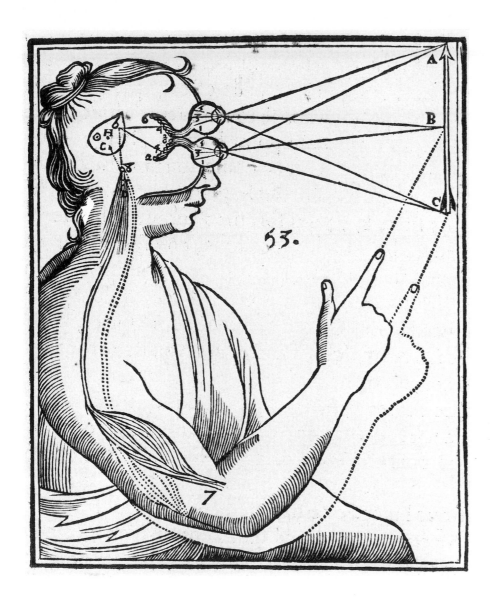

I N THIS DIAGRAMMATIC EXPLANATION of vision, Descartes placed the eyes one above the other. Light rays coming from an object (the arrow, ABC) enter the lenses, then proceed to the retinas and on to the optic nerves and the pineal gland in the center of the brain. Impulses from the pineal gland activate the muscles of the arm and hand, which generate the pointing gesture.

Anatomical studies in Descartes's era were limited by relatively crude dissection procedures, and examination of delicate, small anatomical structures was hindered by the poor quality of microscopes available at the time. Not until the nineteenth century, with its technological advances, was it learned that the optic nerves cross over to opposite sides of the brain before they reach the visual cortex, at the rear of the brain.

The Process of
Visual
Perception

1664

GIOVANNI ALFONSO
BORELLI
1608–1679

# Mechanics of the Human Body

1680

BORELLI STUDIED PHYSICS in Galileo's class at Pisa and became a professor of mathematics at the universities of Messina and, later, Pisa. He was introduced to the study of anatomy by a colleague, the physician and microscopist Marcello Malpighi (see page 43).

In the course of his work, it became evident to Borelli that the science of mechanics could be applied to the study of human and animal motion. His *De Motu Animalium* (On Animal Motion), a book of mechanical analogies, may be regarded as one of the most notable examples of the use of illustration to understand natural phenomena. Borelli's observations of muscular contraction and relaxation, and the load-bearing demand on the bones of the skeleton, are expressed as diagrammatic abstractions.

In this illustration:

Fig. 1 describes the conjunction of two levers (or bones), IFS and HDR, at pivot point C.

Fig. 2 shows how elastic bands (muscles) attached to the levers (at D and F) and to the pivot (B) might bring the levers close to each other.

Fig. 3 shows the elastic bands attached externally to the levers so that they can be "expanded."

Fig. 4 is a sketch of a twin-lever system, in which the two levers are of unequal lengths.

Figs. 5 and 6 demonstrate the muscle and bone configurations in two humans carrying different loads. The center of gravity for each load is delineated by the delicate vertical line that meets the ground at E. Significant portions of the skeleton of each figure are exposed, so that Borelli can demonstrate the lever systems pictured in Figs. 1 through 4.

Figs. 7 and 8 are studies of pulley arrangements, and Figs. 9 and 10 demonstrate the actions of the muscles that enable a human to hold a weight in an outstretched arm.

In *De Motu Animalium*, Borelli expressed his belief that "since the scientific understanding of all these things . . . is based mainly on geometry, it is correct to suppose that God used geometry in the creation of animal organisms, for this is the only science which enables man to read and understand God's handwriting in the animal world."

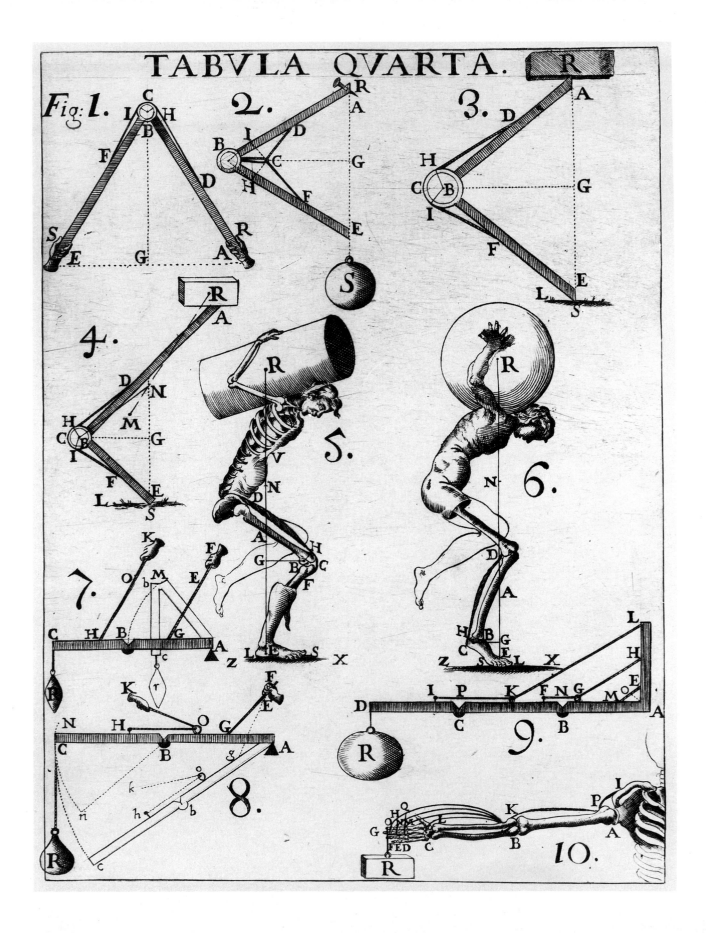

Camelopardalis.

GASPAR SCHOTT
1608–1666

# Camelopardalis

1667

BY THE MIDDLE of the seventeenth century, books of reports and descriptions of botanical and zoological exotica had become common reading matter for educated Europeans. This drawing, by an anonymous illustrator, is from a popular compendium of natural history by Gaspar Schott, a Jesuit scholar. The same animal is also illustrated in an earlier encyclopedia of natural history compiled by the Swiss physician Konrad von Gesner (1516–1565). Schott had access to scientific reports through his contacts with contemporaries such as Athanasius Kircher (see page 206), Christian Huygens, and Robert Boyle (see page 89).

The animal represented here, called a camelopardalis, looks *almost* like a giraffe, and in Schott's Latin text for this illustration he refers to an assertion by Pliny that the camelopardalis is the offspring of a camel and a panther!

Schott was not a scientist but an avid, industrious compiler—a popular encyclopedist. His *Physica Curiosa* describes and illustrates angels, demons, monsters, freaks, exotic animals, meteors, thunder, and lightning. It ends with a listing and denunciation of superstitions.

Haeckel, a physician and later a professor of biology at the University of Jena in Germany, was one of a number of late-nineteenth-century biologists who developed a theory—*Naturphilosophie*—that nature was purposeful and that it produced exquisite, symmetrical organic forms intended for man's aesthetic appreciation.

Haeckel went so far as to claim that protoplasm itself was gifted with a soul. With this bias, he "adjusted" his illustrations of specimens to demonstrate what he and his fellow *Naturphilosophen* may have wished to see. He invariably emphasized this precise symmetry of structure—even though such symmetries did not always exist in the specimens themselves. Subsequent biologists, however, more persistent in their search for objective accuracy, consider many of his studies pleasing but inaccurate reproductions of organic life.

# Specimens of Sea Urchins

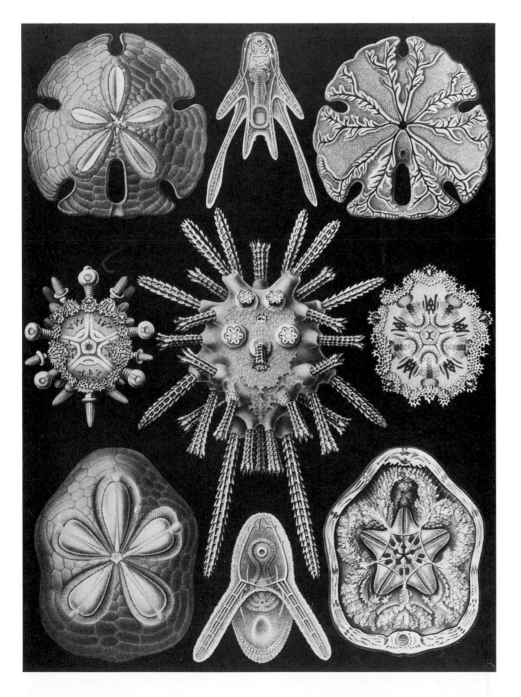

# The Human Fetus

THE FIRST OF THESE TWO ILLUSTRATIONS, presenting the birth of a child as analogous to the blooming of a flower, is from a copperplate engraving prepared about 1601 under the supervision of Giulio Casserius, a highly esteemed professor of anatomy at the University of Padua. Casserius had intended this and several other plates to illustrate a text on gynecology that remained incomplete at the time of his death. The illustration was first used by Casserius's pupil and successor Adrian Spigelius (1578–1625) in his book *De Formato Foetu*, which was published in 1626 with a dedication to Casserius.

The second illustration, from Jane Sharp's *Compleat Midwife's Companion*, was quite evidently copied, crudely, from Spigelius's book. The frequency of such "unauthorized" uses of previously published illustrations testifies—at the very least—to the expanding need for useful medical texts. The identity of

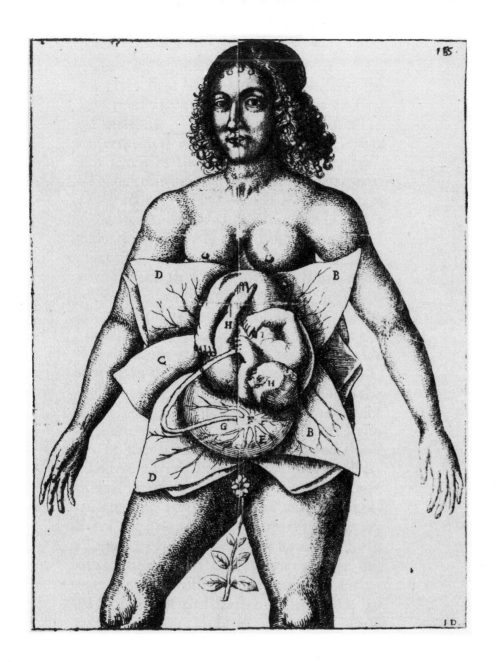

Jane Sharp is uncertain, although some historians of medicine suggest that this may have been the *nom de plume* of an English male physician.

Until the beginning of the sixteenth century, the medical profession often relied upon the writings of the second-century Greek physician Soranus of Ephesus for gynecology, obstetrics, and pediatrics. A French physician, François Mauriceau (1637–1709), published the first relatively reliable account of normal labor and postnatal treatment of the mother and child. In the lying-in room, usually filled with people scurrying about at various tasks, books like Mauriceau's would provide guidance to the midwife as well as some assurance to the mother. Well into the seventeenth century, the practice of obstetrics was mainly the province of women.

# The Human Fetus
## 1671

*Induction*

# III
# Methodology

The business and design of the Royal Society is: To improve
the knowledge of natural things, and all useful Arts,
Manufactures, Mechanick practices, Engynes and Inventions
by Experiments—(not meddling with Divinity, Metaphysics,
Moralls, Politicks, Grammar, Rhetorick, or Logick). . . .
In order to the compiling of a complete system of solid
philosophy for explicating all phenomena produced by nature
or art, and recording a rational account of the cause of things.
—ROBERT HOOKE[1]

I N ALL ERAS, AND IN EACH DISCIPLINE, experimentation reflects the scientist's desire to observe or experience the operation of cause and effect in order to verify or reject a hypothesis.

In science, the word "elegant" implies precision and simplicity, as well as the sense of coming closer to the truth. One of the most elegant experiments in history was conducted by Galileo Galilei (see page 22), at the age of twenty, while he was a student of philosophy and medicine at the University of Pisa.

Galileo arranged a series of pendulum experiments using strings of different lengths and balls of different weights in order to determine the time it took each string and ball to travel back and forth along an arc.

From these simple experiments, using the barest minimum of tangible resources, Galileo calculated the relationship between the length of a pendulum and the frequency of its oscillations. His formulation of the results is recognized as a basic law of mechanics.

# The Astronomer in His Observatory

1587

THE ASTRONOMER DEPICTED HERE, Tycho Brahe, was the last of the astronomers who made celestial observations with the naked eye. Brahe had studied law and philosophy at the University of Copenhagen, but after observing an eclipse of the Sun in 1560 he decided to study mathematics and astronomy. He also dabbled for a while with alchemy, and had considerable skill and success as an astrologer.

Tycho's first major contribution to astronomy was his description of the appearance of a new star and its implications for astrology, which appeared in a book, *De Nova Stella* (Concerning the New Star), which was published in 1573. He postulated that the nova he had observed demonstrated that Aristotle's idea of a fixed, unchangeable universe was no longer tenable. Instead, the universe must be seen as a dynamic system in which the celestial bodies are in continuous motion and in changing spatial relations with each other.

The publication of Tycho's book brought immediate fame to the twenty-six-year-old astronomer. He then decided to move to Germany, where the most advanced astronomical research was being conducted. To dissuade him from leaving, Frederick II, king of Denmark, sponsored a series of lectures by Tycho on astronomy and subsidized the construction of an observatory to be directed by him, on the island of Hven, situated between Denmark and Sweden. The buildings were completed in 1580 and were equipped with the finest available astronomical instruments. Several of those instruments are represented in this illustration.

Tycho's position in this engraving by Jan Blaen emphasizes his importance in the management of the tasks conducted in his observatory. Seated in the boundary of his great quadrant, Tycho points to the window on the left wall to identify the subject of his studies: the heavenly bodies. The great quadrant is inscribed with angular indexes extending from 0° (at the horizontal plane) to 90° (at the vertical plane). In the distant rooms, astronomers work with a variety of instruments: (upper left) a quadrant, rotatable about a vertical axis, with a movable sighting arm; (upper right) an altitude-sighting device; (middle rooms) conference tables and a celestial globe, showing the positions of stars; in the basement rooms, Tycho's alchemical ovens and retort apparatus. Books on astronomy and Brahe's observation records occupy two wall shelves, above the niche in which the model of Earth is situated. Two assistants make adjustments of the sighting angles, and a third sits at a desk recording Tycho's observations.

Tycho's observations were remarkably accurate—correct to two minutes of arc, which we know to be approximately the theoretical limit of unassisted visual measurement. His tables of observations of the motions of Mars and other planets provided Johannes Kepler with the data that proved crucially important in his corroboration of Copernicus's heliocentric scheme of the universe.

# QVADRANS MVRALIS
## SIVE TICHONICVS.

EXPLI-

# Observation of Sunspots

SCHEINER, A JESUIT PROFESSOR of Hebrew and mathematics at the University of Ingolstadt, claimed to have observed spots on the surface of the Sun in March 1611. Large sunspots had been observed previously but it was then believed that they were small satellite bodies rotating around the Sun. Scheiner's announcement was unusual because he claimed that the spots were surface phenomena on the Sun itself.

In the illustration, Scheiner is seated at a table holding a divider with which he plots the positions of the sunspots on a map of the Sun. The assistant adjusts the telescope and reads off the sunspot positions projected on an opaque screen. On the wall behind Scheiner hang three astronomical devices: an astrolabe, a quadrant, and a world map. The engraver has signed his name on the stool at the lower left of the illustration: "David Widman, Sculpt."

Scheiner's claim to have been the first to identify the sunspots as surface phenomena on the face of the Sun was challenged by Galileo, who asserted that he had made the same observation two years before but had not announced it publicly because he had continued his observations to make sure that the spots were surface manifestations, and not small satellite moons, as originally believed. Despite Galileo's scathing challenge to Scheiner's claim of priority, the Vatican supported Scheiner.

Immissione Refractoria composita.

Christoph Scheiner
Rosa Ursina Book III
Science Museum
London

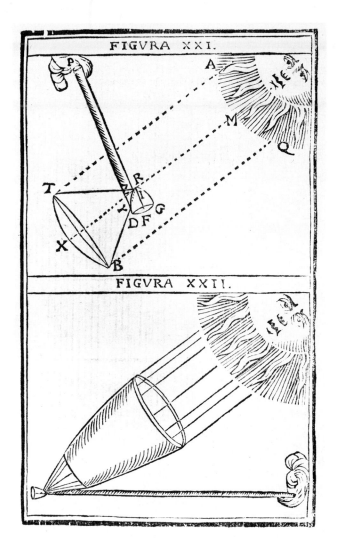

CAVALIERI, WHO JOINED the Jesuit order in 1615, became a skilled mathematician and geometer. His 1632 treatise deals with the use of mirrors, the geometry of conic sections, light, heat, cold, sound, and other "marvelous lore." This illustration describes his optical construction for the collection of heat rays from the Sun. The rays would then be focused to ignite cloth and wood, that is, the sails and hulls of enemy ships.

This use of the Sun's rays to start fires was known to both the Chinese and the Olmecs as early as 1000 B.C. The Roman historian Lucian reported that Archimedes had set fire to the Roman ships besieging Syracuse in 212 B.C. by directing the Sun's rays with mirrors. Such mirrors would have been assembled as a mosaic, to form spherical or parabolic reflectors. Cavalieri, eighteen centuries later, proposed the use of "burning mirrors," which would have been even more practical given the new glass-making technology of his period.

Fig. XXI: A concave mirror, TXB, faces the Sun along the axis XRM. The mirror focuses the reflected rays at R, where a small convex parabolic mirror, RDFG, directs the rays to ignite material in a cylinder, producing smoke at P.

Fig. XXII: A large concave parabolic primary mirror and a small convex parabolic secondary mirror concentrate the heat rays (along the horizontal path at the bottom of the illustration), demonstrating another version of the burning mirror.

The Geometry
of Burning
Mirrors

1632

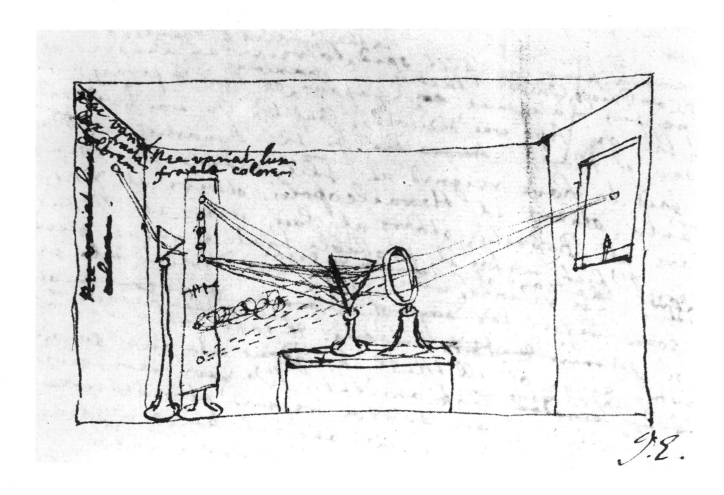

# Experiment on Light and Color

1665–66/1704

IN HIS FOREWORD to a 1952 reprint of Newton's *Opticks*, Albert Einstein paid this tribute to the great English scientist: "In one person he combined the experimenter, the theorist, the mechanic, and not least, the artist in exposition . . . his joy in creation and his minute precision are evident in every work and every figure."

Newton's studies in optics began in 1665, the year of his graduation from Cambridge University. His interest in experimenting with light and color may be traced to his observation of the color fringes he noted at the edges of his telescope lenses, which confused and sometimes obscured the field of vision.

In 1672 Newton sent the Royal Society a letter describing his work involving the use of a prism to analyze white light (sunlight), which the Society published in its *Philosophical Transactions* of that year. In it Newton described, in a meticulously written text (illustrated by his drawing, above) his procedure for demonstrating that white light "in itself is a Heterogeneous mixture of differently refrangible [refractable] Rays." The prism was positioned to allow a small circle of sunlight to fall upon it; the refracted rays appeared as bands of colors: red, orange, yellow, green, blue, and purple.

Newton did not rest with this discovery. He placed a second prism in the path of the spectral rays, and the colors recombined to produce a white ray of light.

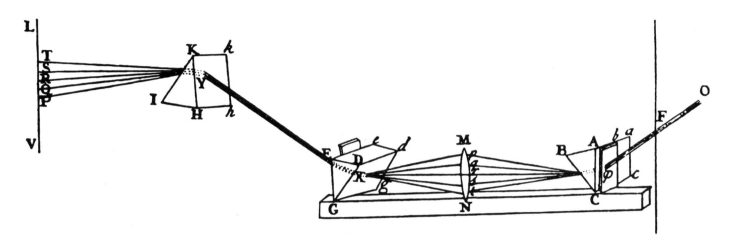

**Fig. 16.**

Newton's letter on light—the first of his scientific publications—provoked a vigorous debate among the society's members and other contemporaries. Newton's reluctance to engage in controversy may account for his delay in the publication of his major work on the nature of light, the *Opticks*, until 1704.

The illustration of the prism and spectrum experiment is described in Book One of Part II of the *Opticks*:

*At the right, sunlight (o) enters the prism through a hole in a window shutter, at F. The rays enter the prism ABC, and refraction by the prism generates the spectrum (p, q, r, s, t) that falls on the double-convex lens, MN.*

*The double-convex lens brings the separated spectral colors to a narrow focus at X, at the face of the second prism, E, D, G. These rays are refracted and produce a reconstituted beam of white light, moving from E to Y. At Y, a third prism H, I, K again bends the white beam to produce a spectrum of colors, T, S, R, Q, P, on a white board, LV.*

*This compounded beam of Light has the same appearance, and is endowed with all the same Properties as a direct beam of the Sun's Light, as far as my Observation reaches.*

## A Reflecting Telescope

1672

NEWTON'S EARLY *refracting* telescopes, like those of his contemporaries and predecessors, employed two lenses to magnify the viewed object: a large "objective" lens to collect the light from the distant object and a small magnifying lens to focus the image produced by the collecting lens for the observer's eye.

Because the edges of lenses behave like prisms, they refract the incoming light and produce an erratic display of color bands around the image of the object. Newton's early experiments with prisms were motivated by his observation of these color aberrations. Knowing that mirrors produced insignificant color aberrations, Newton developed a telescope truly novel for his time: a *reflecting* telescope utilizing mirrors. This is one of Newton's drawings for his revolutionary design, attached to an explanatory letter he sent to the Royal Society in early 1672.

A concave mirror (AV) is fixed to one end (at the left) of the telescope tube. Light from the observed object enters the tube at the opposite end (F), and is reflected and focused by its curvature to form an image on a small flat mirror positioned within the tube at D. The flat mirror is set at a 45° angle to direct an image to the observer's eye (drawn at the upper right at F) outside the tube.

The concave collecting mirror may be adjusted for optimum focusing by means of the screw threaded into the telescope support at M. The flat mirror's position may be adjusted for optimum focusing by sliding the inner cylinder (held by the ring HI) toward or away from the convex mirror. The telescope is mounted on a cradled sphere (S) to permit sighting at any desired viewing angle.

The concave collecting mirror was positioned approximately $6^{1}/_{3}$ inches from the angled, small plane mirror, and the system provided a magnification factor of approximately 38.

In the lower left of his drawing Newton showed how an ornamental crown atop a weathervane 300 feet away appeared when viewed by the reflecting telescope (A). By comparison, the ordinary refracting type of telescope produced the smaller image of the crown (B).

Immediately upon circulation of the announcement of Newton's revolutionary invention he was besieged with letters from eminent astronomers and telescope makers, requesting further technical information and suggesting improvements to his design. The concave collecting mirror remains a dominant feature of optical astronomical telescopes to this day.

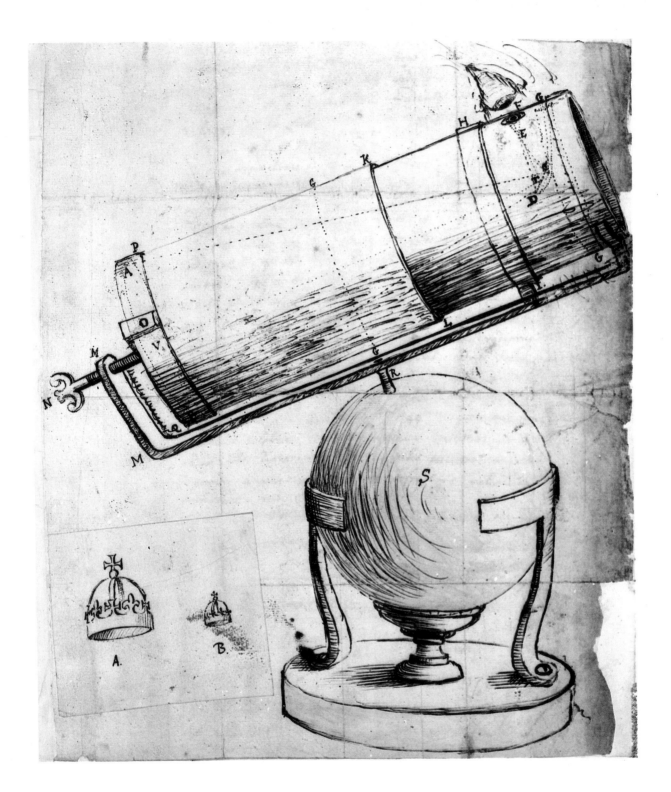

# The Solar
# Spectrum

FRAUNHOFER WAS A SELF-TAUGHT glassmaker and optician in Munich who became widely known for the high quality of his glass and optical instruments. In 1814, while testing his prisms in sunlight, Fraunhofer observed that the spectrum of refracted colors was marked by dark lines. Newton had not noted such lines in his prism experiments, probably because of the poor quality of the glass.

Fraunhofer carefully painted the spectral colors and recorded the positions of the dark lines, labeling them from A to I. Repeated tests confirmed his observation that the dark lines always appeared in the same positions in the spectral display. Above his record of the spectrum, the relative intensities of the colors were indicated by a graph.

When Fraunhofer studied the spectra of starlight by placing a prism at the focal point of his telescope, he found these spectra patterns differed from those in sunlight, with differently spaced dark lines. He was unable to explain the presence of these lines, and his reports were treated as of little importance. It was not until thirty-nine years later that Fraunhofer's dark lines were recognized as indicators of specific chemical elements in the incandescent bodies observed by the spectroscope.

In 1859, the German physicist Gustav Kirchhoff (1824–1887) reported that chemical elements, when heated to incandescence, produced individual spectra marked by similar dark lines. For example, incandescent sodium produced a spectrum marked by a pair of dark lines that correspond to the position of Fraunhofer's "D" line. Kirchhoff concluded that the Sun's light must pass through sodium vapor on its path to Earth, and therefore sodium must be an element in the Sun's chemical composition. With this discovery of the presence of Earth's elements in the Sun, the new science of astrophysics was founded.

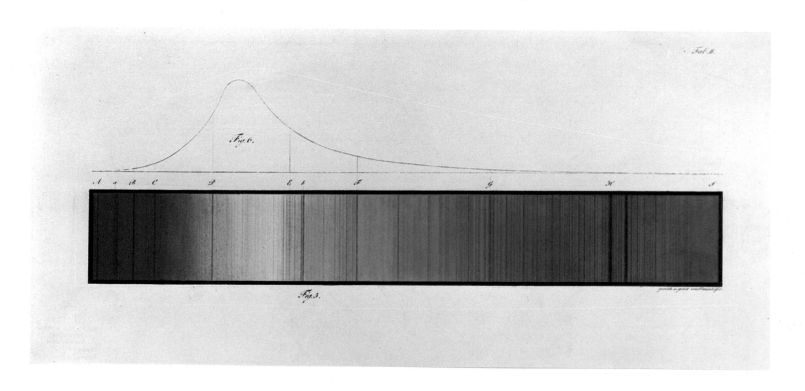

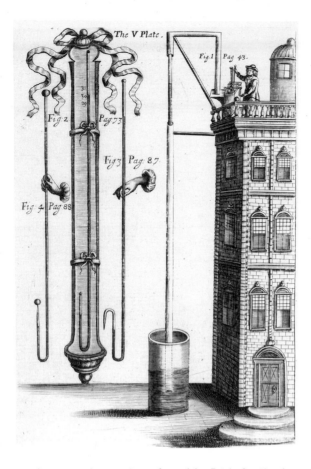

Robert Boyle was born into an aristocratic and wealthy Irish family. As a child he displayed the attributes of genius and at the age of eight was sent to Eton, having already learned to read and speak Greek and Latin. At the age of fourteen he studied the works of Galileo, and by eighteen he had absorbed the writings of Descartes. Educated by private tutors, Boyle was never subjected to the institutionalized science teaching of the great universities.

Experimental science often appeals to the inquisitive, individualist spirit, and Boyle became an avid and brilliant experimentalist who argued that all experiments should be reported as completely and as soon as possible so that other scientists could repeat and corroborate the conclusions. This conviction distinguished Boyle as one of the founders of the modern approach to scientific endeavor.

In accordance with these principles, Boyle carefully supervised the illustrations of his experiments, which are models of clarity and precision, making his experiments easily repeatable. Two of these experiments, illustrated here, were designed to prove that the height to which a fluid could be forced to rise by pressure or suction must vary inversely to the fluid's specific gravity. ("Specific gravity" is the ratio of the weight of a given substance to the weight of an equal volume of a reference substance, usually water.)

At the right (Fig. 1), Boyle stands on the roof of a four-story house, pumping water from a barrel to a height of 33 feet, the maximum to which it could be raised.

At the left (Figs. 2, 3, and 4), Boyle's barometer, a glass tube containing mercury, described as 8 feet long, demonstrates the same law as the water experiment.

The water rose because its specific gravity is lower than that of mercury. The air in the barometer tube was gradually compressed until an equilibrium occurred. The expansion and compression of air, as Boyle observed, was similar to the expansion and compression of coiled metal springs when subjected to an external force. Boyle coined the term "the spring of the air" to describe this effect.

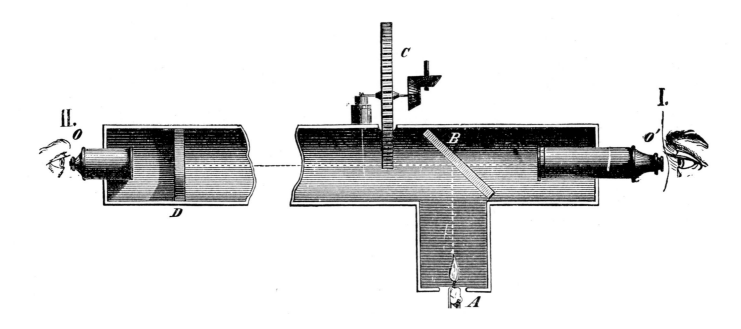

## Measuring the Velocity of Light

1849

Fizeau, the son of an eminent Paris physician, studied medicine but became a physicist instead. His dominant interest was the study of light, and at the age of thirty he devised an ingenious experiment intended to measure its velocity.

The velocity of light had been approximated by the astronomical observations and calculations of Olaus Roemer (1644–1710) in 1676, and by James Bradley (1693–1762) in 1725. Galileo had tried to measure the velocity by flashing lights between two hilltops, but his attempt was thwarted by the inadequacy of his apparatus and the lack of a precise clock.

In 1849, Fizeau devised an optical system in which a rotating toothed disk would interrupt a light beam. (The mechanical-optical system is depicted in the figure above.) This device was positioned on a hilltop 5 miles distant from an observation position (at $O$), at the left of the diagram.

A source of light was positioned at $A$ and directed at a half-silvered mirror ($B$). The observer at $O$ set up his telescope to be directly in line with the light coming from $B$.

Fizeau had arranged a counter to measure the rotational velocity of the toothed disk ($C$). When the rotational velocity reached a specific rate, light passed through each gap in the toothed disk and was reflected back to the observer at $O'$. Fizeau then rotated the toothed disk faster, until the interruptions of

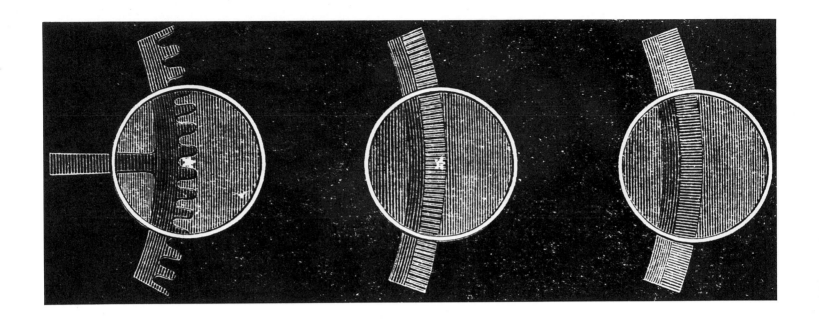

the teeth blocked the light beam reflected from $D$. In the illustration above Fizeau demonstrates how the increase of the rotational velocity caused a "narrowing" of the gaps between the teeth until the light beam was eclipsed.

Because the rotational velocity of the toothed disk could be measured, and the number of teeth was a constant, Fizeau could calculate how long a time was required for a gap to be replaced by a tooth. That brief time would be equal to the time required for the light beam to travel 5 miles from the light source, at $B$, to the reflecting mirror at $D$, and return to the first mirror at $B$. Despite the relative simplicity of his apparatus, Fizeau was able to calculate the velocity of light at approximately 195,000 miles per second. His calculation proved to be only about 5 percent higher than that obtained from later, more refined experiments.

In 1882 the American physicist Albert Michelson (1852–1931) arrived at the figure of 186,320 miles per second. Michelson continued to refine his experimental approach, and in 1933, after his death, studies of his data established the velocity at 186,271 miles per second. Later experimenters defined the velocity of light at 186,282 miles per second. Such information is of crucial importance to astronomy, and Fizeau is honored for his original, ingenious method, which served as a model for future experimenters.

# "Magdeburg Spheres"

1654

G UERICKE'S MOST FAMOUS, successful experiment, the "Magdeburg Spheres" experiment, which was observed by the German emperor Ferdinand III, is illustrated in this elegant drawing. Two heavy metal hemispheres (Fig. I) were fitted with greased gaskets (Fig. II) and then joined to make a sphere (Fig. V). After the sphere was evacuated of air, two teams of horses were whipped to pull at the two hemispheres (Fig. III). The hemispheres could be separated only after air was allowed to reenter the sphere.

Guericke's demonstrations showed that air had weight and density. Several years later Robert Boyle (see page 89) and Robert Hooke (1635–1703) (see page 42) improved on Guericke's vacuum pump. Their experiments established the basic properties of air: that it is a gas whose compressibility is inversely proportional to pressure; and that its volume is inversely proportional to pressure.

ACCORDING TO ARISTOTLE's principles of physics, if an object were to be set in motion by a continuing, propulsive force, its speed would increase as the surrounding medium's density decreased. The extension of this idea led to the notion that in a vacuum—a space devoid of matter—the object would move at an infinite speed. Aristotle could not encompass the possibility of infinite speed, so he concluded that the "medium" that envelops Earth could never be empty of matter, a concept that was expressed as "Nature abhors a vacuum."

Guericke, a German engineer and mayor of Magdeburg, decided to challenge Aristotle's theory. His early experiments, in 1646, using small vessels evacuated of air by a pump he designed, demonstrated that it was indeed possible to "create" a vacuum. He showed that if a bell were placed under a jar from which all the air had been removed, its ringing could not be heard; similarly, candles would be immediately extinguished, and animals could not live.

Three of Guericke's subsequent experiments continued this line of exploration:

Fig. I: Water was gradually pumped out of the filled barrel, with the expectation that the evacuated space could not contain air after the water was removed. The experiment failed, because only a small amount of water could be pumped out before air rushed through the cracks between the barrel staves into the partially evacuated barrel.

Fig. II: Guericke had a metal sphere constructed of two carefully joined hemispheres. The pumpers labored vigorously to evacuate the air from the vessel but the thin metal of the hemispheres collapsed with an explosive sound.

In another experiment (above), Guericke attached a glass bottle containing only air (the vessel on the left windowsill) to the metal sphere. The sphere was partially evacuated of air, and when Guericke opened the connecting valve (just above the glass bottle), the rush of air from the bottle into the sphere was so sudden that the bottle was shattered by the implosion.

OTTO VON GUERICKE
1602–1686

# "Nature Abhors a Vacuum"

1641

# How Water Is Drawn up the Trunks of Trees

1727

HALES WAS A CLERGYMAN by profession and a chemist and botanist by avocation. During this period, dabbling in the sciences was a conventional pastime for Englishmen having some degree of leisure, and botany was a favored—and useful—scientific endeavor.

Hales was, however, much more than an amateur. He had mastered Isaac Newton's mechanics, and employed a similarly rigorous, quantitative approach in his botanical experiments. These contributed significantly to the understanding of rates of plant growth, the use of air for the nourishment of plants, the distillation of fresh water from ocean water, and the use of sulfur dioxide as an insecticide in grain cultivation. Hales also invented the first practical device for the measurement of blood pressure. His original and important reports to the Royal Society earned him election to this entity in 1717.

Hales's 1727 *Vegetable Staticks* was the last book to receive Newton's imprimatur as the Society's president (he died later that year). Hales's expository text resonates with echoes of Newton's literary style—clear, definitive, and logical. He explained the experiment illustrated here:

EXPERIMENT XXI.

*August 13. In the very dry year 1723, I dug down 2 1/2 feet deep to the root of a thriving baking Peartree, hand layed bare a root 1/2 inch diameter* n *(Fig. 10). I cut off the root at* i, *and cut the remaining stump* i,n *into the glass tube* d,r, *which was an inch diameter and 8 inches long, cementing it fast at* r; *the lower part of the tube* d,z *was 18 inches long and 1/4 inch diameter in bore.*

*Then I turned the lower end of the tube* z *uppermost, and filled it full of water, and then immediately immersed the small end* z *into the cistern of mercury* x; *taking away my finger, which stopped up the end of the tube* z. *The root imbibed the water with so much vigor, that in 6 minutes time the mercury was raised up the tube* d,z *as high as* z, *viz. 8 inches.*

*The next morning, at 8 o'clock, the mercury was fallen to 2 inches height, and 2 inches of the end of the root* i *were yet immersed in water. As the root imbibed the water, innumerable air bubbles issued out of* i, *which occupied the upper part of the tube at* r *as the water left it.*

The illustrator/engraver recorded his initials, "S.G."

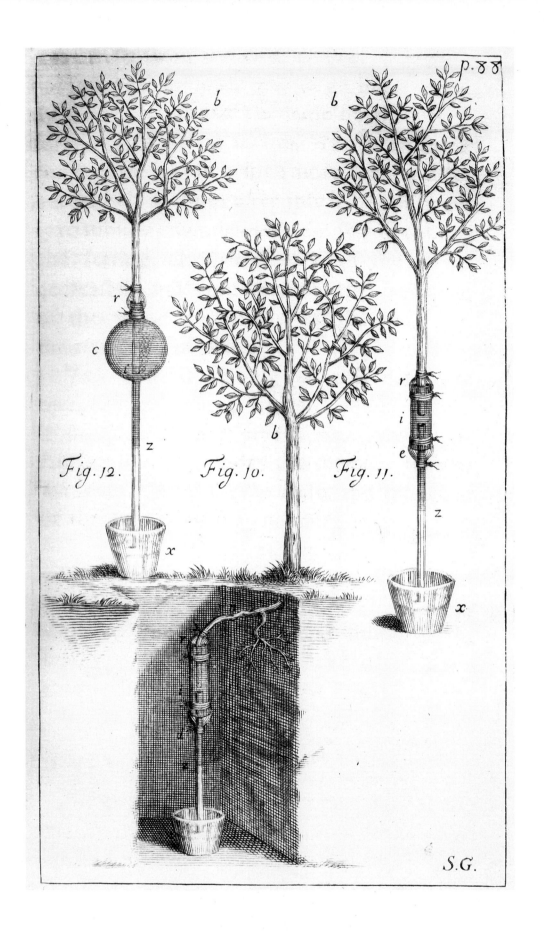

Fig. 12.  Fig. 10.  Fig. 11.

S.G.

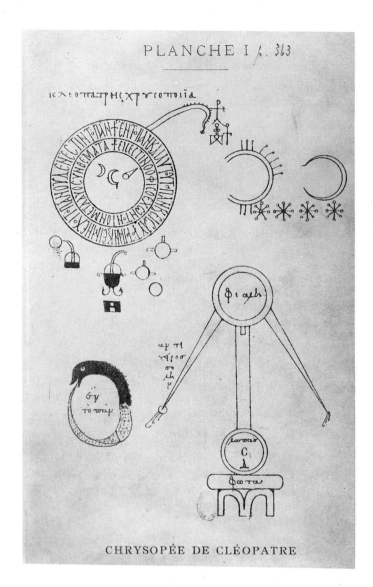

PLANCHE I p. 363

CHRYSOPÉE DE CLÉOPATRE

# Chrysopeia (Gold Making)

FOURTH CENTURY A.D.

"CLEOPATRA" WAS A WOMAN ALCHEMIST who may have used that pseudonym to avoid persecution. The persecution of alchemists is supposed to have begun when the practice was centered in Alexandria. At this time, Theophilus, archbishop of Alexandria, ordered the destruction of the Temple of Serapis, where the study of medicine and alchemy flourished; he based his action on the biblical curse put on any search for knowledge that might equip man to rival the Creator.

Cleopatra's book on gold making was written sometime during the fourth century A.D., and was preserved in a manuscript of the tenth and eleventh centuries. This illustration is her chart for the gold-making procedure.

At the upper left, the Greek text in the circular bands reads: "One is all, by him is all, and for him is all, and in him is all. The Serpent is one; he has two symbols, good and evil." At the center of the circular bands are the alchemical symbols for silver, gold, and quicksilver (mercury). Directly below the circular bands are drawings of vessels, like retorts, used in the alchemist's laboratory. The Serpent is seen consuming its tail, divided in darkness and light, the symbol of eternal recurrence. To the right of the Serpent, Cleopatra has drawn a "cosmic oven," with a heating furnace below a double-spouted retort. The seven- and eight-branched stars at the upper right symbolize both the god and the element Mercury.

Cleopatra left no record of a successful experiment in gold production.

*Methodology*
96

UNTIL THE EARLY YEARS of the twentieth century, ownership of mines and hoards of precious metals was a critical measure of a ruler's power. Scientists and technicians who had mastered the experimental and engineering techniques of mining and metallurgy were highly esteemed, and occasionally honored by appointments to positions on the ruler's technical staff. Lazarus Ercker was such a metallurgist; he was designated chief superintendent of mines and "control tester" for the kingdom of Bohemia in 1567.

The evidence of Ercker's qualifications is to be found in his book, *Mineralischen Ertz und Bergwerks Arten* (On Mineral Ores and Mining Techniques), which was published in 1575. Ercker's book, with Agricola's *De Re Metallica* (see pages 98–99) and Biringuccio's *Pirotechnia*, were the indispensable handbooks for mining engineers through the eighteenth century.

Gold miners occasionally uncover veins of mercury—"liquid silver" or "quicksilver"—which is often found in combination with other precious minerals. The ores are separated from these "amalgams" by a succession of processes shown in this illustration.

A worker (M) attends a furnace at the rear of the processing room. He heats the ore to extract the gold, which will be formed into briquets. In the middle of the room another worker (F) pulverizes the amalgam using a mortar and pestle to extract the mercury, which will be purified by passage through a series of vessels. In the foreground, a third worker (G) squeezes mercury through a leather bag to remove sedimentary particles.

# Processing Gold and Mercury Ores

1575

# Mine Ventilation

1556

AGRICOLA's *De Re Metallica* (On Metals) is one of the classics in the history of science and technology. Published in 1556, it served as a basic textbook in the mining profession for at least two centuries. (In 1912 it was translated from the Latin into English by Herbert Hoover—then known only as a world authority on mine engineering—and his wife, Lou Henry Hoover, a metallurgist.)

Agricola received a medical degree at the University of Ferrara, after studying philosophy and the natural sciences at Leipzig, Bologna, and Padua. He established his first medical practice in Joachimstal, a small, thriving mining city in Saxony. His patients included many miners who suffered illnesses unique to their work, and Agricola's interest was eventually drawn to the study of the mining profession itself. In 1531, Agricola moved to Chemnitz, a larger city, where mining dominated the economic life. By 1546, his fame as a physician was honored by the duke of Saxony, who appointed Agricola mayor of Chemnitz.

*De Re Metallica* was the result of some twenty years of study, interviews, and personal observations of the mining profession. The book summarizes virtually all of the sixteenth-century practical lore of mining: prospecting; assaying ores; mine construction; mine ventilation systems; the classification of minerals by the criteria of solubility, homogeneity, color, and hardness; and the effects of erosion—all treated with meticulous clarity. The underlying viewpoint is that of a physician's pragmatism: Agricola states that "those things which we see with our eyes and understand by means of our senses are more clearly to be demonstrated than if learned by means of reasoning."

For the 586-page book, Agricola hired artists to execute 291 illustrations of the various mining activities "lest descriptions which are conveyed by words should either not be understood by men of our own times, or should cause difficulty to posterity." The original drawings used by the woodcut engravers were made by Basilius Wefring of Joachimstal, where Agricola had begun his medical practice. Seven of the woodcuts were signed by Rudolph Manuel Deutsch, a Swiss engraver and painter; only one is signed by another engraver, Zacharias Specklin. The remaining 283 engravings are unsigned. The work of illustrating the book took five years and delayed its publication until 1556, one year after Agricola's death.

Three types of ventilation machines are described in this neatly composed illustration. At the top, a man and a horse turn the toothed wheel (P), which in turn lifts the tops of a pair of bellows through the cams. In the middle, a horse (feeding from the basket) turns a wheel (H) with his forelegs to pump the bellows situated behind the structure at G. At the bottom, a man treads on pedals to force air from the bellows to the crouching miner.

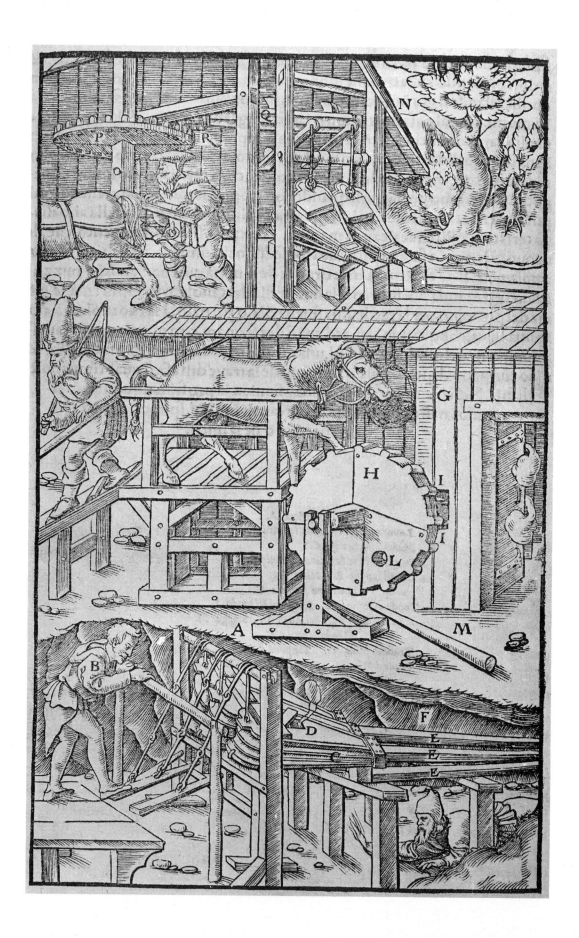

## Magnetizing an Iron Bar

1600

GILBERT, ONE OF THE MOST prominent physicians in London, was appointed, in 1601, practitioner to Queen Elizabeth I and, after her death, to King James I. Like many other physicians of his time, he was curious about scientific matters beyond the practice of medicine.

Gilbert's fascination with magnetic phenomena began during his student days at Cambridge University, and they engaged his attention to the end of his life. His book *De Magnete* (On Magnetism), published in 1600, was the most comprehensive treatment of the subject since the investigations of Peregrinus (born about A.D. 1240) almost 400 years before. *De Magnete* is unique in that it reports the results of Gilbert's numerous experiments and dispels many of the superstitions and fantasies that had accumulated about the subject of magnetism. Galileo praised Gilbert as a pioneer—like himself—in the experimental approach to scientific investigation.

The clarity and precision of the illustrations in *De Magnete* are typified by this woodcut: the intense experimenter hammers a heated iron bar, which is placed on the anvil so that its ends point to Earth's magnetic north (*septentrio*) and south (*auster*) poles. When the iron bar cooled, it was magnetized. Gilbert concluded that Earth itself could be considered a magnet, with lines of magnetic force extending from each pole. (The true positions of Earth's magnetic poles were later charted as magnetic inclinations—at some distance from Earth's geographic poles—by Johan Carl Wilcke in 1766.)

AFTER SEVERAL YEARS of practice as a physician and anatomist in Paris, Guidi was commissioned to organize the first medical faculty of the College of France, where he taught until his death. Guidi was also the author of three books on surgery and medicine.

In this illustration Guidi demonstrates a simple, although discomforting, method for treating an injured spine by reduction of pressure on the vertebrae. The bindings around the patient's legs, hips, torso, and head were to allow the fullest possible extension of the spine.

According to the great German medical historian Karl Sudhoff, the illustrations for Guidi's and other sixteenth-century medical texts have their origins in early Greek manuscripts.

The book was printed on a press owned by Guidi's friend Benvenuto Cellini; the illustrations were drawn by two Renaissance artists, Jan Santorinos and Francesco Primaticcio. We can therefore assume that, for at least several hundred years in Europe, treatment for such disorders remained unchanged.

## Straightening the Spine

1544

COMMENT. III.          279

f iiij

# Removal of a
# Skull Fragment

# Resetting a
# Fractured Arm
# Bone

1517

SOME OF THE EARLIEST EXAMPLES of medical illustration by woodcuts are to be found in Gersdorff's *Feldtbuch der Wundartzney* (Fieldbook of Wound Surgery), published in Strasbourg in 1517. It contains numerous illustrations of the treatment for fractures, amputation procedures, and antisepsis by various methods—all based on Gersdorff's forty years of experience as an army surgeon.

The device illustrated below is intended for the extraction of a bone fragment from the brain following a skull fracture. A long pointed screw is attached to the embedded bone fragment, which may be extracted by turning the butterfly nut directly under the wheel-headed screw handle.

The illustration at right, from the same book, offers an explicit demonstration of the traction procedure for resetting a fractured arm bone, a procedure that is essentially similar to modern practice.

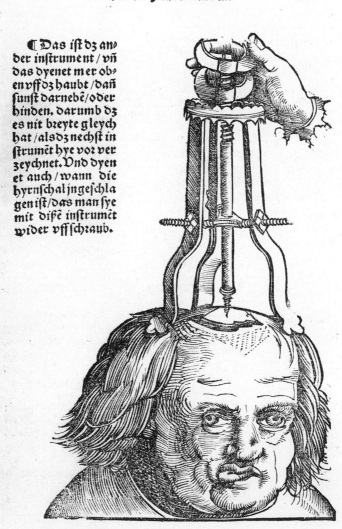

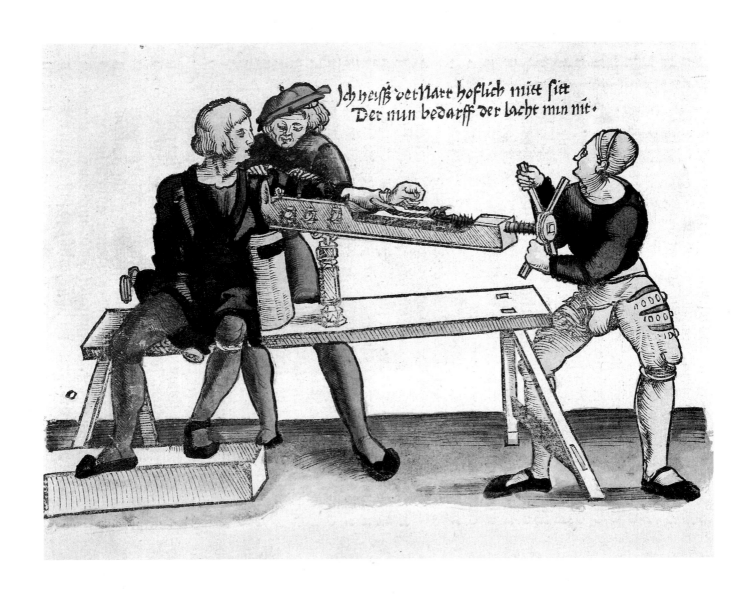

Ich neyſß der Narr hoflich mitt ſitt
Der nun bedarff der lacht min nit·

# Obstetrical Procedure

1580

ONE OF the most neglected aspects of medical practice, until the mid-eighteenth century, was obstetrics. Many women who experienced normal labor succumbed to puerperal fever or convulsions.

As a rule, women in labor were attended only by midwives. Jacob Reuff's book on pregnancy and birth for the instruction of physicians and midwives was read aloud at the onset of labor, for the guidance of both the mother-to-be and the midwife.

In this illustration, the woman in labor is seated in the standard birth chair. At the rear of the room, two astrologers plot the horoscope of the child as it is born.

B ARTISCH WAS BORN to a peasant family in Königsbrück, a few miles from Dresden, Germany. His family's impoverished circumstances prevented his pursuit of an academic training in medicine, but he became a successful barber-surgeon in Dresden. He performed cataract surgery proficiently and claimed success in treating strabismus (crossed eyes) by the method illustrated here.

The mask was perforated with eye slits positioned to urge the eye muscles to assume normal lengths and tensions. The duration of this treatment would, of course, vary with the severity of the patient's condition. The book in which this illustration appeared, *Augendienst* (Treatment of the Eye), is believed to have been written by a scribe, since Bartisch was unable to write.

GEORG BARTISCH
1535–1606

Mask for
Correcting
Crossed Eyes

1583

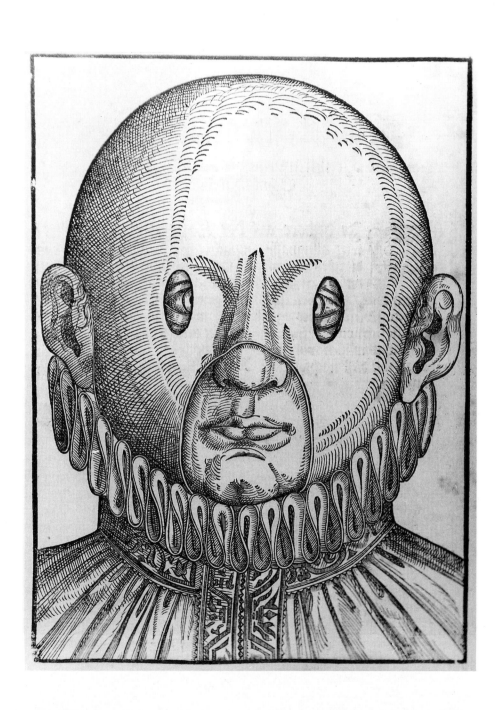

# Oral
# Thermometer

1625

S ANCTORIUS, A PHYSICIAN especially interested in the application of physics to the study of human ailments, practiced in Padua. His is the first drawing known of a practical oral thermometer, made of glass tubing, which he invented.

The device required the patient to maintain contact with the instrument for at least 20 minutes in order to obtain a reading. The vial at the bottom contained mercury, like those of contemporary thermometers, and graduations on the tube provided quantitative measures of the patient's body temperature.

The true and lively Pourtraicture of Valentine Greatrakes Esq:
of Affane in y County of Waterford, in y Kingdome of Ireland
famous for curing several Deseases and distempers

For many centuries, healing by stroking a patient was considered to be an effective treatment because it made use of the supposed phenomenon of "animal magnetism." An early record of a cure by touching is found in a chronicle written by Helgald, an eleventh-century monk, in which Robert the Pious (996–1031) wrought such cures. The personal power of healing by the laying on of hands was an attribute of the classic gods, and also of Jesus. It became one of the divine rights of kings. English and French monarchs practiced this treatment until the seventeenth century. The so-called Royal Touch was considered especially beneficial for scrofula, the swelling of the lymph glands of the neck, an ailment that occasionally subsides without treatment.

Valentine Greatrakes was a soldier in Cromwell's army during the invasion of Ireland. Greatrakes's cures of disoriented and depressed soldiers came to the attention of Cromwell, who gave Greatrakes permission to practice the method. Eminent scientists, such as Robert Boyle (see page 89), testified to the efficacy of Greatrakes's treatment. This illustration shows him in the process of curing a boy. The figures outside the window represent patients arriving for treatment.

Laying On of
Hands: "Animal
Magnetism"

1670

*Methodology*

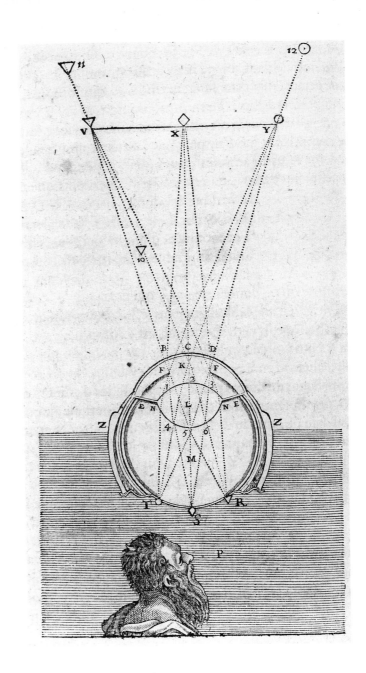

RENÉ DESCARTES
1596–1650

# An Analysis of the Eye

1637

RENÉ DESCARTES SHOWED, in his *La Dioptrique*, how refraction of light rays by the eye's lens produces an inverted image on the retina. (See also his other work on perception, page 71.) The object viewed is the horizontal line, marked V, X, and Y. After entering the eye and passing through the iris (F, K, F), the lens (L) refracts the rays so that the image is inverted at the retina (T, S, R). Descartes shows the inversion by transposing the *object* marks—triangle, diamond, and circle—to their opposite positions at the retina.

He arrived at this finding by a simple experiment: after removing an eye from the carcass of an ox, he scraped out the retina of the eye so that it became transparent. Holding the ox eye in front of his own, he could see an inverted image of the scene before him on the transparent rear surface of the ox's eye.

Such observations and experiments provided some physical basis for the understanding of visual perception. Subsequent investigators learned that the inverted image received by the retina is reinverted, point by point, in the brain's visual center. In the visual cortex of the brain, the image assumes the same geometrical arrangement—top-to-bottom and side-to-side—as the actual viewed object or scene.

JENNER, A PHYSICIAN WHO PRACTICED in the farming region of Gloucestershire, is believed to have gotten the idea of vaccination from a chance remark of a dairymaid: "I can't take smallpox for I have already had cowpox." (The actual word "vaccination," first used by Pasteur in the nineteenth century, is derived from the Latin for cow, "vacca.")

In 1788 Jenner began to notate his observations of patients afflicted with the dreaded smallpox; in May 1796 he decided to attempt his first experiment.

It was from a blister like this on the hand of a milkmaid who had contracted cowpox that Jenner extracted the cowpox fluid. He then injected it into the arm of a healthy eight-year-old boy, James Phipps.

Eight weeks later, Jenner injected smallpox serum into the boy's arm. The boy did not contract smallpox. Jenner injected the smallpox serum again into the boy's arm, several months later, but the boy continued to display no signs of the characteristic rash or pockmarks of smallpox. By 1798 Jenner had immunized twenty-three people successfully and recorded his findings in a small book. The book establishes Jenner's thesis that an inoculation with cowpox protects the patient from smallpox. Jenner's work was taken up by physicians throughout Europe and eventually achieved worldwide recognition as the best method for combating the devastations of smallpox.

# Inoculation Against Smallpox

1796

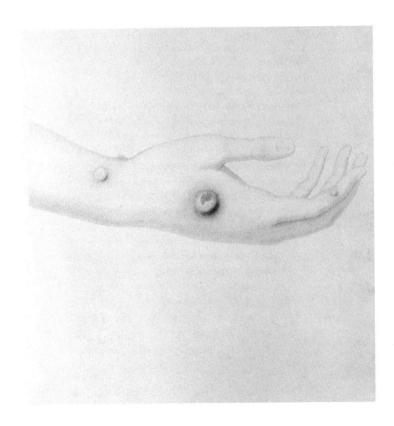
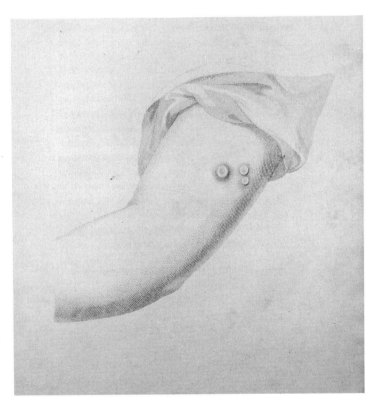

# On the Motion of the Heart and Blood

1628

THE ERRONEOUS TEACHINGS of the physician and writer Galen (c. A.D. 130–200, see pages 36 and 168) on the circulation of the blood persisted for fourteen centuries before William Harvey conducted his experiments. Galen's influence was supported by church doctrine, and most physicians hesitated to challenge his ideas by experimental verification. It was Harvey's experimental conclusions that triggered the eventual demise of Galen's authority.

Harvey was educated in medicine at the universities of Cambridge and Padua. Sixteen years of medical practice in London, from 1602 to 1618, brought him renown as a sensitive diagnostician and effective clinician, and he was appointed court physician to King James I in 1618. After James's death, Harvey remained in the service of James's son, the ill-fated King Charles I, beheaded in 1649. During his service at court, Harvey had both the leisure and material support for numerous experiments, involving the vivisection of a snake, dogs, a deer, chicks, sheep, and other farm animals.

By 1615, he had developed a clear understanding of the circulation of the blood, supported by his skill in dissection, his meticulous quantitative analysis, and his mechanistic view of life processes. Thoroughly aware of the revolutionary impact of his discoveries, Harvey patiently verified each of his proofs during the following twelve years. In 1628 he published the full results of his work in *De Motu Cordis et Sanguinis in Animalilbus* (On the Movement of the Heart and Blood in Animals), a book that is now regarded as the major contribution to seventeenth-century medicine and biology.

Galen had declared that blood flowed in a to-and-fro motion, powered by the dilatation of the heart and arteries; that blood flowed through pores in the heart's septum, the tissue that divides the heart into two ventricles; and that blood was supplied by the liver.

Harvey's experimental investigations and conclusions may be summarized as follows: the blood flows only in one direction, because of the valves in the heart and veins. As both ventricles of the heart contract and expand simultaneously there is no pressure difference between them, and thus the blood cannot flow through the pores in the septum.

From the dissection of cadavers it was known that the human heart has a capacity of about 2 ounces of blood. In life, pumping at about 65 beats per minute, the hearts pumps about 8 lbs. of blood every minute. Multiplied by the number of minutes in a day, the quantity of blood is obviously far too great (11,520 lbs.) for the body to produce from ingested food, as was previously thought. Harvey severed the main artery of a sheep and measured the amount of blood expelled in a unit of time. He postulated that the blood must circulate in a closed system, out of the right ventricle through the body, and returning to the left ventricle. In this vivid drawing, Harvey demonstrated his proof that the blood undergoes "a motion in a circle":

Figure 1: When the arm is tied off above the elbow (A), nodes—blockages—appear at the sites of the valves in the veins (B, C, D, E, F).

Figure 2: When the blood is pressed out of the vein, between O and H, and a finger is placed at H, the vein remains empty.

Figure 3: When a second finger is then pressed down along the vein toward O, the vein remains empty.

Figure 4: If a finger is placed at L, and a second finger presses along the vein from L to N, the vein continues to remain empty.

Therefore, Harvey asserted, the blood must flow through the veins back to the heart.

The ultimate connection between arteries and veins, Harvey suggested, would be found in the capillaries, even though he was not able to observe them. (Capillaries were eventually seen by Marcello Malpighi [see page 43] under his microscope, several years after Harvey's death.) As he expected, Harvey's radical explanation of the blood circulation system was vigorously denounced by some contemporary anatomists and physicians.

WILLIAM HARVEY
1578–1657

# On the Motion of the Heart and Blood

1628

THE ERRONEOUS TEACHINGS of the physician and writer Galen (c. A.D. 130–200, see pages 36 and 168) on the circulation of the blood persisted for fourteen centuries before William Harvey conducted his experiments. Galen's influence was supported by church doctrine, and most physicians hesitated to challenge his ideas by experimental verification. It was Harvey's experimental conclusions that triggered the eventual demise of Galen's authority.

Harvey was educated in medicine at the universities of Cambridge and Padua. Sixteen years of medical practice in London, from 1602 to 1618, brought him renown as a sensitive diagnostician and effective clinician, and he was appointed court physician to King James I in 1618. After James's death, Harvey remained in the service of James's son, the ill-fated King Charles I, beheaded in 1649. During his service at court, Harvey had both the leisure and material support for numerous experiments, involving the vivisection of a snake, dogs, a deer, chicks, sheep, and other farm animals.

By 1615, he had developed a clear understanding of the circulation of the blood, supported by his skill in dissection, his meticulous quantitative analysis, and his mechanistic view of life processes. Thoroughly aware of the revolutionary impact of his discoveries, Harvey patiently verified each of his proofs during the following twelve years. In 1628 he published the full results of his work in *De Motu Cordis et Sanguinis in Animalilbus* (On the Movement of the Heart and Blood in Animals), a book that is now regarded as the major contribution to seventeenth-century medicine and biology.

Galen had declared that blood flowed in a to-and-fro motion, powered by the dilatation of the heart and arteries; that blood flowed through pores in the heart's septum, the tissue that divides the heart into two ventricles; and that blood was supplied by the liver.

Harvey's experimental investigations and conclusions may be summarized as follows: the blood flows only in one direction, because of the valves in the heart and veins. As both ventricles of the heart contract and expand simultaneously there is no pressure difference between them, and thus the blood cannot flow through the pores in the septum.

From the dissection of cadavers it was known that the human heart has a capacity of about 2 ounces of blood. In life, pumping at about 65 beats per minute, the hearts pumps about 8 lbs. of blood every minute. Multiplied by the number of minutes in a day, the quantity of blood is obviously far too great (11,520 lbs.) for the body to produce from ingested food, as was previously thought. Harvey severed the main artery of a sheep and measured the amount of blood expelled in a unit of time. He postulated that the blood must circulate in a closed system, out of the right ventricle through the body, and returning to the left ventricle. In this vivid drawing, Harvey demonstrated his proof that the blood undergoes "a motion in a circle":

Figure 1: When the arm is tied off above the elbow (A), nodes—blockages—appear at the sites of the valves in the veins (B, C, D, E, F).

Figure 2: When the blood is pressed out of the vein, between O and H, and a finger is placed at H, the vein remains empty.

Figure 3: When a second finger is then pressed down along the vein toward O, the vein remains empty.

Figure 4: If a finger is placed at L, and a second finger presses along the vein from L to N, the vein continues to remain empty.

Therefore, Harvey asserted, the blood must flow through the veins back to the heart.

The ultimate connection between arteries and veins, Harvey suggested, would be found in the capillaries, even though he was not able to observe them. (Capillaries were eventually seen by Marcello Malpighi [see page 43] under his microscope, several years after Harvey's death.) As he expected, Harvey's radical explanation of the blood circulation system was vigorously denounced by some contemporary anatomists and physicians.

J ENNER, A PHYSICIAN WHO PRACTICED in the farming region of Gloucestershire, is believed to have gotten the idea of vaccination from a chance remark of a dairymaid: "I can't take smallpox for I have already had cowpox." (The actual word "vaccination," first used by Pasteur in the nineteenth century, is derived from the Latin for cow, "vacca.")

In 1788 Jenner began to notate his observations of patients afflicted with the dreaded smallpox; in May 1796 he decided to attempt his first experiment.

It was from a blister like this on the hand of a milkmaid who had contracted cowpox that Jenner extracted the cowpox fluid. He then injected it into the arm of a healthy eight-year-old boy, James Phipps.

Eight weeks later, Jenner injected smallpox serum into the boy's arm. The boy did not contract smallpox. Jenner injected the smallpox serum again into the boy's arm, several months later, but the boy continued to display no signs of the characteristic rash or pockmarks of smallpox. By 1798 Jenner had immunized twenty-three people successfully and recorded his findings in a small book. The book establishes Jenner's thesis that an inoculation with cowpox protects the patient from smallpox. Jenner's work was taken up by physicians throughout Europe and eventually achieved worldwide recognition as the best method for combating the devastations of smallpox.

Inoculation
Against
Smallpox
1796

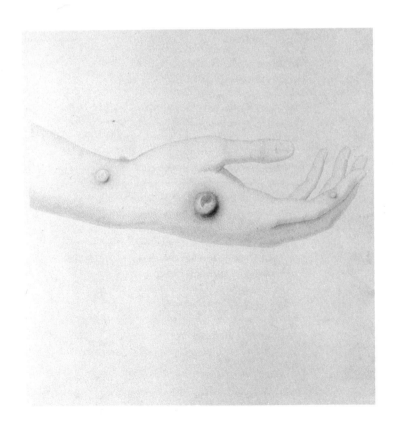
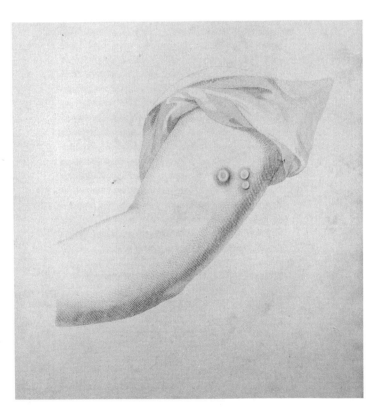

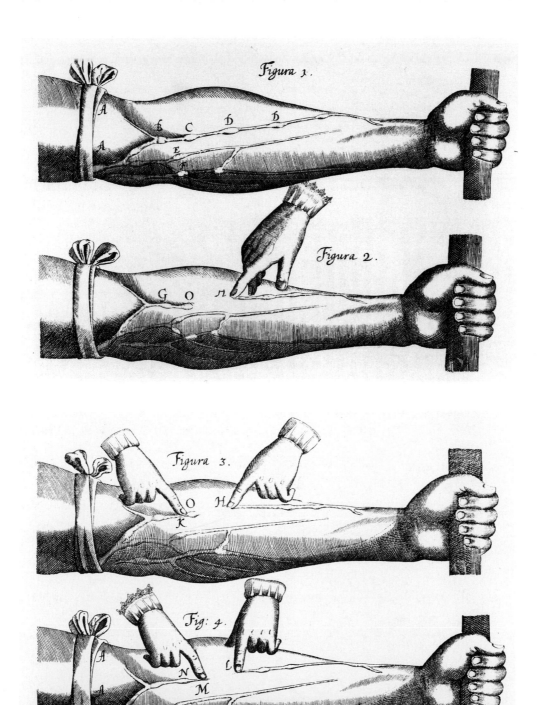

# An Electrical Generator

1672

ELECTROSTATIC PHENOMENA have been observed in everyday life for thousands of years; these include lightning, the sudden stiffening and sparking of hair as it is combed, crackling streaks of light from the tops of ships' masts, and the unique attracting power of substances like amber.

Some investigators, notably Robert Boyle (see page 89) and William Gilbert (see page 100), began to study electrostatic charges but were defeated by the seemingly mysterious and inexplicable causes of the phenomena. It was Guericke whose curiosity was sustained and who had the ingenuity to devise a causative agent—an electrostatic generator—for the first time.

Guericke's device was technically quite simple. He had noticed that pieces of sulfur displayed an attracting power similar to amber. Guericke made a ball of sulfur by melting it and pouring it into a spherical glass container. When the sulfur had cooled, the glass shell was broken and an iron rod was inserted to provide a rotational axis.

To generate the electrostatic charge, the sulfur ball was lightly touched by Guericke's dry hand as the ball was rotated. The charged ball could then be transported for demonstrations, as in Fig. VI, where the sphere attracts a falling feather, faintly visible at *a*.

Guericke investigated both the attraction and repulsion powers of his generator. He tried simple manipulations, by momentary contacts of the charged sphere with bits of paper, feathers, threads, etc., and learned that attraction and repulsion could be predicted from the manner and number of such momentary contacts. He also noted that roaring and creaking sounds could be heard when the charged sulfur ball was held close to the ear, and that it could "exercise its virtue through a linen thread an ell [45 inches] or more in length, and there attract something."

Guericke's published investigations initiated an avalanche of experiments in electrostatics during the eighteenth century. The distribution of reports, illustrations, and diagrams contributed importantly to the eventual mastery of the secrets of electricity.

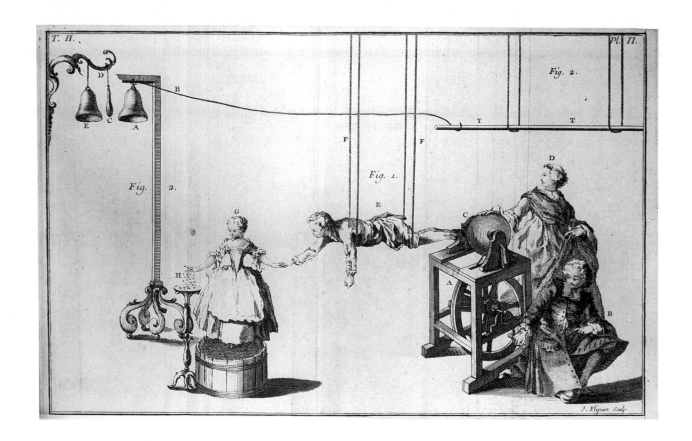

WATSON, A BRITISH PHYSICIAN, conducted a number of experiments involving human beings as conductors of electrical charges. His findings were published in Paris, in 1748, in a book that contained a number of startling illustrations of his potentially dangerous experiments, like the one reproduced here. Such experiments prepared later investigators for their studies of animal electricity, even though the dangers of severe electric shock were as yet not fully appreciated.

In Fig. 1, a young man (B) turns a crank that rotates a glass sphere (C), while the sphere is lightly touched by the woman (D). The electric charge is transmitted from the glass sphere to the shoes of the suspended boy (E), who is held by silk ropes (F, F) above the ground. The boy's hand touches the left hand of the girl (G), who stands on a tub of dried tar (known to be an insulator). She holds her hand just above the surface of a pedestal strewn with chaff (H). The electric charge on the girl's hand attracts the chaff, which moves up and away from the pedestal surface.

Another demonstration, labeled Fig. 2 (at upper left and right), shows a gun barrel (T, T) that has received an electric charge. The charge is transmitted by a wire (B) from the gun barrel to a bell (A). The charge on the bell momentarily attracts the suspended clapper (C), which then swings between the two bells (A and E) and produces a jingling sound.

The illustration, which was engraved by J. Flipart, was Plate II of Watson's book on the properties of electricity.

Aside from the antic charm of the demonstration, the illustration shows the importance of insulating materials like the silk ropes and the tub of dried tar. Watson continued his experiments in electrostatics and recorded several observations of the distances traversed by electric charges: 1,200 feet across the Thames River; an 8,000-foot circuit at Stokes-Newington, using Earth itself as a conductor. Watson's longest transmission was a 4-mile circuit by which he attempted to determine the transmission speed of the electric charge. It was reported as "nearly instantaneous."

SIR WILLIAM
WATSON
1715–1787

# Electrostatics Demonstration

1748

## The Leyden Jar

1745

BENJAMIN FRANKLIN
1706–1790

## Experiments and Observations on Electricity

1751

I N 1744, IN BOSTON, Benjamin Franklin attended a demonstration of electricity given by a Dr. Spencer, a traveling British lecturer. Franklin had received reports on the progress of the electrical science from a London friend, Peter Collinson, and Dr. Spencer's lecture so impressed him that he decided to embark upon his own investigations of the dazzling, newly discovered phenomenon. By this time Franklin had gained considerable means, from his publishing and printing ventures, and he turned to electrical experimentation with his usual enthusiasm and concentration.

Franklin purchased Dr. Spencer's electrical demonstration apparatus in 1746 and repeated the demonstrations for his own edification and satisfaction. By July 1747 he was able to report to Collinson the results of an original investigation and conclusion. This, the first of Franklin's numerous contributions to the science of electricity, described the efficacy of a pointed metal rod "in drawing off and throwing off the electrical fire."

Among the devices Franklin had purchased from Dr. Spencer were several "Leyden jars"—so-called because their inventor, Musschenbroek, was a professor of mathematics and physics at the University of Leyden, in Holland, at the time of the invention, which Musschenbroek reported in January 1745.

In this illustration, Musschenbroek (at the right) generates an electric charge by rotating a glass sphere while touching it with his fingertips. The charge travels through the iron bar suspended horizontally at the center to a loop of wire that leads downward to the water in a glass jar, the Leyden jar.

The young man at the left (reportedly named Cuneus, a student working with Musschenbroek) supports the jar in his right hand, which was moistened with water. The young man's left forefinger draws a powerful electrical shock when it approaches the iron bar. The Leyden jar was the first device capable of *storing* electrical energy, and was very instrumental in advancing eighteenth-century electrical science; it is now called a "condenser" or "capacitor."

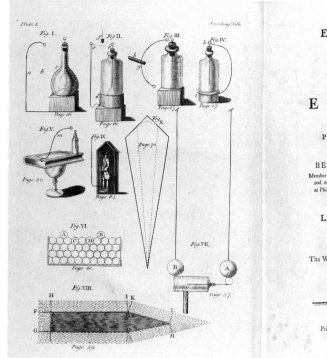

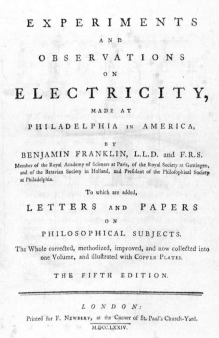

EXPERIMENTS

AND

OBSERVATIONS

ON

ELECTRICITY,

MADE AT

PHILADELPHIA IN AMERICA,

BY

BENJAMIN FRANKLIN, L.L.D. and F.R.S.

Member of the Royal Academy of Sciences at Paris, of the Royal Society at Gottingen, and of the Batavian Society in Holland, and President of the Philosophical Society at Philadelphia.

To which are added,

LETTERS AND PAPERS

ON

PHILOSOPHICAL SUBJECTS.

The Whole corrected, methodized, improved, and now collected into one Volume, and illustrated with COPPER PLATES.

THE FIFTH EDITION.

LONDON:
Printed for F. NEWBERY, at the Corner of St. Paul's Church-Yard.
M.DCC.LXXIV.

Franklin's experiments involved frequent use of the Leyden jar, which appears several times in the frontispiece to his book on his investigations. Franklin was the first to determine that the electric charge was stored in the glass of the jar and not in its outer or inner conductor (i.e., the metal wires or the inner fluid). He also demonstrated that the magnitude of the stored charge was dependent upon the thickness of the glass of the jar.

In Fig. IX of the frontispiece (the second picture from left in the second row of pictures), Franklin's "sentry box" experiment is illustrated. A metal rod 30 feet in height and sharply pointed at its tip terminates at the other end in a stand that is insulated from the ground within the sentry's shelter. The man inside could draw sparks from the rod by means of a wire loop attached to a wax handle. This, of course, was the basis for Franklin's development of lightning rods, which became widely known and used in colonial America as well as in Europe. It was this discovery that brought Franklin to the front ranks of electrical scientists, and was responsible for his election to the British Royal Society.

In the picture at upper right, the scene of Franklin's famous kite experiment of 1752 is reconstructed. The kite carried a pointed wire to attract electrical charges from the storm clouds; a silk thread, attached to the pointed wire, conducted the clouds' electrical discharges to a metal key near the end of the kite's cord. Franklin put his hand near the key and drew a spark. Then, by placing the key in contact with a conductor in the Leyden jar, Franklin was able to store the electrical charge in the jar.

# Lightning Kills Professor Richmann

1753

GEORG RICHMANN, a Swedish physicist at the Imperial Court at Saint Petersburg, attempted to duplicate Franklin's lightning rod experiment. When lightning struck the vertical rod, at the left of the illustration, Richmann drew an electric spark almost 12 inches long to the collector held in his hand.

Since Richmann had not taken the precaution of insulating himself from the ground by standing on a material like tar or wax, the spark leaped from the collector to his head. Richmann's body completed the circuit for the lightning's electrical discharge to the ground, and he was killed instantly. The artist who drew this impressive picture, after the fact, was Gilbert. The name of the engraver is illegible.

Sokolov, Richmann's companion (seen as the figure behind Richmann), was also struck by the same electrical discharge, but he survived.

To my illustrious friend Sir William Crookes of whom I always think and whose kind letters I never answer!
June 17. 1901.                    Nikola Tesla

SEEMINGLY INDIFFERENT to the spectacular display of artificial lightning in his laboratory, Tesla sits in a chair at left, calmly reading. The photograph was made sometime during 1899 in his Colorado Springs laboratory.

The large, cylindrical coiled structure at the left and the smaller coil at the right are Tesla's high-frequency, high-voltage oscillators, now called "Tesla coils." Tesla's research had led to the development of an alternating current apparatus in which electric currents, at high voltages and low current levels, could be transformed into low voltages at high current levels. (This system became the basis for Tesla's highly efficient electric power transmission system, which eventually succeeded in replacing Thomas Edison's uneconomical direct current power distribution system.)

In 1899 Tesla decided that his laboratory in New York City was no longer physically safe for his alternating current experiments, which had produced currents at four million volts, generating arcs that leaped to the laboratory's walls, floor, and ceiling. Leonard Curtis, of the Colorado Springs Electric Company, offered Tesla a site and all the electric power he would need for his experiments, and the pictured laboratory was the first to be installed at Colorado Springs.

Colorado Springs, which is subject to almost daily lightning storms of great magnitude, provided Tesla the opportunity to do some research on natural lightning, and his work at the laboratory there advanced his theoretical and engineering knowledge significantly. One monument to his innovative genius and to his diligent laboratory work is the tall electric power transmission masts that carry the cables for electrical power grids throughout the country.

# Artificial Lightning

1899

*Methodology*

Tab. II.

LUIGI GALVANI
1737–1798

Animal
Electricity

1791

*Methodology*
118

Galvani, a physician and professor of anatomy at the University of Bologna, observed that the muscles of dissected frogs' legs twitched when touched by his metal scalpel. When he applied a spark from a Leyden jar to a frog's muscle, it also twitched.

Galvani then decided to learn whether animal tissue itself generated electricity. He placed several frog-leg muscles, attached by brass hooks, outside the window of the laboratory. The muscles rested on the iron framework of the window. During a thunderstorm, Galvani observed the muscles twitching. However, he also observed that the muscles would twitch even when the day was clear and calm. Galvani therefore concluded that the muscles themselves generated electricity. Although this conclusion eventually proved to be incorrect, Galvani persisted in his belief in "animal electricity."

The error in Galvani's theory became evident three years later, when his friend Alessandro Volta (see page 119) demonstrated that two different metals, immersed but not touching each other in a salt solution, produced electrical currents. The brass hooks and the iron framework of Galvani's window had completed an electrical circuit through the moist frog tissues, which reacted to the current by twitching.

Galvani's 1791 book on animal electricity, *De Viribus Electricitatis in Motu Musculari Commentarium* (Commentary on the Effect of Electricity on Muscular Motion), contains several illustrations, meticulously drawn and ordered. Note the free-floating hands holding the curved wires, which served to complete the electrical circuit between the small voltaic piles (batteries) and specific points on the frog's legs. Such illustrations were intended to enable colleagues and other experimenters to repeat Galvani's experiments and verify the conclusions.

# The Voltaic Pile

1800

GALVANI SENT REGULAR REPORTS of his animal-electricity experiments to Volta, a professor of physics at the University of Pavia. Volta's chief interest, for most of his professional life, was the study of electricity. In 1794 he began the series of experiments that led not only to disproving Galvani's "animal-electricity" theory but also to the invention of one of the most important devices in the history of electricity, the "voltaic pile," or electric battery.

Volta's great experimental achievement is illustrated in these four figures. In fig. 1, bowls of salt solution are connected to each other by metal strips, alternately of zinc and copper. A wire, or another conductive connection, inserted in the two outermost bowls would produce a steady flow of electric current. Volta concluded that the electric currents Galvani had termed "animal electricity" were in fact generated by the presence of two dissimilar metals in the salt solution of the frog tissue.

Figs. 2, 3, and 4 illustrate Volta's ingenious use of small plates of copper and zinc with disks of paperboard moistened in salt solution. The sequence of copper, zinc, and paperboard could be extended to form a powerful battery, as seen in fig. 4. The connectors marked *C* complete circuits of the battery piles. For this invention, Volta received numerous decorations and honors, including the ribbon of the French Legion of Honor.

# Determining the Speed of Electric Current

1803

ALDINI'S EXPERIMENT was designed to determine the speed with which electric current was transmitted in a wire conductor from the west jetty in Calais harbor to the Red Fort (at left). With a voltaic pile consisting of eighty plates of silver and zinc as the electrical source, the circuit was completed by connecting the pile to an overhead wire that crossed the intervening waterway and ended at a small shed at the fort. There the wire was attached to a dissected animal, in the small hut at the left, that was expected to register the electric shock.

The observers on the jetty watched for a signal from the man near the shed. Virtually simultaneously with the closure of the circuit the animal's muscles twitched. Aldini could only conclude that the current traveled with "astonishing rapidity." This experiment was reported in Aldini's *Essai sur le Galvanisme*, published in 1804. The artist responsible for this drawing was Legrand, and the engraver was Blanchard.

Legrand del.                                                                 Blanchard Sculp.

FARADAY WAS EMPLOYED by the British Royal Society from 1813, first as a laboratory assistant to the eminent chemist and physicist Humphrey Davy, then as a lecturer and experimenter, and beginning in 1825 as director of the laboratory. In the summer of 1831 Faraday began a series of experiments in electromagnetism that were to lead to the electrification—literally—of Western industrialized societies.

The voltaic pile, or battery, which provided experimenters with electric current, depended on the effectiveness of the electrodes (e.g., the zinc and copper strips) and the conducting solution, or electrolyte (e.g., salt solution). As electric current was drawn from the battery, the electrolyte and the electrodes deteriorated. The battery became weaker and eventually had to be reconstructed.

By 1831 Faraday, after studying electromagnetic phenomena for almost ten years, decided to determine whether an electric current could be generated from magnetism. The reverse phenomenon—the production of magnetism in the space around conductors carrying electric currents—had been discovered by Hans Christian Oersted (1777–1851) in 1820.

Faraday formed a coil of 220 feet of copper wire and connected the ends of the wire to a galvanometer, a device that measures the flow of electric current (illustration left). He then thrust a cylindrical iron magnet into the coil of wire and observed that the galvanometer registered a flow of current. When he pulled the iron magnet out of the coil, the galvanometer again registered a current flow—but of the opposite polarity. Faraday explained this observation by suggesting that the *relative motion* of either the iron magnet or the coil was responsible for generating the electric current.

A very large permanent magnet had been installed in one of the Royal Society's laboratory rooms (illustration right). Faraday devised a copper disk, 12 inches in diameter, which was fitted with an axle and a hand crank and mounted on a carriage. The rim of the disk was positioned between the poles of the magnet. Strips of copper were placed in contact with the axle and the rim of the disk, and the conductive strips were connected to a galvanometer (seen atop the large magnet).

When Faraday rotated the copper disk, an immediate indication of electric current was observed in the galvanometer. When the direction of rotation was reversed, the galvanometer again indicated a flow of current, but with reversed polarity. Both rotations generated electric current in the copper disk—but only while the disk was in motion.

Faraday's vivid pictorial imagination led him to the idea that magnetic "lines of force" emanated from the magnet's poles outward into space and that the rotating copper disk had cut into those lines of force. In September 1831 he spent ten days in an exhaustive series of trials and repetitions of the experiment. By the end of November 1831 Faraday was able to report to a meeting of the Royal Society that he had succeeded in producing a continuous electric current by "electromagnetic induction." Electricity could now be produced for as long as needed by moving a conductor in a magnetic field.

# Electricity from Magnetism

1838

*Methodology*

# The "Edison Effect"

1880

Edison was one of the most prolific inventors of his time and is credited with the phonograph, telegraph, and carbon telephone transmitter. In 1879, after trying several thousand different materials, Edison found one that would glow at white heat when conducting electric current in an evacuated glass bulb: it was a scorched cotton thread. This new incandescent electric light glowed for forty continuous hours in his early trials; it was refined and adapted for public street lighting within a year.

One year later, while searching for methods to improve his lamp, Edison sealed a metal wire into a light bulb, close to the filament ("small horseshoe"). The wire was connected to an external metering circuit. When the filament incandesced, Edison observed that an electric current flowed from the inserted wire. Although he could not imagine a use for this device, Edison patented it in 1884 and published the discovery in several technical journals. The phenomenon became known as the "Edison Effect."

Edison had unwittingly invented the electronic device now called a "diode": the glowing lamp filament became a "cathode," producing a stream of electrons moving through the vacuum to the metal wire, called the "anode."

John Fleming (1849–1945), an electrical engineer working in the British electric-light industry, studied Edison's invention and in 1904 developed the electron vacuum tube now known as a "rectifier." By polarizing the inserted wire, or "plate," positively, it would attract large quantities of the negatively charged electrons emanating from the filament. If an alternating current (in which the electric charge continuously shifted from negative to positive) was applied to the filament, current flowed only during one-half of each alternating cycle. Alternating current could thus be converted to direct current.

The rectifier (Fleming called it a "valve") is a basic component of immeasurable importance for all aspects of radio communication as well as for all electronic measurement and computing instruments. Since 1948, when the transistor was invented, the rectifier principle has been very successfully adapted to transistor devices.

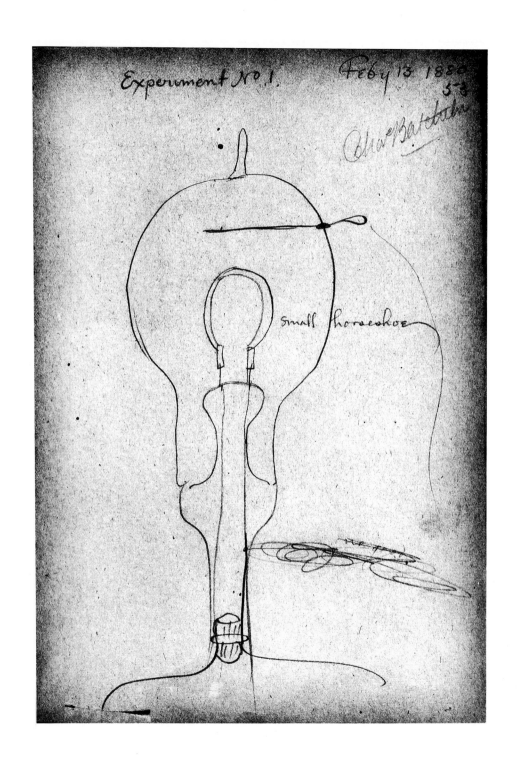

# X-Ray Study of a Crystal

1912/30

X RAYS, DISCOVERED BY Wilhelm Conrad Roentgen in 1895 (see page 139), pass invisibly through certain substances and are obstructed by others. Röntgen recorded this phenomenon in a series of photographs that provoked wide interest, especially in the medical profession. The nature of these new rays was subjected to intensive investigation by physicists, who eventually determined that X rays were electromagnetic waves, like light.

The established method for determining the wavelengths of visible light involved the interference, or diffraction, of a light beam by means of a ruled grating placed in the light beam's path. Gratings were usually made of optical glass plates on which fine, parallel lines were incised at regular distances from each other. The shorter the wavelength of the light, the closer the grating lines had to be. As many as 60,000 straight, parallel scratches, like slits, could be incised on a piece of glass 4 inches square. Interference or diffraction measurement had enabled physicists to determine the wavelengths of visible light, from the infrared (longest wavelengths) through the spectrum to the ultraviolet (shortest wavelengths). Knowing the distance between adjacent slits and the angle of the bent, transmitted light, they could compute the wavelength by means of a simple mathematical equation.

When conventional optical gratings were placed in the path of X rays, the X rays simply passed through unobstructed.

In 1912 Max von Laue (1879–1960), a German physicist at the University of Munich, suggested that a natural crystal might provide an effective grating for X-ray studies. Von Laue knew that crystal molecules have close, lattice-like configurations, and he intuited that a crystal's three-dimensional structure would present a much finer and more regular grating than those produced by conventional mechanical rulings on glass plates. In fact, crystals were found to provide gratings about 1,000 times finer than mechanically ruled gratings.

When a thin sliver of a copper-sulfate crystal was placed in the path of the X-ray beam, a photographic plate recorded a distinct interference pattern. The illustration at left is a photographic positive image; the black dots indicate regions in which the X rays could not penetrate the crystal's molecular lattice. In 1914 von Laue was awarded the Nobel Prize in physics for this discovery.

Eighteen years after his first experiment, he made a copy of the 1912 photograph and joined the dark points together by drawing "zonal" curves. This diagram is von Laue's interpretation of the spacings within the copper-sulfate crystal.

X-ray crystallography was responsible for the institution of a new branch of physics. It provides a method for investigating the atomic structure of matter, as well as the nature of short-wave radiations; the fields of biology and chemistry, as well as physics, have benefited considerably by its application.

It was an X-ray crystallograph of a DNA crystal, made by Rosalind Franklin in Maurice Wilkins's laboratory at Kings College, London, that provided James Watson and Francis Crick with the fundamental insight into the double-helix bonding in the DNA molecule (see page 222).

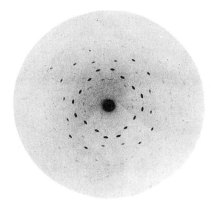
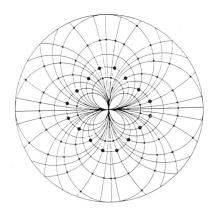

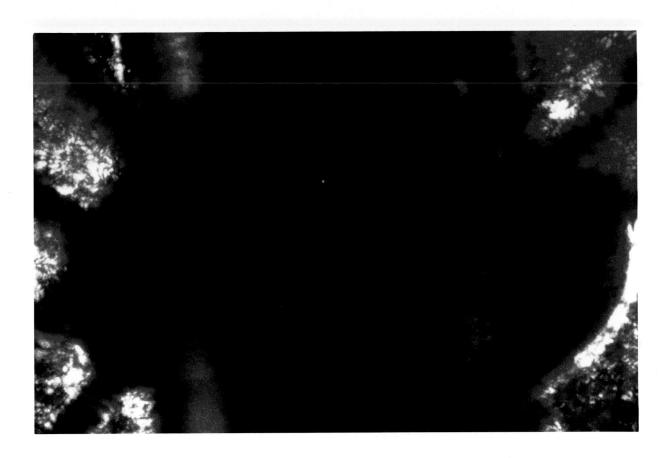

WHEN AN ATOM gains or loses one or more electrons or protons, it becomes electrically charged and is called an "ion." The ion is unstable and can achieve equilibrium only by combining with oppositely charged ions. (The term "ion," the Greek word for "wanderer," was first used by the nineteenth-century British philosopher and historian of science William Whewell [1794–1866], who also coined the terms "scientist" and "physicist.")

At the University of Washington the physicist Hans Dehmelt and his colleagues developed an extraordinarily sensitive apparatus for the manipulation and study of atomic particles. Their apparatus is a refinement of the "Penning electron trap," named after a 1940 invention by the Dutch physicist Frans Michael Penning.

Isolation of a single particle is accomplished by spraying the interior of the trap with a stream of electrons. The trap is then gradually evacuated of electrons, while the radiation emitted by the electron cloud is monitored. Dehmelt and his colleagues refined their technique to the extent that, in 1973, they were able to report the observation of a *single electron* in the trap, isolated from surrounding matter.

More recently, the Penning trap was further developed with the collaboration of Wolfgang Paul, of the University of Bonn. This illustration is a photograph of a single barium ion, which is seen as the small blue-green, seemingly immobile spot in the center. The bright streaks at the perimeter of the photograph are reflections of light from the metal and glass structure of the Dehmelt/Paul trap.

Dehmelt and Paul shared the 1989 Nobel Prize in physics for their contribution to precise measurement of the characteristics of atoms, for example, their magnetic properties, the quantum jumps—or change in energy levels—and the effects of temperature changes on their behavior.

HANS DEHMELT
B. 1922

# Atomic Particle in a Penning/Paul Trap

1986

*Methodology*

125

# IV
# Self-Illustrating
# Phenomena

. . . to hold, as 'twere, the mirror up to nature . . .
—WILLIAM SHAKESPEARE, *Hamlet* III.ii

T HE OBSERVATION of a repeated pattern provokes the scientist to seek the cause of the phenomenon. The alternating rings of light and dark wood fibers in the cross section of a tree trunk reflect the experience of annual growth. These rings also show the cyclical effects of climate during the tree's lifetime. In such an instance, Nature itself provides a significant image that can be deciphered.

Scientists have also found ways of making phenomena illustrate themselves. In 1839, Louis Daguerre announced that he had developed a process that was to become known as photography. Both scientists and artists were immediately captivated by the innovation. Today, photographic instruments, electrical sensors, and computer graphic displays, such as CAT or PET scans, are conventionally accepted resources that can be interposed between the phenomenon and the investigator to capture the event for analytical study.

Phenomena leave many other trails that enable scientists to discover how they function and interact with other forces.

CALIFORNIA
INSTITUTE OF
TECHNOLOGY

The
Andromeda
Nebula

1962

THE GERMAN ASTRONOMER Simon Marius (1573–1624) was the first to name the Andromeda Nebula, which is the only galaxy—a star system—that can be seen without a telescope. Marius used Greek mythological figures, like Io, Europa, and Ganymede, to identify celestial bodies. Andromeda was an Ethiopian princess who was rescued from a monster by Perseus, who made her his wife. A northern constellation, Andromeda lies between the constellations Pegasus and Perseus.

Until 1912 the Andromeda Nebula was considered to be a part of the galaxy in which we live—the Milky Way. In the mid-1920s the American astronomer Edwin Hubble (1889–1953) determined that Andromeda is an "extragalactic nebula," at least 800,000 light-years distant from our own galaxy. More recently, the Andromeda Nebula was recognized as considerably larger than our own Milky Way. We are able to see it only from an oblique direction, which accounts for its seemingly elliptical form; to us, its shape resembles a circular plate with a bulge in its center.

The yellow light of the nebula's central part comes from old stars with low surface temperatures. The blue light of the outer regions comes from the gases and dust of newly formed hot stars. X rays have been detected in the halos—the regions beyond the new blue stars—but they do not reach into Earth's atmosphere.

Because X rays generate intense electromagnetic activity, astronomers have been able to detect very powerful radio emissions from Andromeda's halo regions. These emissions are now known to originate from bubbles of hot gases whose elements correspond closely with those in the halos that surround our Milky Way.

# Halley's Comet

Comets—great spheres of carbon dioxide, methane, or water ice—develop "tails" as they approach the Sun, whose heat partially vaporizes their surfaces. When this happens, they become visible to observers on Earth. Even as late as 1910, such sudden appearances were responsible for the belief that comets were omens of impending catastrophes.

The time required for a comet to complete its elliptical orbit around the Sun can range from as little as five years to many centuries, depending on how elongated the orbit is. Halley's Comet is named after the British astronomer Edmond Halley (1656–1742), who correctly calculated the recurrence of its appearances every 76.3 years. It is estimated to be 9 miles long and 5 miles wide.

This image was recorded during the comet's most recent reappearance, on March 13, 1986, by the NASA Halley Multicolor Camera installed on the Giotto spacecraft. The image, taken at a distance of approximately 12,400 miles from the comet's path, was color-coded to indicate the range of light levels, from white to black.

The white-hot "cone" of the comet—its nucleus—can be seen slightly above and to the left of the center of the photograph: it is the white ellipse resembling an enlarged eye in a small, orange-colored fish. Below the nucleus, the comet's tail—composed of dust and gases—extends to the right in shades of green, orange, and white, ending in the white diffused area just below the cone.

As a comet moves away from the Sun into the outer solar system, its tail is seen to precede, rather than follow, the nucleus.

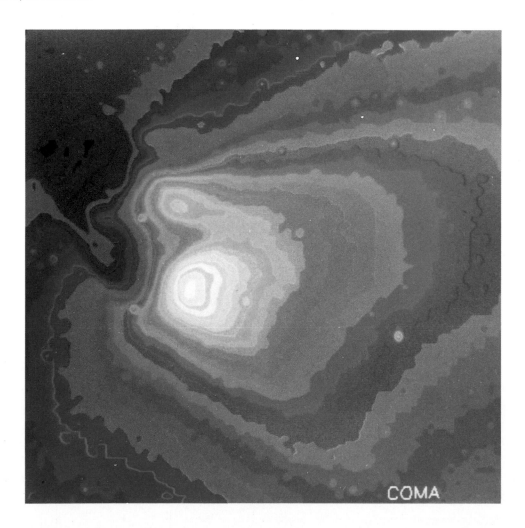

COMA

## Fossil Fish

65,000,000–37,000,000 B.C.

THIS FISH, OF THE SPECIES *Zebrasome deani*, was trapped in a sudden, massive geological upheaval sometime during the Eocene era. It was a period of violent volcanic disruptions in the oceans and on land, marked by the recession and redistribution of large bodies of water and the emergence of the European continent.

Caught in a sudden undersea volcanic eruption, the fish was impressed in a vein of lava. Its soft tissues disintegrated while the bones and outer skin engraved their shapes into the cooling stone of the Monte Boca region in Italy.

The Danish physician and anatomist Nicolaus Steno (1638–1686) was the first to begin a systematic study of fossils as an aspect of geology in his book entitled *De Solido* (On Solids). It is now known that fluorine accumulates, from ground water, in the skeletons of living animals at a predictable rate. Measurement of the fluorine content of an animal's bones and the use of the carbon-dating technique offer a fairly reliable measure of the age of a geologic site. Fossil discoveries enable geologists to trace the history of Earth and the evolution of its multitude of life forms.

ANDREW DOUGLAS (1867–1962), an American astronomer who had become interested in archaeology, hypothesized that variations in the Sun's radiation and historical records of general climatic conditions could indicate the age of organic relics—like woods, stones, and earths—at archaeological sites. In Arizona, where the prevailing dry climate preserves ancient trees, Douglas studied the patterns of their annual rings, which he was able to correlate with seasonal variations in climate and solar activity.

By 1920 Douglas had developed a system for the approximate dating of archaeological sites. His method, called "dendrochronology," can be used to date relics as old as 3,000 years. Here is how it works: two consecutive bands of tissue are formed in each year of the life of a tree; the two bands, one light and the other dark, together are called an "annual ring." In this photograph of a section of a fir tree, more than sixty such rings can be counted. The narrow rings are records of slow growth, and the wide rings records of rapid growth. Splits in the tree trunk are the marks of violent climatic disturbances or electrical storms. By comparing these variations with variations in rainfall, temperature, etc., recorded for a given period, an archaeologist can estimate the dates of events that occurred at the sites.

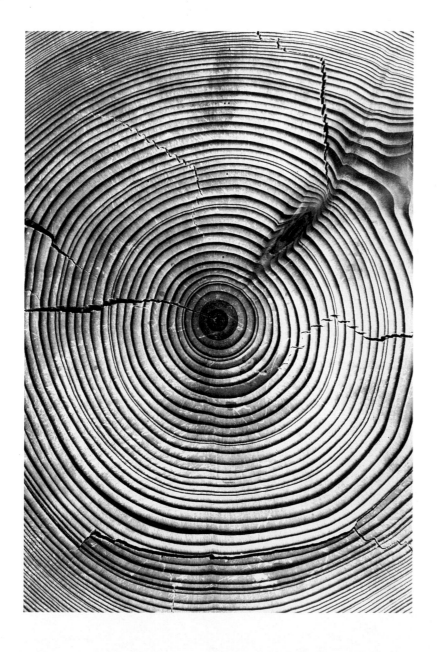

NASA

# A Solar Flare

1973

IN 1859 RICHARD CHRISTOPHER CARRINGTON (1826–1875), a British astronomer, recorded his observations of an unusual burst of light erupting from the Sun's surface. The eruption lasted about five minutes before it subsided and disappeared. Carrington noted that he might have seen the result of the collision of a large meteor that had fallen into the Sun.

Carrington's speculation was proved incorrect about seventy-five years later, when the American astronomer George Hale (1868–1938) analyzed the Sun's spectrum. Hale's research with his spectroheliograph demonstrated that solar flares originate from the Sun's internal turbulence. These flares produce violent electromagnetic disturbances in outer space, which severely affect radio transmissions and electrical systems on Earth.

This photograph of a solar flare was made on December 19, 1973, by the U.S. National Aeronautics and Space Administration. The gigantic loop of incandescent matter—one of the largest solar flares ever photographed—spans more than 367,000 miles across the Sun's surface. The dark granular spots peppering the Sun's surface are fire storms of short duration, averaging 1,000 miles in diameter.

WILLIAM BICKEL

B. 1937

# A Lightning Stroke and Its Spectrum

1989

TUCSON, ARIZONA, is the site of frequent lightning storms. This lightning stroke and its spectrogram were photographed simultaneously on a single frame of color film. The spectrogram (visible at the right side of the photograph) was produced by using a diffraction grating placed directly in front of the camera lens as a filter.

Bickel, a professor of physics at the University of Arizona in Tucson, devised this photographic technique to study the nature of high-intensity electrical discharges. Analysis of the spectrogram revealed the presence of nitrogen (green), oxygen (blue), and hydrogen (red) in the atmosphere pierced by the stroke. The brightness of the spectral lines indicates the relative amounts of each element present at the instant of the flash. The widths and the spectral lines provide information about temperature, electron densities, and the electric and magnetic fields generated by the stroke.

The temperatures in the vicinity of the stroke ranged from 6,000° Kelvin to 30,000° Kelvin (approximately 8,000°F to 40,000°F), according to data derived from studies of the intensity of the nitrogen band in the spectrum. Kelvin's temperature scale assigns zero to -273° centigrade, which is "absolute" zero—the lowest possible temperature attainable. The Kelvin scale then is divided by degrees equal to those on the centigrade scale.

Electric currents in this lightning stroke may have been as high as 20,000 amperes. Currents as high as several hundred thousand amperes have been recorded.

The brilliant light from a lightning stroke is due mainly to the effect of the electric current's excitation of air molecules in the vicinity of the stroke. A typical lightning stroke viewed by the naked eye is often the sum of a swift succession of several strokes occurring at intervals of a few milliseconds.

Several different forms of lightning can be seen in this photograph: the glow of the discharge within the heavy cloud; the branching strokes emanating from the main bolt; and a smaller, unbranched bolt, at the right of center.

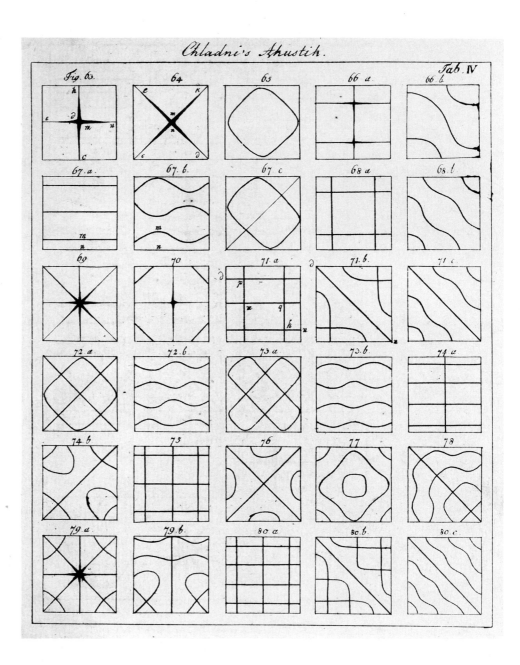

ERNST CHLADNI
1756–1827

# Vibration Patterns

1787

*Self-Illustrating Phenomena*

134

CHLADNI RECEIVED A LAW DEGREE from the University of Leipzig in 1782 and was expected to succeed his father as a lawyer, but turned instead to scientific studies. Chladni, an educated amateur musician, applied his scientific bent to the study of acoustics, and his book *Discovery of the Theory of Pitch* (1787) was the first general treatise on the science of acoustics.

Chladni illustrated his book with the diagrams of vibratory motions of thin metal plates. For these experiments, he covered the plates with thin layers of sand. The plates were then set into vibration by drawing a violin bow across various points on the plate's edges. In the regions that remained motionless, nodal lines and patterns formed where the sand shifted away from the areas that were vibrating.

Chladni analyzed the sand patterns, classified them according to their geometric shapes, and noted the corresponding pitch for each. By this means he was able to determine that a vibrating plate produces a series of tones (the fundamental pitch and its harmonics) that are analogous to the harmonic series of a vibrating string.

THIS EXTRAORDINARY DRAWING by the brothers Weber, a physiologist and a physician, illustrates their observation of the phenomenon of wave interference and its effect on the wave's transmission. Drops of mercury were allowed to fall through a paper funnel into a circular dish of mercury. As each drop fell, the surface of the pool of mercury was disturbed and produced the pattern showing the wave's onset, its propagation to the sides of the dish, and the wave's reflections and interferences. By controlling the rate of fall of the drops, the Webers could draw this pattern of the crests and troughs of the wave.

Of particular interest are the changes in the shape of the reflected wave front and the heart-shaped lobes near the right edge of the mercury pool. The brothers recognized this as a focal position. If, for example, the sides of the dish were mirrored, and a small, blinking light were to replace the mercury drops, the heart-shaped lobe would be the position where the reflected rays would merge; or, if an orchestra were to play in a circular concert hall, in the same location as the drop position, the audience situated at the focal position would experience an overwhelming sound intensity.

The painstaking observation this diagram required makes it one of the great achievements in scientific illustration. Such phenomena are now observed and recorded by sophisticated photographic apparatus in the study of architectural acoustics, sound reproduction, and aerodynamics.

ERNST HEINRICH
WEBER
1795–1878
AND
WILHELM WEBER
1804–1891

# Wave Analysis

1825

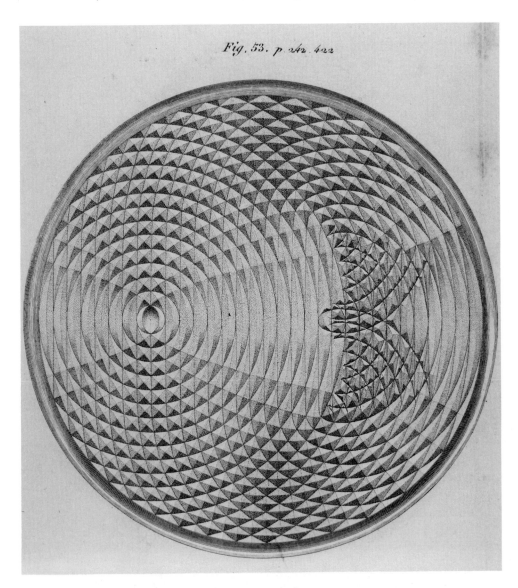

Fig. 53. p. 42. 422

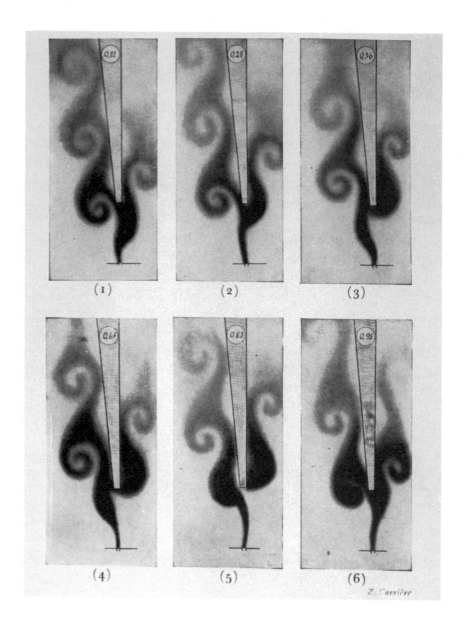

(1)　(2)　(3)

(4)　(5)　(6)

Z. Carrière

ZEPHYRIN CARRIÈRE
B. 1876

# Eddies Formed at the Lip of an Organ Pipe

SIX STAGES IN THE DEVELOPMENT of air eddies inside and outside the wall of an organ pipe were recorded by the French physicist and mathematician Zephyrin Carrière. A continuous airstream flowing out of the pipe's orifice, at the bottom of each picture, was mixed with smoke to make the phenomenon visible. The wedge-shaped structure above the orifice is the "lip" of the organ pipe; the interior of the pipe is at the right side of the lip, and the general room atmosphere is at the left.

The continuous airstream is split by the lip into two alternating eddies, inside and outside the pipe wall. The eddies were recorded at six successive intervals after the onset of the airstream: at 0.22 seconds, 0.28 seconds, 0.34 seconds, etc.

It is the pulsing airstream within the pipe that produces the air vibrations that are sensed by the ear as a tone of a specific pitch. The dark spiral eddies are the sites of momentary air compressions that are followed by rarefactions; the specific pitch and timbre are determined in part by the length of the pipe and in part by the configuration of the lip itself.

Such acoustical studies have been refined and adapted for investigations of fluid dynamics, most notably in the field of aeronautical physics.

FOR THESE CHLADNI pattern photographs (see page 134), shiny plastic particles ("glitter") were used to reveal the node formations—the regions of no vibration—on three violin back "plates." The belly and back plates of well-made violins are not of uniform thickness. They are carved so that, usually, the centers of the plates are slightly thicker than their edges. The violin maker taps the plates and listens to the tones produced by the taps. By thinning certain regions, the plates can be tuned for an optimum pitch, the "tap tone."

Hutchins developed a method for refining the tuning—and graduation—procedure. The entire inner surface of the plate is first covered with a fine layer of glitter. The plate, suspended about two inches above a loudspeaker, is forced into vibration by a tone produced by an audio frequency oscillator and amplifier. Sound energy from the loudspeaker drives the plate into vibration. The glitter is disturbed by the vibration and is redistributed in clusters, forming Chladni patterns. The glitter clusters are generally either curved or straight, and identify the regions of no vibration, called "nodes." The specific shapes of the nodal patterns are related to the graduated thickness of the plates.

In this illustration, three violin backs are compared. At the left, the smooth top and bottom arches are characteristic of a properly graduated plate. When tapped, this plate will produce a clear, ringing tap tone. The violin back in the center displays a thickened nodal pattern. This plate will require additional thinning in the indicated nodal regions. The nodal pattern in the violin back at the right extends to the upper edges of the plate. When tapped, this plate will sound very dull and will require careful additional graduation.

The system developed by Hutchins is now used by violin makers in Europe and America with considerable success.

CARLEEN HUTCHINS
B. 1911

# Violin Backs Tested by Chladni Patterns

1965

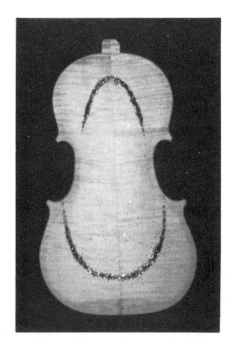
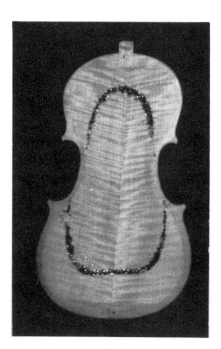
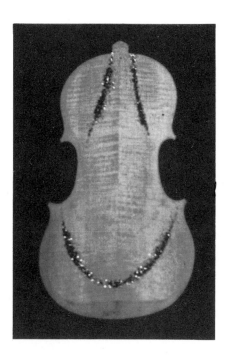

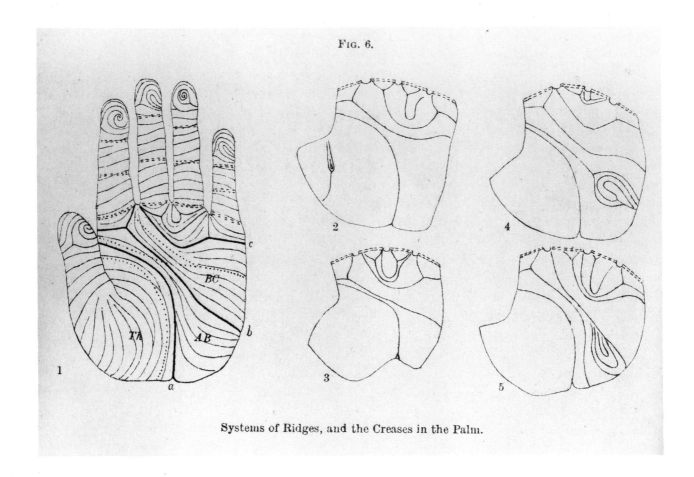

FIG. 6.

Systems of Ridges, and the Creases in the Palm.

SIR FRANCIS
GALTON
1822–1911

# Hand and
# Finger Prints

1892

GALTON WAS A CHILD PRODIGY who was able to read by the age of three and who began to study Latin at the age of four. He studied medicine at Cambridge University, but decided against entering the profession. Driven by his developing interest in biology and anthropology, Galton turned to the study of heredity in hand and finger prints.

The impression of a lightly inked hand or finger on paper serves as a distinct, inimitable identification mark. Hand and finger prints were used for identification purposes as early as 1818, when Thomas Bewick, an engraver and publisher, thumbprinted the cash receipts for his English translation of *Aesop's Fables.* Hand prints of Hindu natives were used as signatures on contracts as early as 1858, and a primitive system of criminal identification by finger printing was instituted by the British in India, in 1878.

Galton adapted this system as a tool for anthropometric classification. He gathered all the early available examples and studies into a book, *Finger Prints,* published in 1892, from which this illustration was selected. The illustration is an example of Galton's characteristically statistical approach to the study of hand and finger prints. The numbers and letters in the illustration are Galton's references to his typology of the ridges and creases in the palm prints. In the beginning of the twentieth century mandatory finger printing of criminals was adopted by the police services in Great Britain and the United States.

CATHODE-RAY TUBES were developed by the British physicist Sir William Crookes (1832–1919) in the late 1870s. These devices were essentially evacuated glass tubes in which the cathode (the negative electrode) produced streams of electrons that traveled in straight lines and cast shadows of objects placed in their path on the end surfaces of the tube.

In 1895, Roentgen, the director of the Physics Institute at the University of Würzburg, in Bavaria, began a series of experiments to study the luminescence of certain chemicals when subjected to cathode rays. On November 5, 1895, he noticed a flash of light that did not come from the cathode-ray tube itself. At some distance from the tube a sheet of test paper, covered with barium platinocyanide, glowed whenever the Crookes tube was turned on. When Roentgen turned off the electric current to the tube, the coated paper stopped glowing.

Because the paper was not in the direct path of the cathode ray, Roentgen thought that the Crookes tube might be producing some kind of spherically radiating energy, penetrating but invisible to the naked eye. Because he did not know the nature of the radiation, Roentgen termed it "X rays."

He devoted the following weeks to concentrated, intensive experimentation. On December 28, 1895, he reported his findings to the Physical Medicine Society of Würzburg. In this paper he described the luminescence he had observed with other materials: "phosphorous, calcium compounds, uranium glass, ordinary glass, rock salt, etc." Roentgen also noted that an observation of special interest was "the fact that photographic dry plates show themselves susceptible to X rays," in other words, that images cast by X rays could be registered photographically.

This photograph of the veins in a human hand illustrates an early use of X rays in the field of medicine. An injection of a liquid dye made the blood vessels opaque to the X rays, registering them as dark lines on the photographic plate.

About a year before his great discovery, in 1894, Roentgen had been appointed rector of the university of Würzburg. In his inaugural address he quoted Athanasius Kircher (see page 206), who had preceded him in the same post some two hundred years before, and whose eloquent words continue to guide all dedicated scientists:

*Nature often allows amazing miracles to be produced which originate from the most ordinary observations and which are, however, recognized only by those who are equipped with sagacity and acumen and who consult experience, the teacher of everything.*

WILHELM ROENTGEN
1845–1923

# X-Ray Photograph of Blood Vessels in the Hand

1895–96

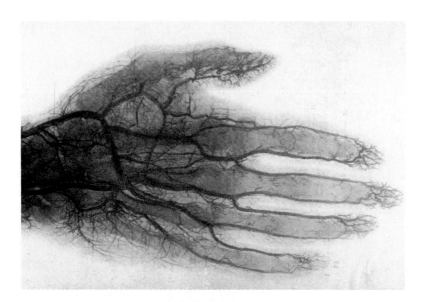

*Self-Illustrating Phenomena*

HAROLD E.
EDGERTON
1903–1990

Stroboscopic
Photograph of
a Milk Splash

1935

Stroboscopic
Photograph of
a Bullet in
Flight

1973

*Self-Illustrating*
*Phenomena*
*140*

Aᴌʟ ᴘʜᴏᴛᴏɢʀᴀᴘʜꜱ ᴀʀᴇ ʀᴇᴄᴏʀᴅꜱ of an object's reflected light captured by the exposure of light-sensitive photographic emulsions for a specific time duration. Nineteenth-century photography, limited by "slow" emulsions and "slow" lenses, necessitated exposure times of at least several seconds, and often more.

In this century, advances in photochemistry, optics, and lighting sources have made photography a versatile, indispensable resource for experimental science. Photography of objects in motion—ranging from atomic particle behavior to nuclear explosions—is routinely dependable and successful.

Harold Edgerton was the pioneer developer of stroboscopic lighting sources, working on them since the mid-1930s. Stroboscopes illuminate objects in motion by flashing on and off at rates of $^1/_{10,000}$ of a second or less. At such exposure speeds, moving objects can be observed in stages otherwise impossible for the naked eye to witness.

In the first of these stroboscopic photographs, made in 1935, a drop of milk falls into a dish of milk. The surface disturbance produces a slight "crater" and the appearance of an instantaneous corona around the rim of the milk dish. The white blob above the dish is another drop of milk about to collide with the surface of the milk in the dish. The flash duration (exposure time) was $^1/_{50,000}$ of a second.

This stroboscopic photograph of a bullet in flight was made thirty-eight years after the milk-drop photograph. The bullet's nose produces shock waves in the air, visible as white lines and eddies behind the bullet. The camera shutter was triggered by the bullet's explosive charge. A candle flame heated the air to make the shock waves visible in the photograph.

The study of shock waves contributes to more efficient designs for rockets, space probe carriers, and reentry vehicles, as well as passenger automobiles and aircraft.

THESE TWO PHOTOGRAPHS (viewing the nose of the plane, and looking down at its body) were made in a wind tunnel of the Lockheed Aeronautical Systems Company in Burbank, California. The scale model of a new aircraft was fixed to receive a brief blast of air, flowing at a velocity comparable to the aircraft's expected supersonic flying speed. Bands of colored oil were applied in stripes before the model was subjected to the air blast.

At certain positions on the aircraft's wings and fuselage the air blast caused visible fringes of color to stream away from the colored oil bands. These regions were analyzed to determine what improvements in the surface configurations of the aircraft's "skin" could reduce the shock wave's effects on the structure.

ERIC SCHULZINGER
B. 1955

# Air-Flow Patterns in the Surfaces of a Supersonic Aircraft

1988

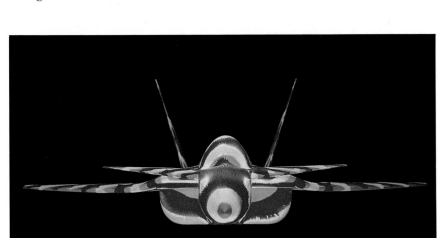

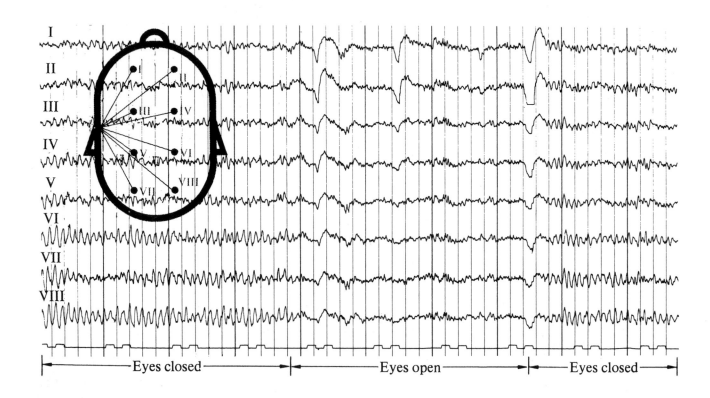

| | | | |
|---|---|---|---|
| ├──── Eyes closed ────┤ | ├──── Eyes open ────┤ | ├── Eyes closed ──┤ |

JULIUS T. FRASER
B. 1923
AND NATHANIEL M.
LAWRENCE
B. 1917

# Electro-encephalograms

1975

E LECTRICAL CURRENTS IN THE BRAIN were first discovered by the English physician Robert Caton, in 1875. A German psychiatrist, Hans Berger, was the first to record brain waves on paper, in 1929, using his young son as the subject. Such graphs display apparent rhythmic variations, which Berger named "alpha" and "beta" waves. Alpha waves have a periodicity of nine to eleven per second; beta waves have a higher frequency of variation.

In this illustration the outline of the top of a human head (showing the ears and nose for orientation) contains eight dots, which mark the positions where electrodes were fastened to the subject's skull. The subject being tested was normal and healthy. The dots are numbered to correspond to the roman numerals at the left of the graphs produced by the recording device.

The most obvious feature of all eight graphs can be seen in the variation of the wave shapes as the subject's eyes opened and closed. Waves recorded from the frontal lobes of the brain show greater amplitudes than those near the center and the posterior portions of the brain.

Electrical brain-wave recording, known as electroencephalography or EEG, has become a routine diagnostic test in neurology and psychiatry. EEG has become important in the study of epilepsy, because different types of epilepsies display characteristically different patterns.

In present-day neurology, the availability of computer analysis makes it possible to correlate a specific stimulus and its recorded electrical-wave response. A flicker of light, or a light tap on the hand, or any other sensory stimulus can now be interpreted by the computer on the response within the brain. Electrical stimulation of the brain, by implanted wires extending into the brain itself, has enabled researchers to map pain centers, emotional centers, appetite centers, and the centers controlling fear and panic reactions.

# Particle Traces in a Bubble Chamber

THE EUROPEAN CENTER FOR NUCLEAR RESEARCH (CERN) is the principal center for particle physics research in Europe. It was established in Switzerland in 1954 by a consortium financed by twelve European countries.

The CERN system uses a proton-synchrotron, a ring structure 656 feet in diameter with an operating energy of 28 billion volts. The device enables physicists to "see" into an atom's nucleus, rather as a telescope allows an astronomer to study heavenly bodies. In the CERN proton-synchrotron, streams of protons, moving at tremendous speeds, are directed at atomic targets. The resulting collisions release smaller particles from the targets.

The small-particle motions leave trails as they pass through a chamber of liquid hydrogen, the "bubble chamber." The trails are photographed, and can be seen as tiny bubbles in the liquid hydrogen. Slower-moving particles produce spiral trails, because of their deflection by the magnetic-field generators positioned around the chamber. Sensitive detectors monitor every aspect of the procedure.

More than 30 fundamental, subatomic particles have been discovered by the CERN and other atom smashers now operating in the United States and Europe. Their research efforts have immeasurably increased knowledge of the structure of matter.

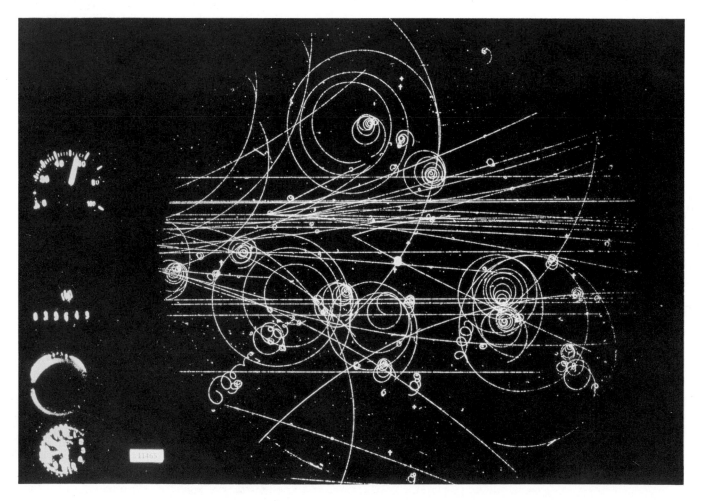

*Self-Illustrating Phenomena*

ALLAN E. KREIGER
B. 1935

# A Damaged Retina

1989

Tʜɪs ᴘʜᴏᴛᴏɢʀᴀᴘʜ ʀᴇᴠᴇᴀʟs the damage in the left eye of a twenty-three-year-old woman who had been hit by a baseball eight years before this examination took place. This blow caused a lesion of the macula (the small area of the retina that is responsible for central vision), which appears as the brown pigment clumping in the center of the photograph. The optic disk (white spot at the left) is normal.

At the time this photograph was taken, the patient's vision was recorded as 20/400, that is, in order to see what a person with normal vision can see at a distance of 400 feet, the patient would have to be at a distance of 20 feet.

The device used to make this extraordinary, detailed photograph is a "fundus camera," whose optical system is designed to record that part of the eye's retina directly opposite the pupil. The magnification on the 35mm slide film was approximately 2.5. The photograph was made by Jay Sands (b. 1942), a specialist in photography of the eye.

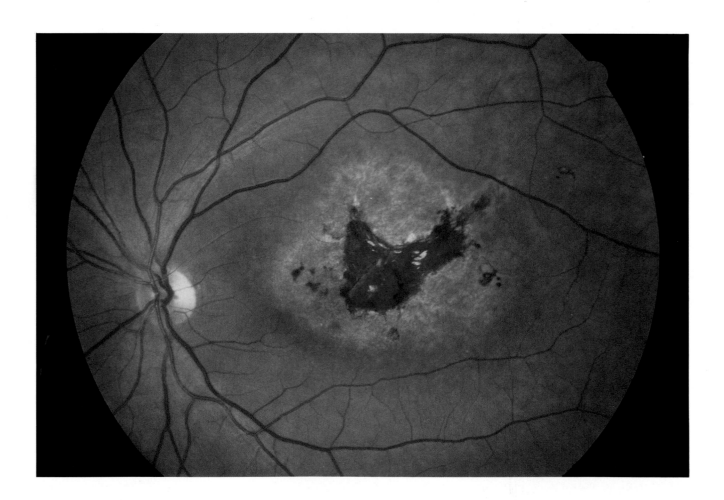

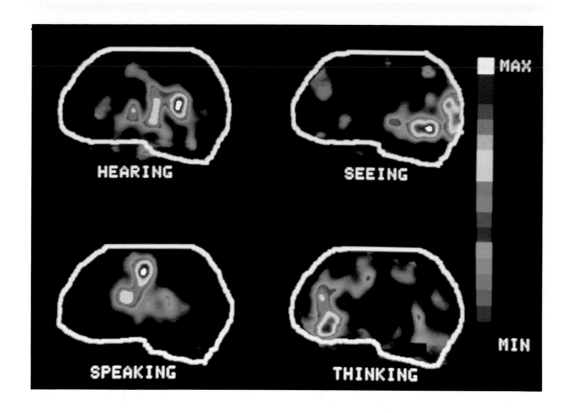

HEARING     SEEING     MAX

SPEAKING     THINKING     MIN

P ET (POSITRON EMISSION TOMOGRAPHY) scans generate images of the distribution of a radioactive substance after its injection into the bloodstream. The original research for this diagnostic procedure was published in 1890 by the British neurologists Sir Charles Sherrington (see page 48) and C. S. Roy. Because of the inadequacy of measurement instrumentation at that time, the information remained dormant until the 1980s. With the availability of very sensitive sensors and measurement apparatus, Posner and his group at Washington University in St. Louis, Missouri, were among the first to develop PET scanning clinical procedures.

In preparation for a PET scan, the patient receives an injection of a short-lived radioactive substance, such as oxygen-15 (which decays completely in 2 minutes) or nitrogen-13 (10 minutes) or carbon-11 (20 minutes). The radioactive substances release positively charged subatomic particles—positrons—from the cell nuclei which are detected by radiation sensors positioned around the section of the body being studied. The information received by the sensors is organized by a computer which then produces an accurate image of the radioactivity levels in the section of the organ under scrutiny—a "tomograph."

In this illustration the four PET scans reveal the sites where hearing a word, seeing it, speaking it, and thinking of it occur in the brain of a normal subject. The computer images are color enhanced in accordance with the "MAX-MIN" scale, at the right, which serves as an indicator of the functional intensity. The patient was positioned facing left for this series.

Since the PET scan's procedure involves the injection of a radioactive substance that flows through the blood circulation system of the entire brain, the scan can detect areas of affected brain function at a distance from the site of major brain damage.

DR. MICHAEL
POSNER
B. 1936

PET Scans
of Left-Brain
Function

1987

*Self-Illustrating
Phenomena*

# V
# Classification

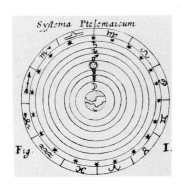

Fig. I.

The process of understanding nature
as well as the happiness that man feels in
understanding—that is, the conscious
realization of new knowledge—seems . . .
to be based on a correspondence,
a "matching" of inner images pre-existent
in the human psyche with external
objects and their behavior.
—WOLFGANG PAULI [1]

P AULI'S "PRE-EXISTENT INNER IMAGES" are the structure into which the scientist fits his observations. The act of classification is an attempt to discover some semblance of order in Nature. Knowledge must be codified and stored so that succeeding observations may be compared, and differences, however subtle, can be investigated and clarified. The encyclopedists recognized these functions as early as the beginning of the first millennium. Pliny the Elder (A.D. 23–79) collected information from some two thousand manuscripts written before his own *Natural History* was published, in A.D. 77. The first true encyclopedia, the *Natural History* offered a grand summary of knowledge available to ancient scientists.

A considerable portion of a scientist's education is devoted to the history of investigation in a particular branch of science. The student memorizes terminology, symbols, early experiments and conclusions, and classifications, which eventually serve as a resource to guide the scientist in further observations and experiments. For example, a newly discovered botanical specimen is studied for its similarities to and differences from known specimens; or the unusual path of a subatomic particle, after collision with another particle, is compared with previously photographed collision traces.

The periodic table of the elements is a chart devised to demonstrate the periodic recurrence of chemical and physical properties of the elements, arranged in the order of increasing numbers of protons in their atoms. The Russian chemist Dmitri Mendeleev (1834–1907) published his chart of the periodic table in 1869. His extraordinary insight led him to provide gaps to be filled by the names and properties of elements as yet undiscovered—elements that he intuited must exist!

## Astronomical Images in the Tomb of Seti I

C. 1290 B.C.

T HIS CEILING PAINTING in the tomb of Pharaoh Seti I, who ruled during the thirteenth century B.C., illustrates the intricate relationship between Egyptian astronomy and mythology. After their deaths, the pharaohs of Old Kingdom Egypt were believed to ascend to the polar sky, where they ruled over the hours of day and night.

The stars visible around the North Pole Star, which neither rise nor set, were believed to be eternal. Pharaoh's soul, or *ba*, was a "living star at the head of his brethren," just as his person in life was the godhead of his subjects. The pharaoh's tomb, which was the vehicle for his journey to the sky, was decorated with symbols of his guides and protectors.

The dark, heavy red dots in the painting represent the stars visible in the Big Dipper and its neighboring constellations. The handle of the Big Dipper extends across the back of the Bull (the Egyptian name for the Big Dipper) to the stars on the floating horizontal figure's eye, shoulder, elbow, and thighs, which form the cup. This horizontal figure holds golden thongs, which are tethered to a post representing the north celestial pole. A female hippopotamus, a Nile goddess, guards the pole.

Sebek, the crocodile god, who must be appeased by sacrifice and prayer, stands in back of the hippopotamus. The god Horus lies horizontally and rests his feet on the anchor pole, helping to support the Bull. Together, Sebek and Horus control the river leading to the Other World. The Nile's benevolence in supporting the recurrence of rich harvests was invoked, in this symbolic fashion, by the Egyptian priests and their tomb painters to affirm the eternal powers of the pharaoh.

At the far right stands the goddess Hathor, wearing the Sun disk on the crown of her head. She represents the principle of motherhood, daily giving birth to the rising sun and nourishing the order of the world. Hathor will protect the soul of Seti I during his voyage to his new abode in the heavens.

Like those of the other pharaohs, Seti I's tomb was intended to be sealed forever. Archaeologists justify opening it because, in all cultures, the study of tomb decorations provides profoundly important information about mankind's intellectual development.

*Classification*
*148*

DURING THE YEARS 622 to 633, Isidore, the archbishop of Seville, published an encyclopedia of etymologies, which was the first compendium of Greek, Arabic, Hebrew, biblical, and general astrological knowledge, arithmetic, and early linguistics. It was so admired and useful to medieval scholars that about a thousand copies have survived in manuscript, many of them beautifully illuminated.

This illustration is from the first printed edition, of 1472. It depicts Adam naming the animals, referring to the biblical account of the origin of taxonomy in the Old Testament: "And out of the earth the Lord God formed every beast of the field, and every fowl of the air; and brought them unto Adam to see what he could call them; and whatsoever Adam called every living creature, that was the name thereof" (Gen. 2:19).

# Adam Names the Animals

c. 633/1472

# Sky Map

A T THE NORTHEASTERNMOST tip of Siberia lies the Chukchi Peninsula, about 20 miles from Alaska across the Bering Strait. The boundary of the Arctic Circle cuts through the peninsula at approximately 67° north latitude, and the North Pole is about 1,500 miles north of the Chukchi coastline.

The ancient Chukchi people called the North Star—an immediate, predominant mark in their night sky—the "Nail Star." It appears at the center of this map of the heavens because it was considered to be the axis of the world of earth and sky.

The two lines intersecting at the North Star divide the sky into four parts. At the lower left is the realm of Dawn, with the image of the Sun disk marking the position of the rising Sun. Inside his igloo-shaped domicile, the Man of Dawn offers a fox to the Chukchi gods in tribute to the benevolence Nature promises for the new day.

At the upper right, in the realm of Dusk, the Man of Evening and his family wear ceremonial costumes to honor the Sea God: the most important food source was the Bering Sea, which borders the Chukchi Peninsula. Nearby, the crescent phase of the Moon hovers. Midway between Dusk and Dawn lies a third realm, Darkness, represented by the animal emerging from a branching tree.

The pair of crudely parallel lines, descending from the region of the North Star toward the realm of Dawn, contains the glowing stars of the Milky Way.

At the top center right, six small stars (four over two) represent the Pleiades cluster. These stars can be seen with the naked eye, and their appearance in the northern sky heralds the approach of spring. In the subpolar temperatures of the Chukchi Peninsula, the advent of a slightly warmer period would be greeted with pleasure, however brief its duration. The inclusion of the Pleiades in the sky map may indicate that the Chukchi were able to correlate their sky observations with imminent changes in their climate.

It has been proposed that this sky map was drawn by an explorer studying the Chukchi people sometime during the late nineteenth century.

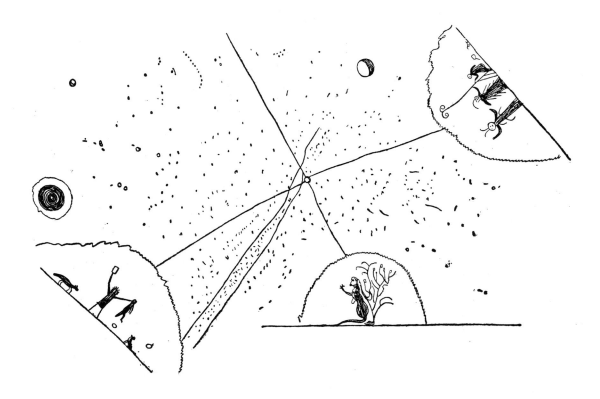

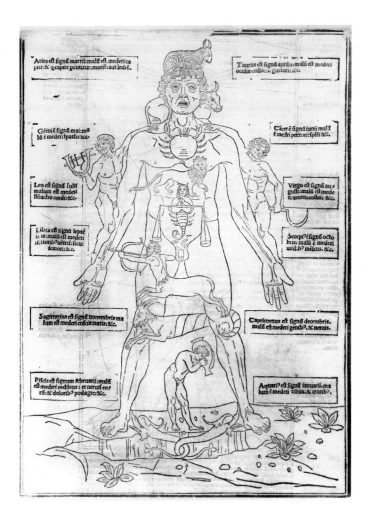

THE CONCEPT THAT ASTROLOGICAL influences determine health and illness arose early in Babylonian, Egyptian, and Greek cultures. The ancients believed that the Sun, the Moon, the stars, and the planets were sentient beings that exerted profound effects on the human condition. For example, health, vigor, and sexual power were supposed to vary with the phases of the Moon. Moonlight was thought to exert a potent force on physical beauty and insanity, as well as to cure various ailments including warts.

Eventually, astrologers (who were often also physicians) catalogued the twelve signs of the zodiac and their influences over parts of the body, as seen in this thirteenth-century Zodiac Man chart.

JOHANNES KETHAM

# Zodiac Man

1522

ARIES: *head, eyes, adrenals, blood pressure*

TAURUS: *neck, throat, shoulders, ears*

GEMINI: *lungs, nerves, arms, heads, fingers*

CANCER: *chest wall, breasts, some body fluids*

LEO: *heart, spine, upper back, spleen*

VIRGO: *abdomen, intestines, gallbladder, pancreas, liver*

LIBRA: *lower back, hips, kidneys, endocrines*

SCORPIO: *reproductive organs, pelvis, urinary bladder, rectum*

SAGITTARIUS: *thighs, legs*

CAPRICORN: *knees, bones, skin*

AQUARIUS: *ankles, blood vessels*

PISCES: *feet, some body fluids*

Christian theologists eventually denounced the practice of astrology, and in 1585, Pope Sixtus V condemned astrology as a heresy. Nevertheless, evidence that astrological principles were operative in mainstream medicine can be found well into the seventeenth century.

# The Constellation Aquarius (The Water Carrier)

c. 1650

B Y THE TIME THIS ILLUSTRATION was painted for a Persian manuscript, astrologers' and astronomers' representations of zodiacal signs as persons or animals had become a convention. From the earliest days to the present, images that represent the twelve signs of the zodiac have been known: this Persian version consists of a ram, a bull, twin children, a crab, a lion, a virgin woman, a balance, a scorpion, an archer, a goat with a fishtail, a water carrier, and a pair of fish.

The similarities among these signs in various cultures have led to speculation about their origins. We know that animal attributes are associated with gods in the religions and religious art of many ancient cultures. The Babylonians, for example, elevated their gods into the heavens, calling constellations the Ram, the Bull, the Crab, the Lion, the Scorpion, the Fish, the Goat, etc., each expressing a primal characteristic in mankind.

The Greeks adopted Babylonian terminology to identify their constellations, although the word "zodiac" comes from the Greek meaning "circle of the signs," as well as "little animal," and Greek mythology is the source for the iconography of Western astrology and astronomy. Islamic artists adapted the imagery of the Greeks to fit their own conventions of dress and attitudes, as with the Greek god Zeus, who appears wearing a turban and carrying a scimitar.

In this illustration of a Persian Aquarius, a youthful male figure holds an upturned vase from which water falls to Earth. The gold dots delineate the stars in this constellation and provide a skeletal outline for the drawing of the hands, shoulders, arms, thighs, and calves of the figure. Note the rush of stars that enhances the representation of water flowing from the vessel held by the carrier. The Persian names of the stars are indicated by tiny red markings.

In Western astrology, Aquarius represents the period when spring displaces winter (from January 21 to February 19 in the Northern Hemisphere). The water symbolizes refreshment and truth.

THIS IS THE FIRST PAGE of the first printed edition of Euclid's *The Elements of Geometry*, published in Venice in 1482. The illuminated capitals, decorative borders, and the precisely executed examples of geometric figures suggest that the publisher, Erhard Ratdolt, was thoroughly aware of the book's potential importance for mathematicians, scientists, and scholars in general. *The Elements* has enjoyed more than a thousand subsequent editions and Euclid's name is now a household word throughout the civilized world.

Euclid is thought to have received his early education in Athens, in Plato's Academy. The latter part of his life was spent in Alexandria, where the great library and university had become the center for scholars not only from Greece, Arabia, and Egypt, but also from Europe. It was here in Alexandria that Euclid assembled and codified the mathematical lore from earlier Greek and Egyptian mathematicians: the theory of numbers, the idea of *ratio* to express relationships between two or more quantities, and, of course, geometry.

The diagrams in the right margin are the geometric figures that Euclid analyzed by his system of postulates, or axioms, which are proved true by rigorous logic. The figures, in descending order, are: the straight line connecting two points; the rectangle; the angle and the perpendicular; the circle and its parts; the three forms of triangles; and the rectangle, square, and parallelogram.

Based upon the construction and analysis of idealized two-dimensional figures, Euclid's geometry became a cornerstone for training in logical thinking.

# Chart of Comparative Cosmologies

EARLY SEVENTEENTH
CENTURY

A FTER THE PUBLICATION of Copernicus's *On the Revolutions of the Heavenly Spheres* in 1543, speculation about cosmology continued among astronomers for at least a century. This chart was prepared for comparative study of the main cosmological systems known to early seventeenth-century astronomers.

The first five figures represent geocentric schemes—that is, with Earth at the center and its moon, the Sun, and other planets in orbit around Earth.

Fig. I demonstrates Ptolemy's scheme, as proposed in his *Almagest* (Synthesis of Astronomy), c. A.D. 150. Earth is at the center of the orbits of the Moon, Mercury, Venus, the Sun, Mars, Jupiter, Saturn, and the outer fixed stars. The outermost border contains the twelve signs of the zodiac, the division of annual time (the year) into successive periods of observation.

Fig. II is a construction of the scheme proposed by Plato (c. 427–347 B.C.) in his *Timaeus* dialogue. It appears to be virtually identical with Ptolemy's scheme, which was devised almost five hundred years later, but the Sun's orbit is placed close to Earth just beyond the Moon.

Fig. III, the Egyptian scheme, differs from the previous two only in its representation of a greater distance between Earth and the Sun.

Fig. IV is Tycho Brahe's (see pages 80–81) proposal (c. 1580), in which distances between the celestial bodies are no longer regular, in an attempt to explain the observation of irregular orbital durations.

In Fig. V, the Semi-Tychonicum scheme, Mars's orbit is shown as intersecting the Sun's orbit around Earth. The Sun, in turn, is represented as having Venus as a satellite, or moon. Jupiter now has at least three moons; and Saturn has two moons.

Fig. VI, the Copernican scheme (1543), places the Sun at the center of the concentric orbits of the planets known at the time. The concentricity of Copernicus's planetary orbits was revised in 1609 by Johannes Kepler, who had mathematically determined that the planets must move in elliptical orbits.

Only the first two cosmological systems, the Ptolemaic and the Platonic, are represented with the zodiac band encircling the systems. Its absence from the remaining examples may be interpreted as a sign of the waning influence of astrology in the general field of cosmology.

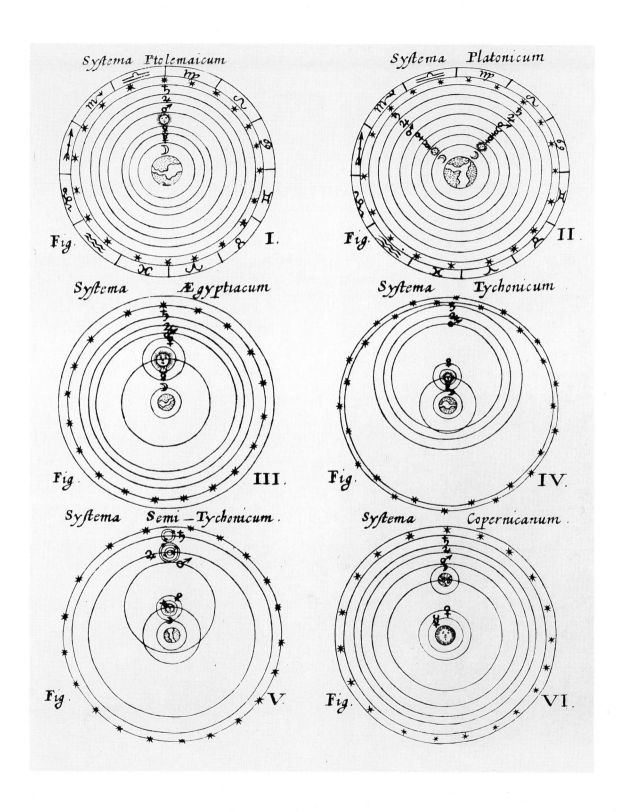

Systema Ptolemaicum

Fig.     I.

Systema Platonicum

Fig.     II.

Systema Ægyptiacum

Fig.     III.

Systema Tychonicum

Fig.     IV.

Systema Semi-Tychonicum.

Fig.     V.

Systema Copernicanum.

Fig.     VI.

# The Surface of Mercury

1974

THIS MAP OF A PORTION of the surface of Mercury was taken by the Mariner 10 space probe March 29, 1974. Mercury, the planet closest to the Sun, has been observed from Earth since man's beginnings in prehistory. Because its orbit around the Sun (of approximately 88 Earth days' duration) is perceived to be much faster than that of the other planets, the Greeks named it Hermes, after the fleet-footed messenger of the gods. It was later called Mercury, the Roman equivalent.

The Mariner 10 spacecraft was directed to make three passes around Mercury at a height of approximately 12,000 miles. The splendid detail of the photographs delineates surface objects as small as 325 feet in diameter. Mercury's surface, like that of the Moon, is scarred by numerous craters and craters within craters caused by meteorite collisions. Some of the cliffs in its craters are estimated to be as high as 6,300 feet above the adjacent valley floors.

The names assigned to craters, mountains, and other features—Beethoven, Bartók, Shelley, Delacroix, Milton, Dostoevski, Mark Twain, et al.—express the whims and fancies of the members of the astronomy community, whose world fellowship allows them the privilege of naming sites they have identified and studied.

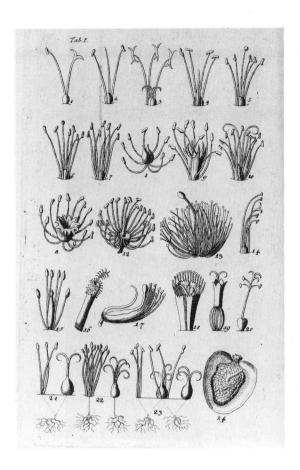

WHEN LINNAEUS WAS about eight years old, he was so passionate about the classification of Nature that he was called "the little botanist" by his parents and friends. Later, Linnaeus studied medicine at the universities of Lund and Uppsala, in Sweden, but was still irresistibly drawn to botanical studies, which he eventually transformed into a major scientific discipline.

In 1732, the University of Uppsala, where he was a lecturer in botany, commissioned Linnaeus to make a study of the flora in Lapland. His explorations covered some 4,500 miles of northern Scandinavia.

In 1735, at the age of twenty-eight, Linnaeus published his great *Systema Naturae*, which was the first book to provide a systematic classification of living things, and which earned Linnaeus the title of the "Founder of Modern Taxonomy." The book originally consisted of only seven large, densely illustrated pages, but by the tenth edition, it had expanded to 2,500 pages describing 8,500 plants and 4,236 animals.

As a concomitant of his classification system, Linnaeus devised binomial nomenclature—still current—in which each type of living organism is assigned a first name, denoting the group (genus) to which it belongs, followed by a specific name or adjective (species). *Homo sapiens* ("Man, thinking") is a well-known example. Linneaus also devised the symbols ♂ and ♀ for "male" and "female."

This chart from *Genera Plantarum* (The Genera of Plants, 1737), delineates the 24 classes of the reproductive systems of plants according to the arrangement of their stamens ("male" organs) and their pistils ("female" organs). The first 15 figures are of plants with isolated stamens. Those numbered 16 to 20 represent plants in which stamens and pistils grow together in the same plant. Figs. 21 to 23 are plants with separate male and female flowers, and Fig. 24 represents plants with hidden reproductive organs.

After Linnaeus's death, in 1778, a British naturalist, Sir J. E. Smith, purchased all his books and collections and moved them to England, where they became the basic library of the English biological association, The Linnaean Society, founded in 1778.

CAROLUS LINNAEUS
1707–1778

# Classification of Plants by Sexual Characteristics

1737

*Classification*

157

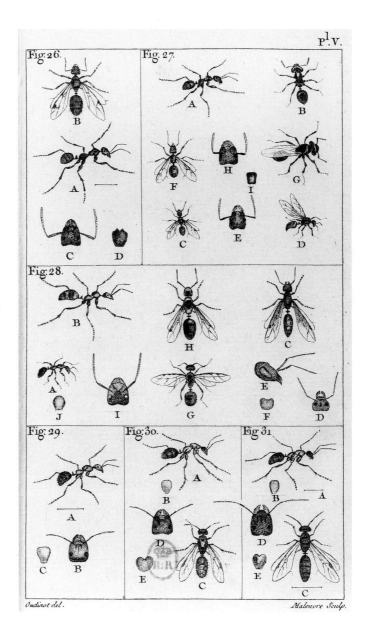

Oudinot del.                                    Maleuvre Sculp.

# Classification of Ants

THESE DRAWINGS ARE some examples of the astonishingly clear and elegant illustrations made by the French illustrator Oudinot for Latreille's *Histoire Naturelle des Fourmis* (Natural History of Ants), published in 1802. In the preface to his book Latreille gracefully acknowledges Oudinot's contribution, and the fact that he was on the staff of the Museum of Natural History. The book actually contains engravings made by Maleuvre based on Oudinot's work.

Latreille was the founder and the first president of the French Entomological Society. He classified the ants he had studied in the south of France and later in the great collections of the Jardin des Plantes, in Paris. He identified approximately one hundred species, of which six are represented here. (Since Latreille's book was published, entomologists have identified more than 5,000 species.)

The three characteristic types of ants are represented in Fig. 27, at top right. A and B is the female worker; C and D is the male: F and G is the egg-laying queen. The male and the queen are shown (in D and G, respectively) as ready for the flight in which they will mate. H, I, and E represent parts of the head and armor.

T HIS PAGE, WITH AN ILLUSTRATION by Don Greame Kelley, from *The Amateur Naturalist's Handbook* by Vinson Brown, charts several *phyla* (main divisions) and classes of animals:

*Protozoa*: one-celled animals

*Porifera*: sponges; animals having no appendages (that is, legs, tentacles, etc.)

*Coelenterata*: simple water animals with small, stinging, explosive barbs for protection; jellyfish, hydras, sea anemones, etc.

*Ctenophora*: "comb" jellies; jelly-like animals with rows of hairy swimming plates

Names and pictures, arranged in charts like this one, are studied and memorized to become part of the firm groundwork of the biologist's education.

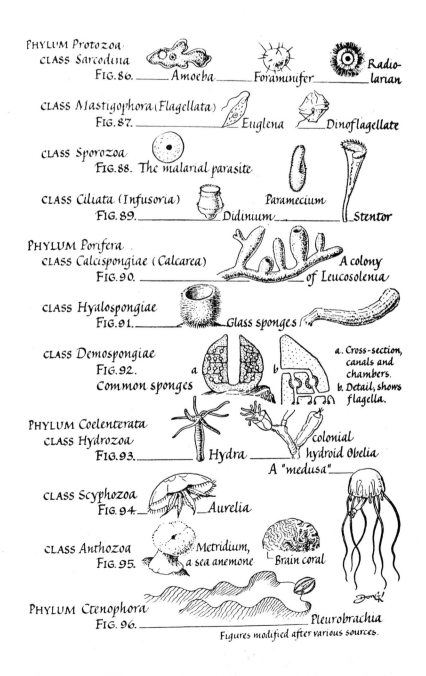

PHYLUM *Protozoa*
CLASS *Sarcodina*
FIG. 86. _____ Amoeba _____ Foraminifer _____ Radiolarian

CLASS *Mastigophora* (Flagellata)
FIG. 87. _____ Euglena _____ Dinoflagellate

CLASS *Sporozoa*
FIG. 88. The malarial parasite

CLASS *Ciliata* (Infusoria)
FIG. 89. _____ Didinium _____ Paramecium _____ Stentor

PHYLUM *Porifera*
CLASS *Calcispongiae* (Calcarea)
FIG. 90. _____ A colony of Leucosolenia

CLASS *Hyalospongiae*
FIG. 91. _____ Glass sponges

CLASS *Demospongiae*
FIG. 92.
Common sponges
a. Cross-section, canals and chambers.
b. Detail, shows flagella.

PHYLUM *Coelenterata*
CLASS *Hydrozoa*
FIG. 93. _____ Hydra _____ colonial hydroid Obelia
A "medusa"

CLASS *Scyphozoa*
FIG. 94. _____ Aurelia

CLASS *Anthozoa*
FIG. 95. _____ Metridium, a sea anemone _____ Brain coral

PHYLUM *Ctenophora*
FIG. 96. _____ Pleurobrachia

Figures modified after various sources.

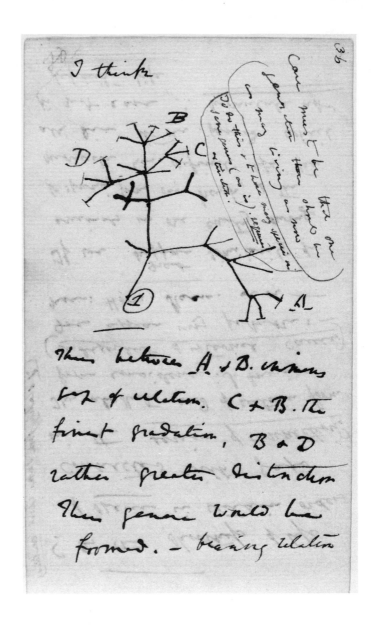

CHARLES DARWIN
1809–1882

# Sketch for an Evolutionary Tree

1870

*Classification*
160

THE TREE IS VIRTUALLY an archetypal symbol that serves as a metaphor for the development of an organic, intellectual, historical, or other process. Darwin's notebooks contain several such tree diagrams with which he speculated on the theory of the evolution of life forms.

This is Darwin's third tree diagram and appears on page 36 of the *First Notebook*. Just above the diagram, Darwin wrote, "I think." Below the diagram is: "Thus between A & B immense gap of relation, C & B, the finest gradation, B & D rather greater distinction. Thus genera would be formed—bearing relation to ancient types."

The marginal note at the right of the tree diagram reads, "Case must be that one generation then should have as many living as now. To do this & to have many species in same genus (as is) REQUIRES extinction."

Darwin's eventual speculations about the *continuous propagation* of an evolved species were followed by his recognition of the impossibility of such an occurrence, which would produce an overwhelming overpopulation. Therefore, he decided that a species must gradually become extinct.

HAECKEL RECEIVED A DEGREE in medicine from the University of Berlin in 1857, practiced for only one year, and then devoted himself to work and study in comparative anatomy as a professor at the zoological institute in Jena. Haeckel, a very competent draftsman and artist, made detailed drawings of the organisms he studied. One hundred of these were collected and published in a book for laymen, *Art Forms in Nature*, in 1904 (see page 75).

Haeckel was the first German biologist to become an active and devoted partisan of Darwinism. His branching "evolutionary tree of life" (shown here with labels in English) elaborates on the theory of evolution. Haeckel carefully partitioned the tree to accommodate the four major groups of phyla: primitive (protozoa), invertebrates, vertebrates, and mammals. The gnarled trunk and branches of the tree reflect his pleasure in drawing.

# The Tree of Life

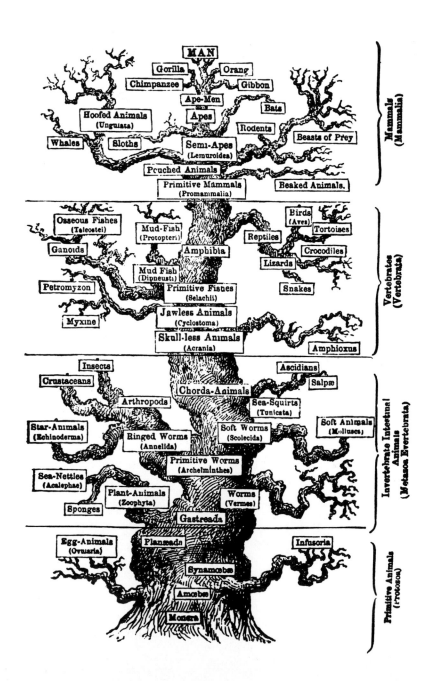

# Evolutionary Tree

1950

R EFINEMENT OF THE EVOLUTIONARY tree continued, as demonstrated in this illustration from de Beer's *Atlas of Evolution*.

Because biologists had become more cautious regarding Darwin's theory of evolution, the branches of this tree were not joined to each other. The linkages between the varieties of species could not be fixed, due to lack of adequate fossil evidence to fill in the discontinuities in evolutionary progression.

De Beer was a director of the British Museum of Natural History, edited Darwin's *Notebooks*, and wrote a biography of Darwin.

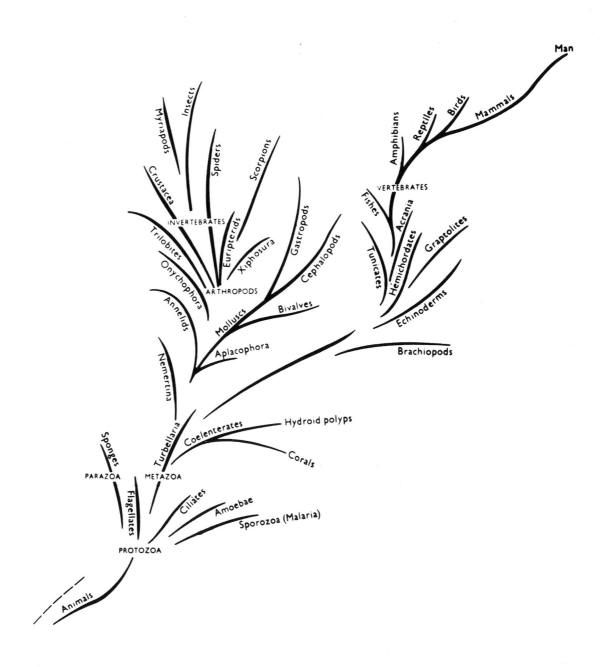

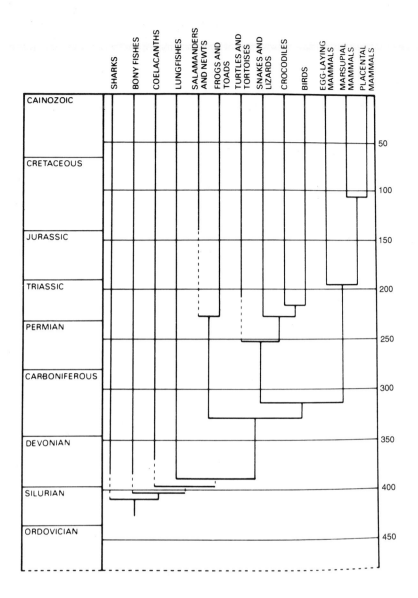

THIS EVOLUTIONARY TREE is even more conservative than de Beer's. The caption for this illustration in the Museum's *Evolution* handbook cautions:

*Solid vertical lines show groups known by fossils; dotted lines indicate "gaps" in the fossil record—periods when the group is inferred to have existed, but no fossils have been found. These gaps might be due to failures in fossilization, or to mistakes in the genealogy, or to wrongly identified fossils; or they could be (and have been) taken to show that the theory of evolution is wrong.*

Nevertheless, examination of this tree reveals an acceptance of the apparent continuity in the evolution of animal life forms, enumerated at the top of the chart: SHARKS, LUNGFISHES, SALAMANDERS, BIRDS, MAMMALS, etc.

Biologists, in the main, continue to be indebted to Darwin's thesis, which created the modern sciences of comparative physiology, comparative pathology, and comparative psychology.

BRITISH MUSEUM OF NATURAL HISTORY

Evolutionary Tree

1978

*Classification*

*163*

# Evolution of
# Homo Sapiens

1970

S IR WILFRED LE GROS CLARKE, a professor of anatomy at Oxford University, was the author of the classic *History of the Primates*, in which this illustration appears. Primates are mammals, including humans, apes, monkeys, and related animal forms such as lemurs and tarsiers, and are unique in having forward-looking eyes, grasping hands with nails at their fingertips, and other features that distinguish them from mammalian vertebrates like dogs, rodents, elephants, bats, whales, etc.

The clarity of this classification of the supposed stages in the evolution of *Homo sapiens* is especially remarkable: the anatomical details of the successive skeletons are precise, and by the juxtaposition of the six forms the illustrator, Maurice Wilson, composed a timeline to produce a quickly memorable image of the evolution to the well-balanced, upright figure of man.

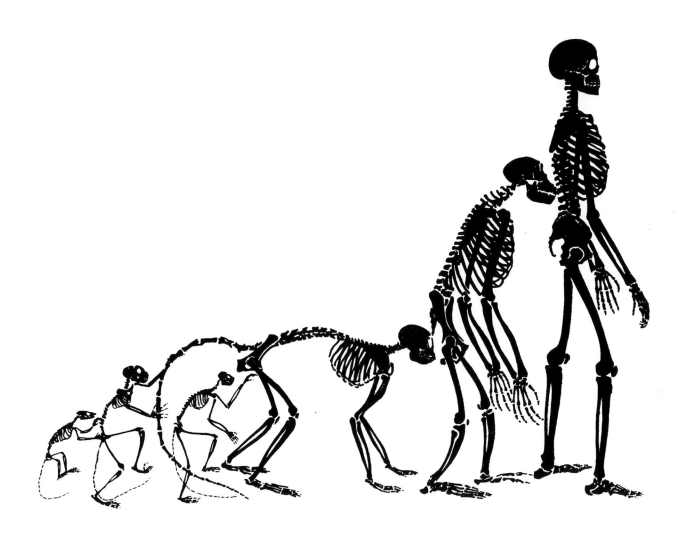

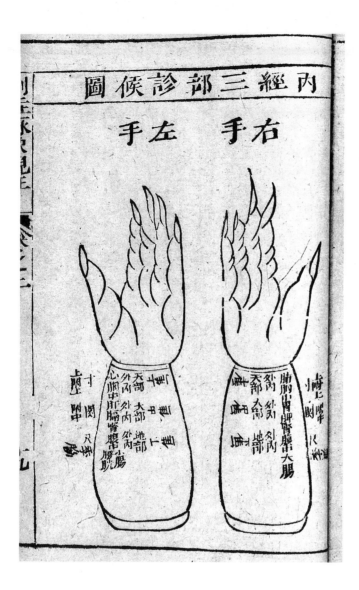

IN ANCIENT CHINESE MEDICINE, practitioners learned to diagnose a patient's ailment by taking the pulse. The physician felt each wrist at three main regions, each of which is associated with a particular organ—such as the heart, the lungs, the liver—or the digestive tract. These main regions are indicated by notations outside the drawings of each wrist.

Each of these three main areas was divided into subzones, which when touched very lightly by the physician's fingertips provided diagnoses of several hundred possible defects. The physician would also note the patient's skin temperature, texture, and dampness, and would compare the patient's pulse rate with his own. The practice continues to this day, and is considered valid by modern physicians who are also acupuncturists.

This chart is reproduced from an edition of *Secrets of the Pulse*, published in 1693, which gives its source as a chart purportedly devised by Pien Ch'iao some time during the sixth century B.C. It probably dates about five centuries later.

## Pulse Chart

1693

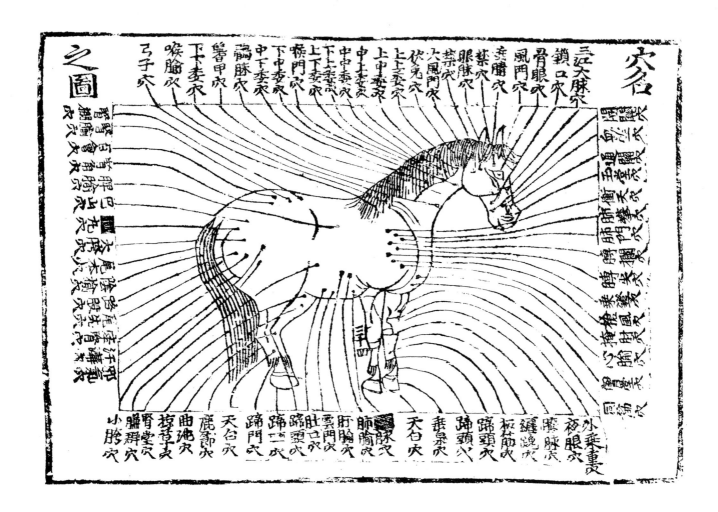

CHINESE

# Veterinary Acupuncture

1399

*Classification*
*166*

THE PRACTICE OF ACUPUNCTURE in China was sustained by oral tradition for several hundred years until, sometime during the third century B.C., it was institutionalized in writing in one of the books of the *Nei Ching* (The Canon of Medicine). The book, entitled *Ling-Hsu* (The Spiritual Nucleus), is devoted to the different techniques of acupuncture.

Acupuncture is intended to restore a normal equilibrium between the inner forces of *yang* (male) and *yin* (female), which are believed to control the health of the body. Very fine needles are inserted into the skin at acupuncture "points" that lie along twelve "meridians." These meridians extend from the top of the head to the soles of the feet. The needles are believed to conduct energy, or the "life force," between certain points along the meridians, each of which is associated with a specific organ in the body.

Domesticated horses were highly prized possessions in Chinese society, and the dependence upon acupuncturists for the treatment of animal ailments attests to their skill in veterinary medicine. This instructional chart, showing eighty points for needle insertions, is from a fourteenth-century book on acupuncture entitled *Ma Niu I Fang* (Medical Techniques for Horses and Cattle).

ACUPUNCTURE TREATMENT has been a dominant medical technique in China for more than two thousand years. The twelve acupuncture meridians encircle the entire length of the body from the top of the head to the soles of the feet, so treatment can be administered to meridians on the front or the back of the body.

   This chart, from a book prepared during the Ming Dynasty (1368–1644), pictures sections of two meridians, one along the arm and the other joining it to a meridian on the torso used in treatment for respiratory ailments.

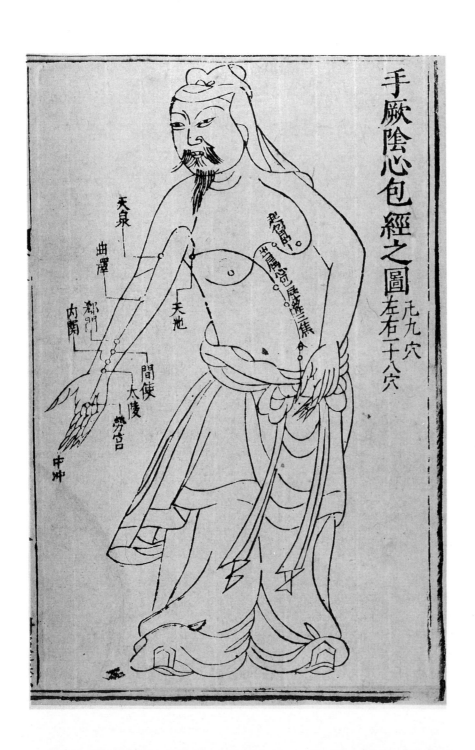

手厥陰心包經之圖 左右二十八穴 凡九穴

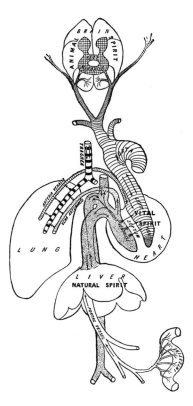

GALEN

C. A.D. 130–200

# Human Physiology

DATE UNKNOWN

Galen (see page 36), the second-century physician who is esteemed in the history of medicine as second only to Hippocrates (c. 340–370 B.C.), is thought to have written some five hundred medical treatises, of which perhaps eighty are extant. No evidence has been uncovered, however, to indicate that Galen, or even an artist employed by him, illustrated his original texts. Thus, all the drawings illustrating Galen's anatomy and physiology may be considered approximate or spurious.

Medical historians are in agreement on Galen's importance as the founder of experimental physiology, but because the dissection of human cadavers was forbidden by ecclesiastic authorities, he based his ideas of human physiology on extrapolations of his dissections of apes, pigs, cows, and dogs. Although this illustration, drawn several centuries after his death, typifies the crudity of Galen's physiology, his authority remained undisputed until there were advances in anatomical observation.

Galen began his medical practice in Rome in A.D. 164. In obedience to Aristotle's dictum "Nature makes nothing in vain," he developed three basic doctrines, the first two of which presented severe obstacles to understanding human physiology until the ban against human dissection was lifted.

The first of these doctrines was "vitalism," in which Galen maintained that the liver introduced "natural spirits" from ingested food into the blood. "Vital spirits" were supposed to be present in the heart's left ventricle, and vital spirits were supposed to be converted into "animal spirits" in the brain.

The second doctrine proposed that the blood passes through invisible pores in the heart's septum (the tissue that divides the heart's ventricles), with the heart acting as a massive, unidirectional pump.

The third doctrine maintained that suppuration (the exudation of pus) was an essential factor in the healing of wounds, because pus contained healing substances in itself.

These doctrines were vigorously supported by ecclesiastic authorities, whose belief in the perfection of the divinity was extended to justify the prohibition of the dissection of humans. In effect, Galen's basic teachings became superstitions. It was not until the early sixteenth century that physicians and surgeons, such as Vesalius (see pages 40–41) and Harvey (see pages 110–11), were able to overcome the intellectual bondage that had hampered physiology for so many centuries.

BVIOUSLY FAR FROM REALISTIC, this drawing by a Persian anatomist shows some bones of the limbs, shoulder, spinal column, and skull. Labels identify the parts of the skeleton, which is drawn in a characteristic "flat display" and may have been intended as a mnemonic diagram for anatomy students.

In a 1907 study of the traditions of anatomical illustration, Professor Karl Sudhoff of the University of Leipzig explained that very few early anatomic illustrations were based on firsthand observation; for the most part, they were copied from sketches in older manuscripts. It was not until Vesalius published his great *De Humani Corporis Fabrica* in 1543 (see pages 40–41) that the study of human anatomy began to be based on accurate, direct observations.

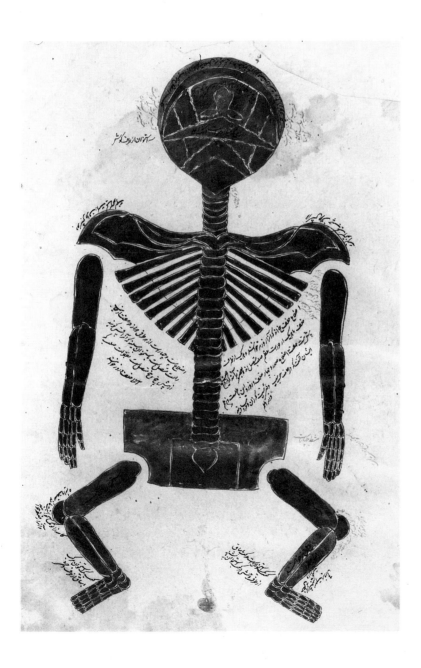

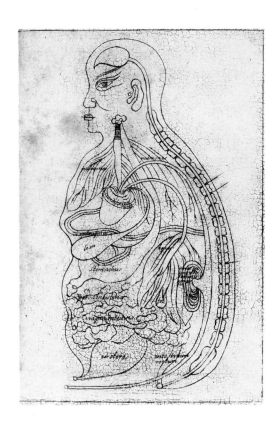

ANDREAS CLEYER
1634–1698

# A Chinese Physiological Diagram

1682

C LEYER WAS A DUTCH PHYSICIAN and botanist employed by the Dutch East India Company. In the course of his service in the Orient, Cleyer acquired a collection of Chinese medical texts and illustrations that had been assembled by Michael Boym, a Jesuit missionary in China. Using Boym's illustrations and adapting his texts, Cleyer produced his own book, *Specimen Medicinae Sinicae*, in 1682. Cleyer's compilation included illustrations and explanations of Chinese herb and root medicines, pulse lore (the diagnosis of illness by touching twelve points on the wrist), and physiological illustrations.

This woodcut diagram is best appreciated as a crude functional exposition, rather than a representational drawing. It indicates the interconnection between the brain and the spinal cord; the relationships (mostly incorrect!) among the lungs, heart, stomach, liver, and bowel; the kidneys, bladder, and several cardiovascular paths. Such diagrams were used for teaching for hundreds of years. According to ancient Chinese medical principles, the heart was the king and director of the human body; the lungs, his executives; the liver, the general. Similar, fantastic analogies were used for the rest of the organs.

In China, until the end of the nineteenth century, human anatomy was described by extrapolations from the study of lower animals and therefore anatomical illustrations were essentially diagrammatic and speculative. An accurate understanding of human anatomy had been hindered by imperial law, based on religious teachings — the successions of Buddhist, Taoist, and Confucian advisers to the Chinese emperors were devoutly committed to the principle of the sanctity of the human body. Coroners were permitted to examine bodies before or after burial, but only to determine superficial signs of wounds, blows, evidence of strangulation, suicide, or poisoning.

The modernization of Chinese anatomical studies came about with medical missions sent by English and American churches to care for their religious teachers in China. Chinese physicians began to study in England and America in the latter half of the nineteenth century, and by the beginning of the twentieth century, collaboration between Chinese and Western physicians provided a realistic foundation for anatomical studies in Chinese medical schools.

*Classification*
*170*

GERSDORFF WAS AN ALSATIAN army surgeon, with several decades of experience in the treatment of wounds that soldiers might suffer in battle. This is one of a number of illustrations for Gersdorff's landmark *Fieldbook of Wound Surgery*, published in 1517. The woodcuts, made by Johannes Wechtlin, were often imitated in later books on the subject.

Wechtlin's illustrations were used for the training of army surgeons, who were permitted to treat only officers. The rank-and-file soldier usually received no surgical attention. This illustration served as a general chart, demonstrating the variety of wounds whose treatment Gersdorff explains. The book also contains the first known picture of an amputation procedure, specific treatments for a variety of gunshot wounds, and recipes for Gersdorff's ointments and antiseptics.

Some medical historians have suggested that Gersdorff's book, written in the vernacular German, may have influenced physicians in favor of more pragmatic, reality-oriented surgical practice. For example, before Gersdorff's *Fieldbook* was published, bullet wounds were considered poisonous and were treated by promoting the exudation of the pus, leaving the bullet in place. He developed special instruments to probe and extract the bullet, after which he applied a styptic of his own formula to check bleeding.

HANS VON
GERSDORFF
D. 1529

# A
# "Wound Man"

1517

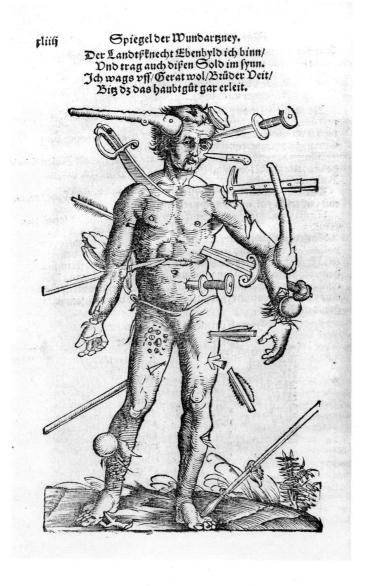

# Personality
# Types

PHYSIOGNOMY, the "science" of discovering inner character from the observation of facial or other physical features, was first described by Aristotle, who compared human and animal characteristics to derive type descriptions: bold, shy, honest, dishonest, etc. Such ideas held currency in Europe until the early eighteenth century. In 1743 the English king, George II, made the practice of physiognomy illegal.

Even in our own times there are many who attempt to read character from faces and head shapes. Specific groups of facial muscles are employed—unconsciously or not—to express emotions, moods, or judgments. Frequent use of those muscles develops lines and wrinkles that may become permanent features of the face. So there is some justification for relating facial expressions with habits of thought or feeling.

This chart, published in Strasbourg in 1531, presents eight examples of personality types, from a book by Johannes ab Indagine, a physiognomist, astrologer, and palm reader of Nuremberg. The woodcuts in Indagine's book were subsequently reproduced many times.

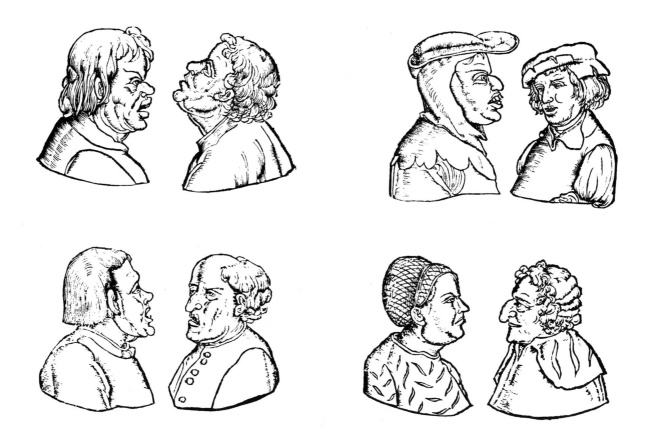

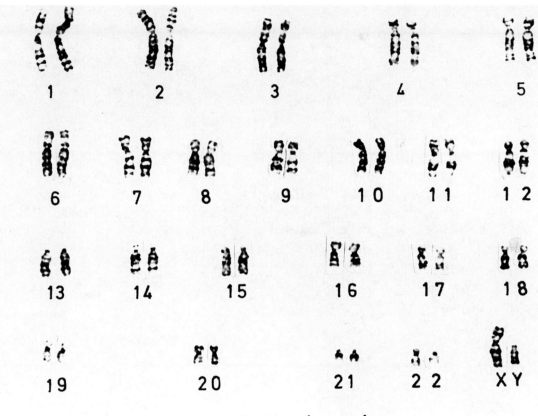

1  2  3  4  5

6  7  8  9  10  11  12

13  14  15  16  17  18

19  20  21  22  XY

Normal male.

Forty-six chromosomes carry all the hereditary material that determines the transmission of physical characteristics from human parents to their children. This discovery was made by two Swedish geneticists, J. Hin Tjio and Albert Levan, in 1956. The chart illustrated here was formulated and executed by a committee at the Denver convention of geneticists in 1960 to standardize the identification of the twenty-three chromosome pairs. It is arranged by order of the specific characteristics of each chromosome found in the cell nuclei.

All cells in the body have two copies of each chromosome type—one inherited from the father and one from the mother.

The female ovum contains only one X chromosome. The male's sperm cell carries either an X or a Y chromosome. In the process of sexual reproduction, if the sperm transmits an X chromosome to the ovum, the combination of the two X chromosomes generates a female child. If the sperm transmits a Y chromosome to the ovum, the X-Y combination produces a male child.

Due to the great improvement in the staining techniques employed for microscopic examination, during the 1920s, biologists and geneticists determined that each chromosome is similar to a string of beads, with the "beads" being the genes. The total number of genes contained in each human chromosome is still unknown, but it must be in the thousands.

Chromosomes
of a Normal
Human Male

1960

*Classification*

# Crystal Systems

THE UNIQUE STRUCTURAL PROPERTIES of crystals were discovered by accident when a French mineralogist, René Just Haüy (1743–1822), accidentally dropped a block of crystal. It shattered into many small pieces and Haüy could see that even the smallest pieces, from inside the block and outward, displayed precisely similar symmetrical shapes.

Crystals are solids having a definite, orderly arrangement of the atoms, molecules, or ions that are unique to the specific substances of which they are composed. In nature, they are formed either from molten matter or by the slow deposition and accumulation of a mineral, as in a geode. Diamonds and other precious stones—quartz, germanium, silicon, and galena—are familiar examples.

The six main crystal structural systems are represented in these illustrations, as they appear in Vinson Brown's charming and informative *Amateur Naturalist's Handbook*. The illustrator, Don Greame Kelley, has taken great care to make his drawings readily comprehensible. With the knowledge of these six systems, crystallographers can classify and understand the mechanical, electrical, and chemical properties of specific crystals. Each system has three axes that vary in their dimensional relationships.

X-ray crystallography, first demonstrated by the German physicist Max von Laue (see page 124), offers the possibility of "looking into" the crystal structure. An X-ray crystallograph enabled researchers to identify the double-helix structure of DNA in 1953 (see page 220).

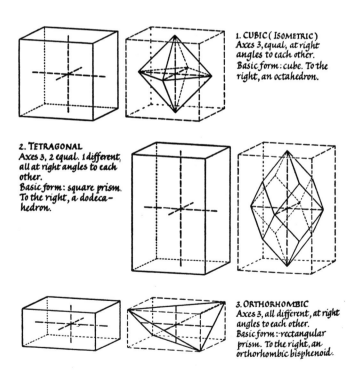

**1. CUBIC ( ISOMETRIC )**
Axes 3, equal, at right angles to each other. Basic form: cube. To the right, an octahedron.

**2. TETRAGONAL**
Axes 3, 2 equal. 1 different, all at right angles to each other.
Basic form: square prism. To the right, a dodecahedron.

**3. ORTHORHOMBIC**
Axes 3, all different, at right angles to each other.
Basic form: rectangular prism. To the right, an orthorhombic bisphenoid.

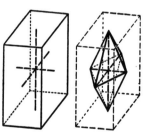

**4. MONOCLINIC**
Axes 3, all different. Two axes are at right angles to each other, but not to the third.
Basic form: inclined rectangular prism. To the right, an octahedron.

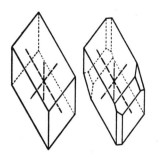

**5. TRICLINIC**
Axes 3, all different, no two at right angles with each other. Most difficult system to determine, but rarest in occurence.
To the right, a typical form.

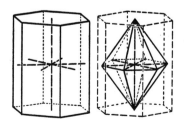

**6. HEXAGONAL**
Axes 4, 3 of equal length, at 60° angle to each other, different from and at right angles to the main axis.
Basic form: 6-sided prism. To the right, a hexagonal bipyramid.

# A Table of the Elements

T HE THEORY THAT ALL MATTER is composed of "indivisible particles"—atoms—had been proposed as early as the fifth century B.C. by the Greek philosophers Leucippus (c. 490 B.C.) and Democritus (c. 480 B.C.). Yet it was not until Dalton published his *New System of Chemical Philosophy, Part I*, in 1808, that a rational explanation of the atomic theory became available to chemists.

Dalton designed the symbols of his table, as did other chemists preceding him, for his personal use. The uniqueness of Dalton's table lies in his assignment of a specific weight (mass) to the atom of each element. By what is reported to have been a "flash of intuition," Dalton perceived that specific *quantitative* relationships characterize the structures of chemical compounds (mixtures of elements).

In his *New System*, Dalton enunciated three major principles: that the atoms of each element are alike and are different from the atoms of every other element; that combinations of different elements are characterized by the proportions of the "weights" (masses) of the specific elements they contain; and that elements can combine with each other in more than a single proportion, provided that the proportions are ratios of whole numbers.

Dalton was of course unable to weigh any of the atoms of the elements known at the time. Instead, he proposed an arbitrary method for assigning weights. Hydrogen, the lightest element, was assigned the weight of 1; the other elements were assigned weights relative to that of hydrogen. As an example, water, composed of hydrogen and oxygen, could be described as having a ratio of 7 (oxygen) to 1 (hydrogen). (This was later corrected to 8:1.) By such proportional analyses of the elements in compounds, he was able to assign nitrogen (azote) the number 5, carbon 5A, phosphorus 9, sulfur 13, and so forth.

Dalton realized that the smallest portion of each compound must consist of a specific number of atoms of each element in the compound. He called that specific number of atoms a "compound atom." We now call it a "molecule."

Dalton's contemporaries found his symbols for the elements too cumbersome for swift notations. Five years after Dalton's book was published a new system was devised by the Swedish chemist Jöns Jacob Berzelius (1779–1848). In Berzelius's system, the initial letter of the Latin name of the element, or the initial plus a second letter, is used as the symbol for the element. For example, oxygen becomes "O"; hydrogen, "H"; silver, "Ag" (argentum); and so forth. Compounds are notated as letters with number subscripts when the molecule contains more than one atom, e.g., water is $H_2O$, ammonia is $NH_3$, etc.

## ELEMENTS

| | | w.t | | | w.t |
|---|---|---|---|---|---|
| ⊙ | Hydrogen | 1 | ⊕ | Strontian | 46 |
| ◑ | Azote | 5 | ✳ | Barytes | 68 |
| ● | Carbon | 5A | Ⓘ | Iron | 50 |
| ○ | Oxygen | 7 | Ⓩ | Zinc | 56 |
| ✪ | Phosphorus | 9 | Ⓒ | Copper | 56 |
| ⊕ | Sulphur | 13 | Ⓛ | Lead | 90 |
| ◉ | Magnesia | 20 | Ⓢ | Silver | 190 |
| ⊖ | Lime | 24 | Ⓖ | Gold | 190 |
| ◫ | Soda | 28 | Ⓟ | Platina | 190 |
| ⦀ | Potash | 42 | ✺ | Mercury | 167 |

# Napoleon's
# Russian
# Campaign

1869

MINARD, A CIVIL ENGINEER, was a French inspector-general of bridges and causeways. This graph—perhaps a scholarly diversion—was drawn by him in 1869. It charts the losses suffered by Napoleon's army in his Russian campaign, from 1812 to 1813.

The thick gray band at the top indicates the size of the French army, beginning with 422,000 men, until it reached Moscow with 100,000 men. The black lower band charts the retreat from Russia, ending with an army reduced to only 10,000 men. Vertical lines extend from the retreat path down to a temperature scale, which records the bitterly cold winter experienced by the ill-fated French army.

Six dimensions of data are displayed on Minard's two-dimensional graph, which is considered one of the most sophisticated hand-drawn displays of statistical information ever made.

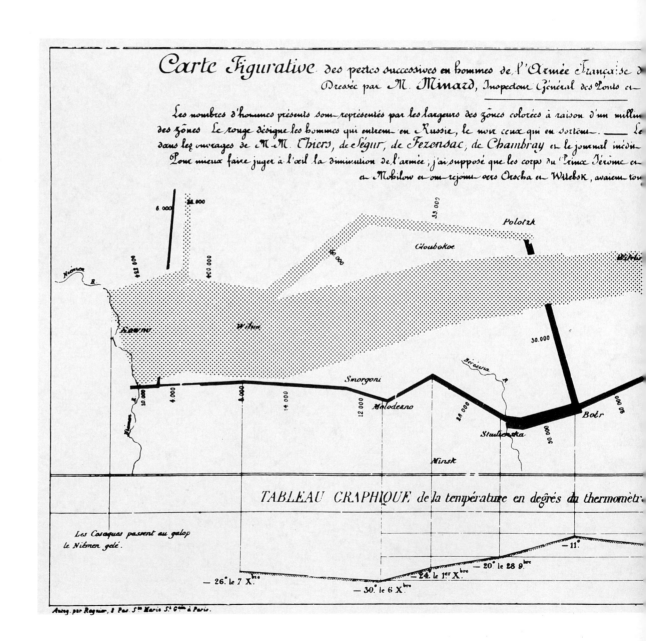

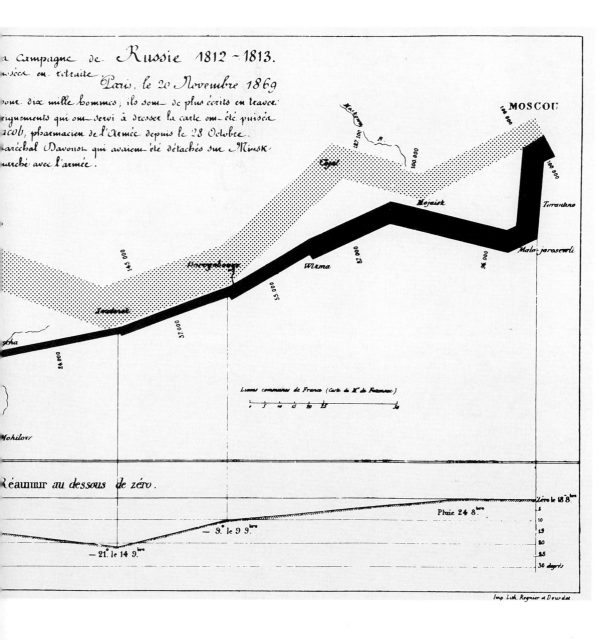

# Chart of
# Weather
# Symbols

1948

THESE SYMBOLS WERE USED for weather charting by meteorologists throughout the United States from the 1920s until 1955, when they were revised and expanded. Modern meteorologists now have a chart containing almost a hundred such symbols, including groups to signify past weather conditions, total cloud covering, and pressure changes, as well as refinements of the older symbols.

The symbols in this illustration display economy and aptness. Many are virtually pictograms, such as those representing gale, lightning, rainbow, thunderstorm, and zodiacal light (the aurora borealis).

| Symbol | Name | Symbol | Name |
|---|---|---|---|
| ⑂ | Aurora | ≡° | Mist |
| O | Clear | ◑ | Partly cloudy |
| ● | Cloudy | ⌒ | Rainbow |
| ⋏ | Dew | V | Rime |
| ●° | Drizzle | ☆ or Ⓢ | Snow |
| ∞ | Dust-haze | ⊠ | Snow on ground |
| ⊞ | Dust-storm | ⊛ | Snow and rain together |
| ≡ | Fog | ⊹ | Snowdrift |
| ⚡ | Gale | △ | Soft hail |
| ~ | Glazed frost | ⊕ | Solar corona |
| ⩶ | Ground fog | ⊕ | Solar halo |
| ▲ | Hail | T | Thunder |
| ⊔ | Hoar frost | ↳ | Thunderstorm |
| ⊢ | Ice crystals | 0 | Unusual visibility of distant objects |
| ↙ | Lightning | ≡: | Wet fog |
| ∪ | Lunar corona | ℳ | Zodiacal light |
| ⊓ | Lunar halo | | |
| ⋈ | Mirage | | |

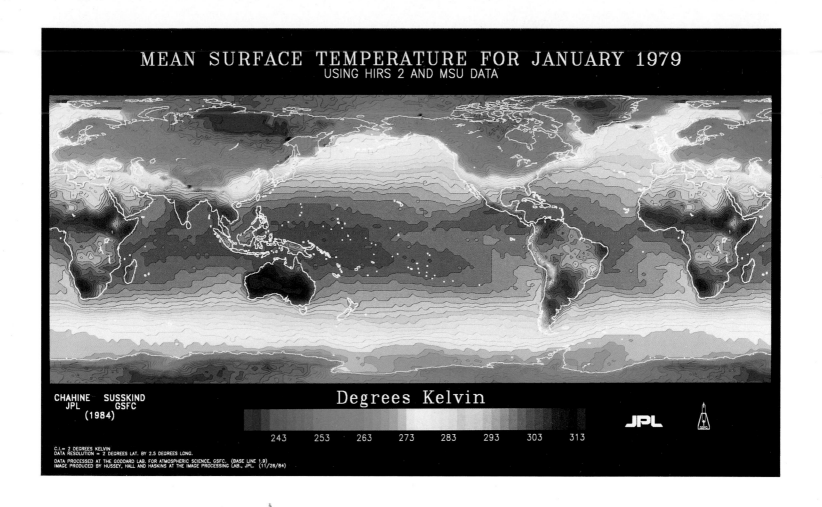

CHAHINE  SUSSKIND
JPL    GSFC
(1984)

C.I.= 2 DEGREES KELVIN
DATA RESOLUTION = 2 DEGREES LAT. BY 2.5 DEGREES LONG.
DATA PROCESSED AT THE GODDARD LAB. FOR ATMOSPHERIC SCIENCE, GSFC. (BASE LINE 1.9)
IMAGE PRODUCED BY HUSSEY, HALL AND HASKINS AT THE IMAGE PROCESSING LAB., JPL. (11/26/84)

THE U.S. NATIONAL AERONAUTICS and Space Administration launched a program for continuous monitoring of Earth's surface temperatures in 1960. This illustration is a computer-processed display of the television data received in January 1979 from the TIROS-N polar-orbiting satellite.

TIROS-N satellites (TIROS stands for "Television and Infrared Observation Satellite" and "N" denotes the specific satellite model) circle Earth in polar orbits, about 500 miles above its surface. The orbits are completed every 100 minutes, as Earth spins below.

Sensors and video cameras on the TIROS-N satellites transmit information about cloud cover, surface temperatures, and atmospheric temperatures. The satellites are also equipped to relay environmental data from buoys, balloons, and unmanned weather stations. Some TIROS satellites carry search and rescue radio equipment to relay signals from ships and aircraft in distress.

A color key, in degrees Kelvin (see page 133), is provided below the map. Note that the hottest temperatures (dark red-brown splotches) prevailed in Africa, South America, and Australia. Measurements such as these have allowed scientists to detect the recent warming trend in Earth's atmosphere.

The data for this global temperature profile were organized and color enhanced at the Goddard Laboratory for Atmospheric Science and the Jet Propulsion Laboratory at Pasadena, California.

NASA

Global
Temperature
Profile

1979

Classification

179

# VI
# Conceptualization

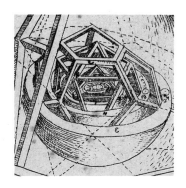

A geometrical-physical theory as such is incapable of
being directly pictured, being merely a system of concepts.
But these concepts serve the purpose of bringing a
multiplicity of real or sensory experiences into connection
in the mind. To "visualize" a theory, or bring it home to
one's mind, therefore means to give a representation
to that abundance of experiences for which the theory
supplies the schematic arrangement.

—ALBERT EINSTEIN[1]

PLATO (c. 427–347 B.C.), in the second part of his *Timaeus* dialogue, presented his theory of matter in accordance with his belief in divine perfection. Observation and experimentation were demeaned as misleading: divine perfection could be comprehended only through the imagination. In Plato's theory, the forms of the fundamental structures of the smallest particles were right-angled triangles. Particles of larger size were formed when those right-angled triangles joined as pairs to make isosceles triangles, and then squares. These, in turn, could combine to make more complex, heavier particles whose structures were in the forms of solid geometric figures: cubes, tetrahedrons, octahedrons, and icosahedrons. Those four solid figures formed the structural units of the four "elements": earth, fire, air, and water.

After some two thousand years of inquiry into the nature of matter, we recognize that Plato's concept, although aesthetically pleasing, is scientifically untenable. But what is intriguing here is the examination of the structural elements of Plato's imaging process in the development of his theory. Plato had engaged in a "thought experiment"—an experiment conducted entirely in his mind.

Isaac Newton regarded the subtle relationship of mathematics to mechanics as the key to the explanation of phenomena. The nineteenth-century Scottish physicist James Clerk Maxwell, attempting to make his mathematical equations relating electric and magnetic phenomena more comprehensible, drew pictures of his imagined "lines of force." Albert Einstein, in his later years, envisioned a "unified field theory" that would accommodate electromagnetism, the space-time structure, and gravitation. Such thought experiments may be generated by dissatisfaction with previously expressed explanations; by new, or faintly glimpsed observations; or by a heightened state of awareness to subtle, intangible discontinuities or incongruities.

In the sciences, the memory of observed phenomena, illustrations, and quantitative and mathematical relationships is subjected to mental scanning, contemplation, and meditation that may produce new insights. It seems that we cannot think about an observation or experience in the objective world without resorting to mental imagery. Some of the images in this section, however, display no reference to objective, visible reality; they arise from the mind's magnificent resources.

THE QUESTION "How did the wonderful universe, the earth and all its marvels, and ourselves come into being?" is primal in the history of scientific thought. Prehistoric science emerged from guesses and imagination. In antiquity, answers to those questions were debated with great intensity; reverberating throughout the society, they became myths.

Ancient Chinese scholars offered the image of P'an Ku as the creator of all things in the universe. It was P'an Ku who gave form to the heavens and the earth. His tears made the great Yellow and Yangtze rivers. His breath generated the winds, his speech was the thunder, and his brilliant scanning gaze was the lightning. P'an Ku, the creator himself, developed like a plant, emerging out of leaves (at center bottom).

The artist who drew this face of P'an Ku chose a particular human countenance to symbolize the generalization of the creator, just as was done in other ancient cultures.

（會圖才三）氏古盤

【盤古】62 バン　天地開闢の初めに出て、此の世に君臨した古の天子の號。路史注に渾敦氏は卽ち盤古といふ。〔三五曆記〕未レ有二天地一之時、混沌如二雞子一、盤古生二其中一、一萬八千歳、天地開闢、清陽爲レ天、濁陰爲レ地、盤古在二其中一云云、天日高一丈、地日厚一丈、盤古日長一丈、如レ

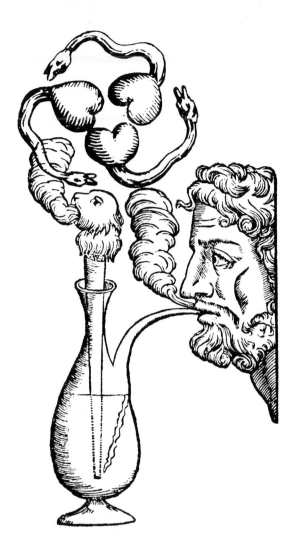

Alchemy, the progenitor of chemistry, was brought to Europe via Greece, from Egypt and the Middle East, sometime during the third century A.D. Sometimes persecuted because of their resistance to church dogma, the alchemists often pursued their work in secret. They directed their practice toward three objectives: the transmutation of base metals into gold; the discovery of a universal cure for disease; and a system for infinitely prolonging life.

In Genesis, the first book of the Old Testament, it was the Serpent who had directed mankind to the knowledge of good and evil by his offer of the fruit of the tree of knowledge to Eve. This early image of Alchemical Man was a cherished symbol, consisting of major elements in alchemy. The emblem can then be read as a testament of the alchemist's dedication to his science: the alchemist, with his own breath and spirit, instills his experimental materials with his total devotion. There will arise from his efforts the three serpents with heart-shaped tails, who will continue to guide mankind's search for compassionate truth.

It is noteworthy that the alchemists accepted some women into their profession. Prominent among them were the priestess who called herself "Isis"; "Mary the Jewess," a Greek woman who invented the slow-heating device now called the "double boiler"; and "Cleopatra," who had written the *Chrysopeia*, on the making of gold (see page 96). The admission of women into a scientific profession (the alchemists were also professional chemists, producing substances for daily life) at such an early time in history is remarkable.

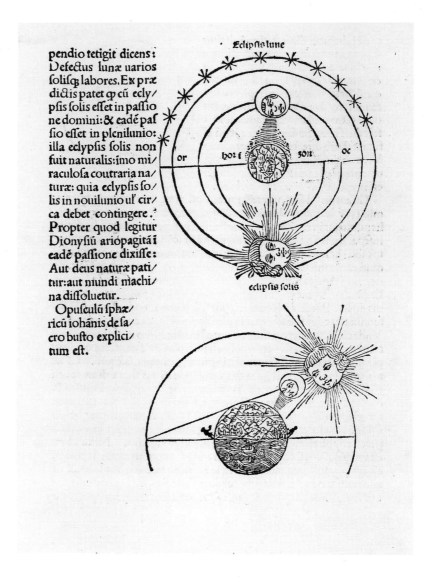

**H**OLYWOOD WAS AN ENGLISH CLERGYMAN who is believed to have lived mainly in Paris, where he taught mathematics and astrology; in scholarly circles he was known as "Sacrobosco" (the Latin equivalent of "Holywood").

Holywood wrote the *Sphaera Mundi* (Spheres of the World) in order to bring information from Ptolemy's *Almagest*, which had been written in Greek, to scholars having no training in that language. Ptolemy (c. 100–170) had compiled virtually all of the knowledge of astronomy of his own time into this encyclopedia, which also included his own observations of the heavenly bodies and diagrams of their orbital motions. The assumption in the *Almagest* is that Earth is at the fixed center of the universe.

Holywood's *Sphaera Mundi* upholds the geocentric theory and also presents simplified proofs of the circular orbits of the planets, explanations of eclipses of the Sun and the Moon, and a proof that Earth is indeed a sphere.

At the top of the first illustration: with Earth at the center of the universe, under certain conditions the path of the Sun's light is obstructed by Earth, so Earth then casts its shadow on the Moon.

At the bottom: at certain times in each year Earth, the Moon, and the Sun are aligned so that the Moon obstructs the light from the Sun. Holywood assures the reader that the Sun does not stop shining; the Moon simply casts its shadow on a part of Earth.

## QuOD AQuA SIT ROTVNDA.

Quod at aqua habeat tumore & accedat ad rotuditate sic patet. Po
nat signu i littore maris & exeat nauis a portu: & i tatu eloget cp ocul⁹
existes iuxta pede mali no possit uidere signu. State uero naui ocul⁹ eiuf
de existetis i sumitate mali: bn uidebit signu illud. Sed ocul⁹ existetis iu
xta pede mali meli⁹ deberet uidere signu cp q e i sumitate: sicut patet p li
neas ductas ab utroqʒ ad signu: & nulla alia hui⁹ rei ca e cp tumor aqʒ. Ex
cludat .n. oia alia ipedimeta: sicut nebulæ & uapores ascedetes. Ite cu aqʒ

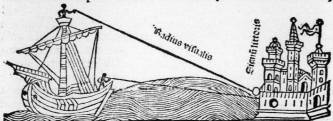

sit corp⁹ hogeneu totu cu ptib⁹ eiusde erit ronis: sed ptes aqʒ (sicut i guttu
lis & rorib⁹ herbaʒ accidit) rotuda naturalif appetut forma ergo & to
## QuOD TERRA SIT CENTʒ MVNDI.  tu cuius sut ptes.

Quod aut terra sit in medio firmameti sita sic patet. Existentib⁹ i su
perficie terræ stellæ apparet eiusde quantitatis siue sint i medio cæli: si
ue iuxta ortu: siue iuxta occasu: & hoc quia terra æqualiter distat ab eis
Si eni terra magis accederet ad firmamentu i una parte cp in alia aliquis
existes i alia pte supficiei terræ cp magis accderet ad firmametu no uide
ret cæli medietate: sed hoc e cotra Ptolemæu & oes phos dicetes cp ubi
cuqʒ existat homo sex signa orint ei: & sex occidut: & medietas cæli se
per apparet ei: medietas uero occultat. Illud ite e signu cp terra sit tacp
cetʒ & puctus respectu firmameti: quia si terra esset alicuius quatitatis
respectu firmameti: no cotingeret medietate cæli uideri: Ite si itelligat
supficies plana sup centʒ terræ diuides ea i duo æqualia: & p coseques
ipsu firmametu. oculus igit existens i cetro terræ uideret medietatem
firmameti. Ideqʒ existes i supficie terræ uideret eade medietate. Ex hiis
colligit cp isensibil e quatitas terræ q e a supficie ad cetʒ: & p coseques
quatitas toti⁹ terræ isensibilis e respectu firmameti. Dicit etia Alfragan⁹
cp mima stellaʒ fixaʒ uisu notabiliu maior e tota terra: sed ipsa stella re
spectu firmameti est cp punctus: multo igit fortius terra cu sit minor ea.

In the second woodcut Holywood demonstrates that Earth's shape must be spherical. At the top of the ship's mast, the sailor in the crow's nest can see the shoreline, but the sailor at the bow of the ship, at sea level, is prevented from seeing the shoreline because of the curvature of the ocean's surface.

Holywood's illustrations of the eclipses are known to have been adapted from an earlier astronomy text, the *Rudimenta Astronomica* (Rudiments of Astronomy). However, the illustration demonstrating Earth's spherical shape may have been drawn by Holywood himself. *Sphaera Mundi* began to be circulated in manuscript copies about 1220. With the advent of the printing press, the book was one of the first astronomy texts to be printed, in 1472. Its reputation was so great that twenty-four more editions were published during the next three decades.

# Machinery of the Heavens

A SCHOLAR, IDENTIFIABLE by his cap and gown, kneels in a landscape abundant with the good works of nature and man. He has pierced the shell of stars to observe the great wheels that move the heavenly bodies. This woodcut illustrates a mechanistic explanation—remarkably prescient when contrasted with the mystical views then current—of the cosmology proposed by the German cardinal Nicholas de Cusa.

Primarily a philosopher and mathematician, Cusa did not engage in detailed astronomical observations and calculations. His book *Reconciliation of Opposites*, which was written in the mid-1440s, offered the first reasoned exposition of a heliocentric cosmology, and questioned the accepted dogma of geocentricity. A half century before Copernicus, and two centuries before Galileo, Cusa theorized that Earth might rotate on its axis while moving in an orbital path around the Sun; that space is infinite; and that the stars were like our own Sun, and might be at the centers of other inhabited universes.

Although his ideas challenged church doctrine, Cusa presented them as philosophical conjectures, and so did not bring censure upon himself. His main argument was based on the supposition that since the universe is infinite, an observer standing anywhere on Earth would see the universe as though he were at its center; and this would also be true for an observer standing on the Moon, or on any of the planets or stars. His statement, that "the fabric of the world has its center everywhere and its circumference nowhere," was echoed some five hundred years later by Albert Einstein, who remarked in 1931 that "all places in the universe are alike."

# The Solar System

Nicholas Copernicus, a canon of the cathedral at Frombork, Poland, had studied mathematics, medicine, and Roman Catholic church law under the sponsorship of his uncle, a bishop. In 1500, Copernicus was invited to attend a conference in Rome on the reform of the church calendar. The conference impelled him to examine the reasons for the frequent corrections of the calendar.

The Julian calendar, established by Julius Caesar in 46 B.C., had provided the basis of the church calendar for more than 1,500 years. It specified a 365-day year for each of three years in succession, to be followed by one 366-day leap year. But by the beginning of the sixteenth century, numerous manipulations and compromises—including alterations limiting the duration of the offices of certain church dignitaries—had skewed the Julian calendar by approximately 11 days.

Such irregularities made it impossible to denote specific dates for the observance of some church holidays, such as saints' days. A devout member of the congregation might not be able to engage in the acts of devotion prescribed for the saint's day—and might therefore put at risk the chance for salvation.

In traditional church practice, the annual calendar was established by the study of astronomers' tables of the positions of the planets in their courses. These tables were compiled in keeping with the notion of geocentricity. However, by 1507 Copernicus had concluded that the calendrical tables could be established more rationally by adopting a heliocentric theory of the planetary orbits: that is, that Earth and the other planets orbit around the Sun. This idea had been proposed by several astronomers long before Copernicus, notably by Aristarchus (c. 300 B.C.), and even closer to Copernicus's own time, by Nicholas de Cusa (c. 1440) (see page 12).

Copernicus's diagram, illustrated here, shows the Sun at the center. Around it move the planets Mercury (VII), Venus (VI), Telluris (Earth) and its moon (V), Mars (IIII), Jupiter (III), and Saturn (II)— all within the heavenly sphere of fixed stars (I). This illustration first appeared in a manuscript that Copernicus circulated among European astronomers and scholars.

The new system was discussed with great interest, but such a radical challenge to church doctrine placed Copernicus in danger of the accusation of heresy. He therefore refrained from publishing his manuscript until thirteen more years had passed. His book, *De Revolutionibus Orbium Coelestium* (On the Revolutions of the Heavenly Spheres), was published in 1543 and dedicated to Pope Paul III. It was received with disfavor by the church and was placed on the prohibited list (the ban was lifted in 1835).

Nevertheless, Copernicus's work was studied by eminent astronomers such as Tycho Brahe, Johannes Kepler, Galileo, and Isaac Newton, whose work led to the confirmation of the heliocentric theory.

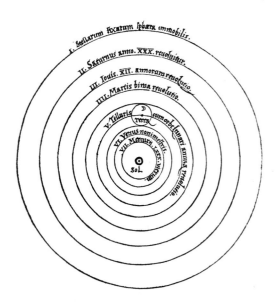

JOHANNES KEPLER
1571–1630

## Model for the Orbits of the Planets

1596–97

WHILE A STUDENT of Lutheran theology at the University of Tübingen, Kepler read Copernicus's *De Revolutionibus Orbium Coelestium* (On the Revolutions of the Heavenly Spheres). Deeply impressed by Copernicus's theory of a heliocentric universe, Kepler, already an accomplished mathematician, turned to the study of astronomy.

In 1594, at the age of twenty-three, Kepler was appointed professor of mathematics and science at the University of Graz, in Austria. Kepler's interests were wide-ranging; he easily absorbed the ideas of the ancient philosophers, mystics, and astrologers. (Emperor Rudolf and members of his court frequently commissioned Kepler to provide them with horoscopes, which were highly prized.)

In his early work as an astronomer Kepler was guided by Plato's concept of a harmonious, mathematically ordered universe. His first published contribution to astronomy, the *Mysterium Cosmographicus* (Mysteries of the Cosmos), 1596, pays tribute to the Greek philosopher. Kepler's scheme of the planetary orbits is based on a combination of Plato's five regular polyhedrons with the hypothesis of "spherical planes" in which the planets travel. This diagram of cosmological structure was devised to illustrate Kepler's idea.

In the drawing, the outermost sphere (a) has been bisected to expose the internal arrangement of the system. In the outermost region, Saturn, the most distant planet known at the time, moves in a circular orbit around the Sun. Saturn's "orbital sphere" is separated from Jupiter's by the interposition of a cube (b; one of the five regular Platonic polyhedrons). Between Jupiter and Mars stands a tetrahedron, or pyramid; Mars and Earth are separated by a dodecahedron; Earth and Venus are separated by an icosahedron; and Venus and Mars by an octahedron. At the center of the system stands the orb of the Sun.

Kepler was unable to correlate his observation records of the planetary orbits with the separation distances demanded by Plato's ideal polyhedrons, so he abandoned that effort shortly after his *Mysterium Cosmographicus* was published. Nevertheless, the book brought Kepler to the attention of his eminent contemporary Tycho Brahe. Recognizing Kepler's mathematical ability, Tycho invited him to work at his observatory in Prague in 1600.

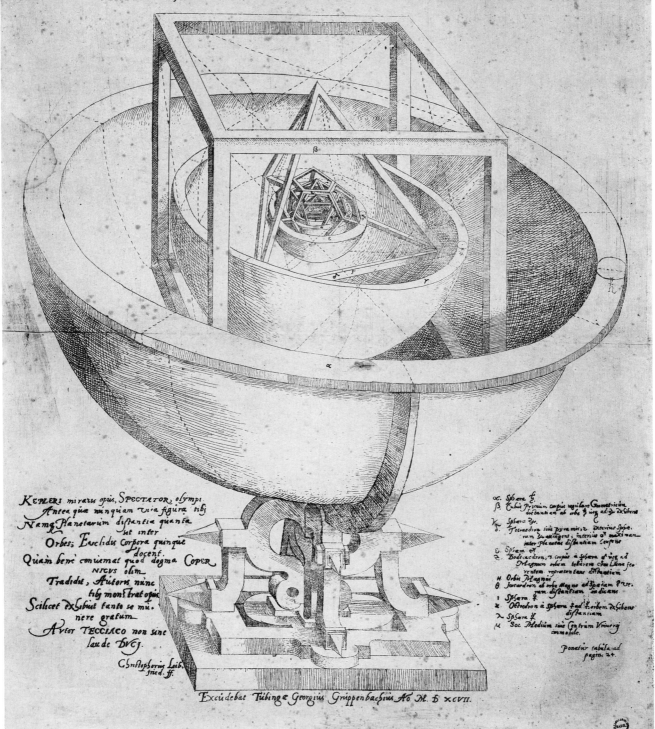

# The Orbit of Mars

AFTER TYCHO BRAHE'S DEATH in 1601, Kepler was appointed "imperial mathematician," in charge of Brahe's observatory. Kepler had been given Tycho's closely guarded tables of his planetary observations, and Kepler embarked on a mathematical analysis of Tycho's data. Tycho had almost daily recorded his observations of Mars's position as it moved across the sky; other astronomers had been content to make such observations occasionally, at astronomically or astrologically momentous times, such as planetary oppositions or conjunctions.

Kepler spent almost eight years in the study of Tycho's Mars tables. His analysis led him to conclude that Mars's orbit must take an elliptical, rather than the commonly accepted circular, path. This diagram shows the orbit of Mars as an ellipse (the broken line) within the conventionally accepted circular orbit. The Sun is at *n*, one of the ellipse's foci.

Because Tycho's tables of Mars's positions were recorded at virtually daily intervals, Kepler could divide the elliptical path into distances traveled per unit of time. Therefore the area traversed by the radial line extending from the Sun to Mars (*n* to *b*) must be proportional to the time required for Mars to move from *b* to *k*. This insight led Kepler to the further recognition that Mars must vary in its orbital velocity as it traverses the elliptical path, speeding up as it approaches the Sun and slowing down as it moves away from it. The changes in orbital velocity were eventually explained by Isaac Newton's exposition of the gravitational attraction between bodies.

A figure of "Victorious Astronomy" decorates the upper right corner of the diagram. It serves as an implicit tribute to Kepler's revolutionary achievement, which dispelled the traditional Platonic theory of circular orbits.

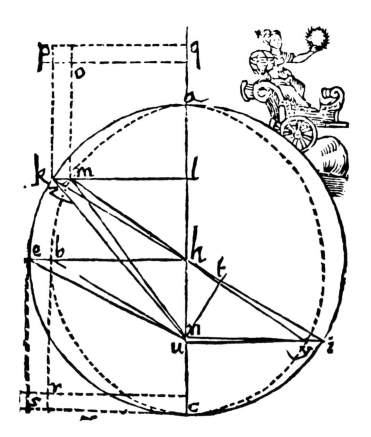

# The Harmonies
# of the World

I N 1619, KEPLER PUBLISHED what he described as his major achievement, *Harmonice Mundi* (Harmonies of the World). The divine law he had been seeking was uncovered at last: the velocities of the planets in their orbits are related to specific musical scales!

Earlier astrologer-astronomers like Gafunicus and Zerlino had assigned single musical tones to individual planets; but Kepler claimed to have realized a specific series of tones for each of the planets known in his time: Saturn, Jupiter, Mars, Earth, Venus, and Mercury—as well as a motif for Earth's Moon, "hic locum habet etiam" (The moon always occupies this position).

Ascending tones correspond to a planet's approach toward the Sun, and descending tones to the planet's movement away from it. Kepler's notations (above) employ musical clef signs that are now outmoded. Transcribed into modern notation, each motif reads as follows:

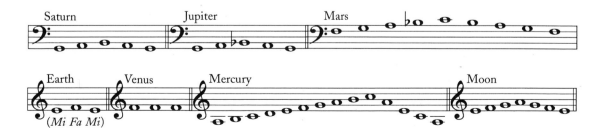

In the marginal fine print at the lower right of the page Kepler notes that the tones for Earth—*Mi, Fa, Mi*—stand for *Mi*sery, *Fa*mine, and *Mi*sery. In fact, the period in which this work was written was marked by violently destructive religious and secular wars.

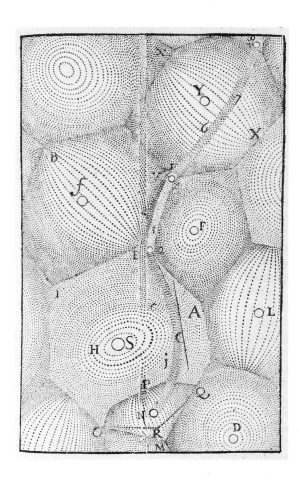

# The Matter of Space

1640

I N HIS *Discourse on Method* (1637), Descartes urged scientists to doubt any conclusion or theory until it had been repeatedly proved by demonstration. But seventeenth-century astronomical technology was too rudimentary to provide instrumentation for the study of the matter of space. Addressing the question of what, exactly, supported the planets in their orbits, Descartes applied his formidable intellect to the construction of an image of the composition of space. This comprised the third part of his *Principles of Philosophy* (1640).

First, Descartes rejected the traditional idea that the planets moved in a vacuum. He proposed instead that the infinite universe must be filled with matter of a special kind, which he named "plenum," and that such matter must be composed of extremely fine particles, all of them in motion. Each particle would impart its motion to its neighboring particles, and their changes in position would form vortices. The planets were transported by the vortices through the plenum.

This illustration from his *Principles of Philosophy* describes his idea. The plenum is represented by dashed lines. Each vortex carries a Sun around which the planets rotate. Several Suns (Y, F, L, D, N, and S) with their satellite planets are indicated, accommodating the idea that our solar system is only one of many in the universe. The slightly darker serpentine path that extends from the bottom center at N to the upper right, at 8 of the diagram, describes Descartes's concept of the motion of a comet as it is borne by the plenum.

Descartes supported the Copernican heliocentric cosmology, and his ideas were widely discussed in European scholarly circles. Isaac Newton studied Descartes's *Principles of Philosophy* while he was a student at Cambridge University, in the early 1660s, and it was Newton's theory of gravitational attraction between bodies in space that effectively disproved Descartes's vortex-plenum theory.

THE MYSTERY OF THE ORIGIN of the solar system has captivated mankind's imagination for thousands of years. But technology, on which experimental efforts must depend, has not yet provided the ultimate resolution of the many questions about the nature of space and matter, the formation of planets, stars, and other astronomical phenomena.

In 1944, C. F. von Weizsäcker, a German astronomer, advanced a hypothesis to explain the origin of the solar system, which is illustrated here. He proposed that the original dust cloud from which the solar system was formed would not be able to rotate as a single system, but would break up into a system of vortices, as Descartes had said (see his vortex-plenum system, page 192). As the energy fields expanded, the vortices would increase in size and matter would coalesce at the boundaries of groups of vortices to form planets. The entire system would, theoretically, generate opposing forces at its outermost reaches, at the enclosing circular path marked by counterclockwise arrows. Note the movement of adjacent vortices (small arrows). The illustration was drawn by James Egleson, based upon suggestions by von Weizsäcker and other physicists.

# Evolution of the Solar System

1944

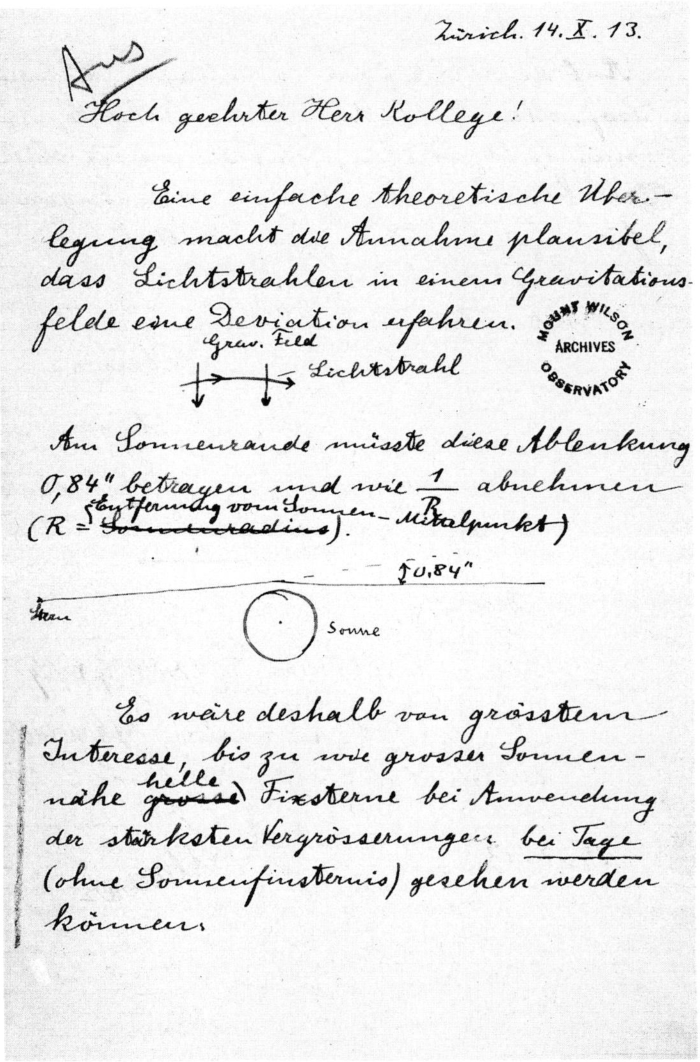

Zürich. 14. X. 13.

Hoch geehrter Herr Kollege!

Eine einfache theoretische Über-
legung macht die Annahme plausibel,
dass Lichtstrahlen in einem Gravitations-
felde eine Deviation erfahren.

Grav. Feld → Lichtstrahl

Am Sonnenrande müsste diese Ablenkung
0,84" betragen und wie $\frac{1}{R}$ abnehmen
(R = Entfernung vom Sonnen-Mittelpunkt).

↑0,84"

Sonne

Es wäre deshalb von grösstem
Interesse, bis zu wie grosser Sonnen-
nähe helle Fixsterne bei Anwendung
der stärksten Vergrösserungen bei Tage
(ohne Sonnenfinsternis) gesehen werden
können.

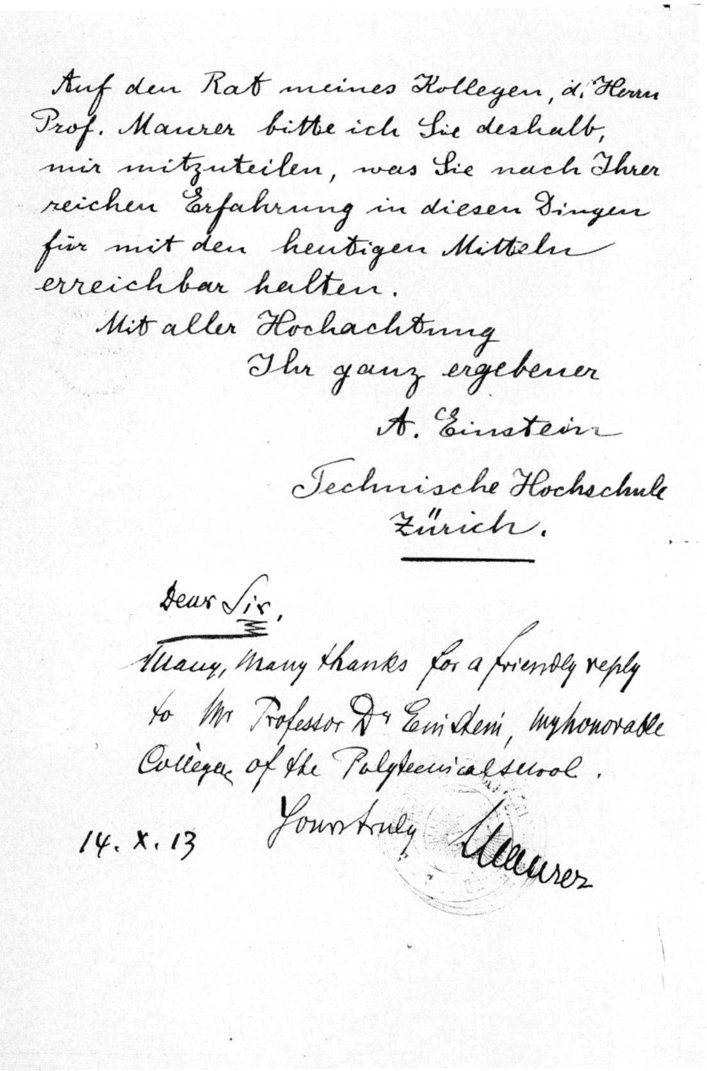

Auf den Rat meines Kollegen, d. Herrn
Prof. Maurer bitte ich Sie deshalb,
mir mitzuteilen, was Sie nach Ihrer
reichen Erfahrung in diesen Dingen
für mit den heutigen Mitteln
erreichbar halten.
Mit aller Hochachtung
Ihr ganz ergebener
A. Einstein
Technische Hochschule
Zürich.

Dear Sir,
Many, many thanks for a friendly reply
to Mr Professor Dr Einstein, my honorable
Colleague of the Polytechnicalschool.
Yours truly

14. X. 13    Maurer

ALBERT EINSTEIN
1879–1955

Gravitational
Deflection of
Light
1913

I N THIS LETTER WRITTEN October 14, 1913, to the great American astronomer George Hale (1868–1938), director of the Mount Wilson Observatory in Pasadena, California, Einstein asks about the possibility of arranging for an experiment using the observatory's telescope, at the time the newest and most sophisticated in the world.

Einstein's purpose was to verify a hypothesis he was exploring for the third part of his "General Theory of Relativity." He believed that light could be deflected by a gravitational field much more noticeably than Newton had suggested almost two hundred years before.

In this letter Einstein drew a diagram to illustrate his idea, noting his calculation of the angle of deflection that must occur as the light from a distant star approaches and passes the Sun: 0.84″ (⁸⁴/₁₀₀ of a degree of arc). However, observation of a star whose light rays were passing close to the Sun would of course be hindered by the Sun's overwhelming brightness. Einstein asked Hale to determine by telescopic observation "within how great a proximity to the Sun bright stars could be seen by daylight, without a solar eclipse."

Because of the outbreak of World War I in 1914, Einstein's hypothesis could not be tested until the spring of 1919. A solar eclipse was to occur on March 29, 1919. The British Royal Astronomical Society organized two observation expeditions, one to northern Brazil and the other to Principe Island, off the coast of West Africa. The astronomer Arthur Eddington (1882–1944), of the Greenwich Observatory staff, a vigorous supporter of Einstein's work, chose to observe the eclipse at the Principe Island station. (It was later reported that Eddington was so preoccupied with the photography of the eclipse that he did not have the opportunity to observe it directly.)

The telescopic photographs confirmed the validity of Einstein's hypothesis. When the photographs of the stars' apparent positions were compared with their actual positions six months previously (that is, when their light was unobstructed in the midnight sky), the angle of deflection of their rays by the Sun's gravitation agreed closely with Einstein's prediction.

The observed position of a star whose light passed close to the Sun was the *apparent*, not the actual position. Einstein's diagram can be amended to illustrate this:

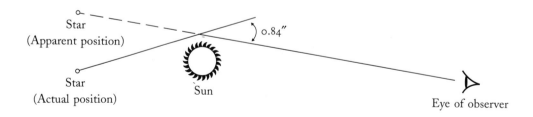

Einstein's idea has led to the recognition of a phenomenon called "gravity's lens." Because there are massive bodies in outer space, starlight must be deflected by the gravitational forces of the intervening celestial bodies. Such deflections are analogous to those produced by optical lenses, and astronomers are studying this phenomenon for the possibility of viewing celestial bodies with magnifications and acuities beyond the capabilities of our most powerful telescopes. Gravity lenses may also affect the paths of other forms of electromagnetic radiations arriving at Earth from outer space.

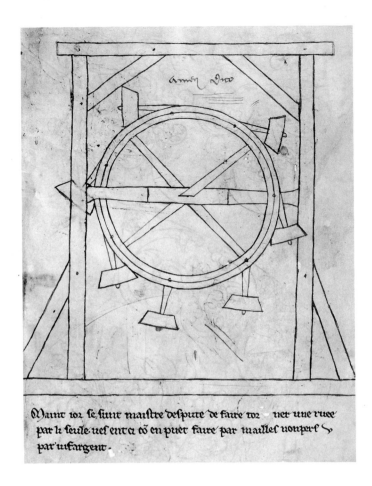

Manet toz se sunt maistre despute de faire toz net une ruee par li seule net enta tô en puet faire par maillet nonparf par usfargent.

Perpetual-
Motion
Machine

1235

THE IDEA THAT A MACHINE could be designed to work perpetually without requiring water, wind, or muscle power was first discussed in a Sanskrit manuscript in the fifth century A.D. In about 1150 an Indian mathematician, Bhaskara II, suggested that a perpetually moving wheel could be harnessed to replace human labor.

Honnecourt was an architect who worked for the Cistercian Order of the Roman Catholic church. He studied and reported on the construction of several cathedrals, such as those at Rheims, Laon, and Cambrai. It is not known whether he was active in their construction or repair, but his sketchbook provides drawings of their structural details and decoration, as well as instructional diagrams for drawing the human figure, the taming of a lion, wrestling maneuvers, and this illustration of a scheme for a perpetual-motion machine.

This machine, he proposed, would turn perpetually after it was given its original impetus, because the weights attached by rods to the rim of the wheel would fall regularly, and so maintain the rotation of the wheel. Note that, in his drawing, Honnecourt places the axle and frame in the same plane as the wheel, even though they would have to be at right angles to each other.

Like all other mechanical perpetual-motion machines, this one is doomed to failure. Energy would be lost due to friction at the axle and at the weight-arm pivots; additional work, from outside the system, would be required to keep the wheel turning. Although no record has been found of any attempt by Honnecourt to build a working model of his machine, his drawing is nevertheless accompanied by this assurance: "Often have experts striven to make a wheel turn of its own accord. Here is a way to do it with an uneven number of mallets and with quicksilver." (The quicksilver—mercury—partially fills each mallet.)

THE ORIGINS OF THE SCIENCE of geology are to be found in the work of miners and metallurgists who documented and illustrated their findings of ores, and in the maps drawn by geographers who measured the features of Earth's surface as accurately as their knowledge of geometry allowed.

Although they are usually invisible, the layerings below Earth's outer crust can be seen in the eroded sides of hills and mountains, which for centuries were thought to be indicators of cataclysmic inner upheavals that had caused the crust to bend. However, theorizing about such causes and mechanisms risked the disapproval of ecclesiastic authority, which taught that the universe was created by God in a gesture requiring only six days for completion.

Descartes, a devout Christian, believed that God's creation of the material world was founded on discoverable mechanical and mathematical principles, a view that neatly accommodated theological canons and his own driving, passionate intellect. In these illustrations, he explains the layered structure of Earth before the emergence of mountains, and the formation of mountains and oceans.

In the upper illustration, E is Earth's crust, which he describes as composed of "earths" and "stones"; a layer of air surrounds the Earth. Under Earth's crust are layers of air (F) and water (D). The interior crust (C) is composed of metals. At numbers 2, 3, 4, 5, and 6 fissures have developed in the dry outer crust. Due to their inaccessibility, Descartes dismissed the interior regions (I and M) as outside the realm of his considerations.

In the bottom illustration, Descartes proposed that when fissures caused the upper crust to weaken and collapse, mountains were created (4-9), allowing water under the crust to form oceans (at 2-3 and 6-7) and portions of the crust to form level plains (at V and 2I).

Descartes explained his theory of Earth's formation in terms of invisible particles of matter in continuous motion, vestiges of the planet's origin as a hot star like the sun.

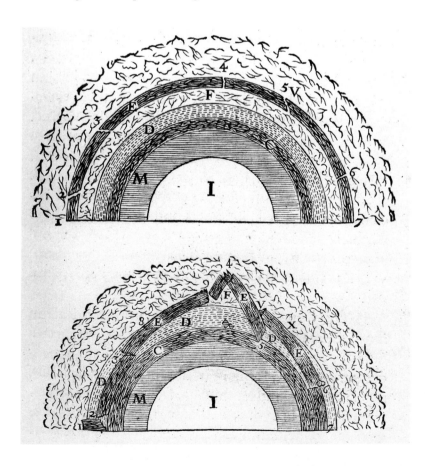

# Rock Avalanche and Water Turbulence

C. 1500

THIS IS ONE OF A SERIES of ten drawings illustrating an imagined "deluge": an avalanche of rocks smashing down a mountainside into a lake causes violent turbulence in the water, which is represented as short streams ending in spiral volutes.

Leonardo's water studies were begun in the early 1490s and continued into the second decade of the sixteenth century. All of them display his characteristic fascination with the conflict of forces of nature. Many of them, especially those of the "deluge" series, are abstractions vividly expressing Leonardo's astonishment and excitement about water in motion.

It is considered unlikely that, even with his extraordinary visual acuity, Leonardo could have actually seen the turbulent forms as he drew them. The visual impression suggests freeze-frame imaging within his own mind.

# Ballistics
Theory

F OR MORE THAN FIFTEEN HUNDRED years the dominant figure in the physical sciences was the Greek philosopher-scientist Aristotle. Transcripts of his discourses, recorded by students at the Lyceum, Aristotle's school in Athens, were collected into approximately 150 volumes. They constituted the basis of the study of physics until Galileo's and Newton's work revised and refuted many of Aristotle's concepts.

Aristotle's physical principles were formulated mainly by reasoning rather than by close observation and experimentation. For example, he maintained that a heavy object would fall more swiftly than a light one, because the "quality of heaviness" is the object's expression of its "wish" to remain at or return to its resting place. Therefore, the path of an object hurled into space would describe a straight line to some maximum height, at which point the object would "wish" to return to earth by a straight, vertical path.

In this sixteenth-century illustration, the path of a cannonball is delineated according to Aristotelian physics. The cannon's inclination is set to the angle ABC. The cannonball leaves the mouth of the cannon and continues in a straight path along the line ABF; at F, the observed maximum height, the cannonball drops vertically along the shortest possible path G, because of its supposed "wish" to return to its natural resting position.

Aristotle's mechanics could not be supported by experiment, which would have required a reliable method for measuring small time intervals. Fairly accurate clockworks were not developed until the seventeenth century by Christian Huygens (1629–1695); Galileo (1564–1642; see page 22) reputedly used his own pulse count for timing his experiments on falling bodies. Nevertheless, Aristotle's rational deductions were sacrosanct for more than fifteen centuries.

# Trajectories of Water Jets and Cannon Shells

C. 1485

I N 1482 LEONARDO ENTERED the employ of Lodovico Sforza, duke of Milan, as artist, architect, and military engineer, and remained in his service until Sforza was deposed in 1499. During those years Leonardo was required to develop weaponry for use in the recurrent wars between provincial rulers. His notebooks contain hundreds of designs that remained secret and were not discovered until late in the nineteenth century.

Leonardo expressed his hatred of war, calling it "beastly madness," but he appears to have accepted its inevitability as an expression of mankind's brutal instincts. His extraordinary faculty for observation enabled him to recognize the fallacy of Aristotle's straight-line rising and falling trajectories. This first illustration stands as one of his elegant analogies for explaining the reality of a phenomenon. Although there is no record that this machine was ever executed, it is possible that Leonardo could have constructed the device for a demonstration.

Three jets of water emanate under pressure from spouts positioned at angles comparable to the inclinations customarily set by cannoneers. Leonardo's commentary reads: "Test in order to make a rule of these motions. You must make it with a leather bag with many small pipes of the same inside diameter, disposed on one line." Leonardo concluded that ballistic trajectories must describe curved paths (see next illustration). Although he did not use the term, they are indeed parabolic, as Isaac Newton was to show almost two hundred years later, in 1687.

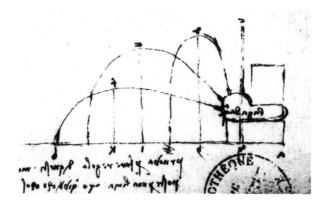

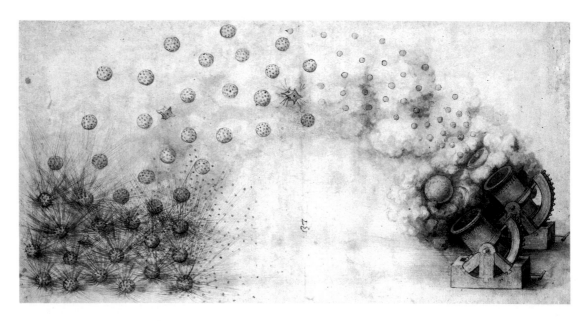

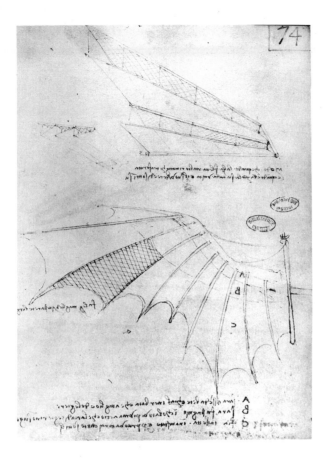

# Wing for a Flying Machine

C. 1490

ASIDE FROM TWO DESIGNS for parachutes, no scientific drawings of flying machines are known from the late Middle Ages and the Renaissance. Leonardo's intensive studies of the possibility of man-powered flight were made during the years of his employment by Lodovico Sforza (see page 200).

With no university education, Leonardo was unable to read Latin, and therefore could not study the works of his scientist predecessors or contemporaries. He was essentially a philosophical experimenter, equipped with an insatiable curiosity and a remarkable talent for drawing.

Leonardo's designs for aircraft were based on his observations of the flight of birds. This illustration delineates several elements he thought to be fundamental: a rigid anchoring bar to be attached to the aviator's body, at the right; a rib structure to provide support for a flexible membrane; a semirigid airfoil for gliding, to be supported by the three ribs adjacent to the anchoring bar; and a flexible wing membrane covering the remaining ribs to produce the up- and downstrokes for lift and propulsion.

As was his custom, Leonardo wrote his identifications and comments in mirror writing. The notes for this design refer to the lateral variations in the thicknesses of the membrane, at A, B, and C.

Leonardo's designs have been analyzed by twentieth-century aeronautical scientists, who agree on his originality but nevertheless conclude that his machines reveal basically untenable assumptions. The salient errors are Leonardo's dependence on the incorrect idea that "a bird makes the same use of wings and tail in the air as a swimmer does of his arms and legs in water"; Leonardo's failure to recognize the overwhelmingly complex control mechanisms to be manipulated in flight; and his belief that, even though a man's muscular power is proportionally much inferior to a bird's, a man might be able to fly if his muscle power could be applied efficiently. This last objection was proved wrong by the spectacular flight of the *Gossamer Albatross* across the English Channel in 1979. The pilot, a highly trained bicyclist, provided the propulsive power by pedaling the aircraft's propeller via a gear chain.

*Conceptualization*

201

# Study for Perspective Drawing

I T IS NOW COMMONLY ACCEPTED that scientific illustration requires that the illustrator be able to draw an object with the appearance of normal perspective. The geometric procedures to achieve that illusion were developed by painters during the fifteenth and early sixteenth centuries. Previously, spatial relationships were generally rendered in a series of flat planes, and relative sizes were indicated by simple gradations of large (close) to small (distant). The cogent illusion of depth on a flat plane distinguishes Renaissance painting and scientific illustration from all previous eras.

Dürer's prodigious talent is visible in this woodblock print from his book on geometrical figure constructions. Dürer entitled this print "The Artist and the Reclining Woman." In it, the artist draws on a sheet of paper marked by grid lines whose six-by-six divisions correspond to those of the vertical grid screen through which he observes the reclining woman. Close to his eye, the pointed apex of a miniature obelisk enables him to sight the vanishing point and see the perspective angles he must observe while drawing the details of the woman's form and drapery. In effect, the artist peers from the tip of a triangle whose base is the background wall at the left of Dürer's illustration.

It is noteworthy that Dürer's expository drawing is itself a demonstration of his skill in projective geometry: *vide*, the angles formed by the grid screen and the back wall of the studio; the angles of the masonry of the window frame and the structure of the drawing table; and the illusion of roundness that he achieves by means of the close contour lines that suggest shadows. The location of the source of light—a critically important factor—appears to be above and slightly left of the center of the vertical grid screen.

I N 1604, DE VRIES, A DUTCH PAINTER, published *Perspective*, a book containing seventy-three drawings explaining his method of perspective geometry.

The vanishing point in this example is placed at the eye level of the figure of the visitor entering the room through the door in the far wall. The horizon line ("Orizon") passes through the visitor's eye, as do the lines converging from the corners of the room. De Vries indicates the correspondence of the dimensional units ("1" through "6") on the square-tiled wall surface with the squares on the floor. The variable open and shut positions of the doors and window shutters are indicated by dotted arc lines.

The two vertical human figures are of equal height (approximately 6½ units), as revealed by the receding grid lines. The supine figure on the floor appears elongated, even though it, too, occupies the same number of tiles. Shadows are convincingly represented by means of cross-hatching throughout the illustration.

As with many others in de Vries's book, this scene has a faintly disturbing undercurrent. Is the supine figure the victim of a crime? Is the man behind the door at the right the criminal? And is the visitor entering the room at the distant door—which is also at the vanishing point of the drawing—the discoverer of the crime?

JAN VREDEMAN
DE VRIES
1527–1607

## Architectural Perspective

1604

*Conceptualization*

DOMENICO FONTANA
1543–1607

# Moving the Obelisk

1586

IN 1585 THE VATICAN APPOINTED a commission to study the possibility of moving a magnificent, 3,000-year-old, 360-ton Egyptian obelisk—the tallest known in the Western world—which had been brought to Rome by Constantine in A.D. 334. It had been moved once from its original site on the Circus of Nero to a position behind the Vatican Sacristy, where it had become a symbol of the triumph of Christian Rome over pagan Rome. Its new proposed location in the plaza in front of the Church of Saint Peter would give it even greater prominence.

The commission received some five hundred proposals for managing the difficult task, from all over Italy as well as from Rhodes and Greece. The renowned architect-engineer Domenico Fontana's plan was deemed the most impressive, and Fontana was chosen to be the chief engineer on the project.

His drawings are an elegant example of the conceptualization of a solution to a grand problem in mechanics—a "thought experiment" in mechanical engineering. Note that flat plans of winches, pulleys, and buildings are combined with skilled perspective views of men and horses at work.

First, the obelisk was encased in a sheath of timbers, to which ropes were attached. (See the side panels, with the obelisk faces marked E, F, G, and H.) Within the circular sacristy Fontana had to place three winches to assist in lowering the obelisk. D, at the top, is the carriage that would carry the obelisk to its new site. Two men—possibly inspectors—are seen at the lower left, observing the men and horses operating a winch.

The labor of 900 workmen and 74 horses was synchronized by Fontana himself, using trumpet calls and bell ringings to control the slow, delicate operation of lowering the massive stone monolith and repositioning it on its new site. The operation began on April 30, 1586, and was successfully completed five months later, on September 28.

Drawings of the plans were engraved by Natale Bonifazio and Giovanni Guerra and were printed by Bartholmeus Grassius to be sold as souvenirs during the spectacular operation. The plans were ultimately published in Fontana's book, *On Moving the Vatican Obelisk*, in 1590, four years after the successful completion of the project. This very rare book is considered to be one of the finest—in format, typography, and engravings—of all engineering records.

Fontana received a very generous reward and was made a noble of the Palatine Court. As the leading architect for the Vatican, he was later employed on several major projects during the rebuilding of Rome, including completion of the dome of Saint Peter's.

CONCORDIA

Scala di palmi 30. serue per il testa

Scala di palmi 40. serue per le quatro state

Scala di palmi 60. serue per la pianta

## ATHANASIUS KIRCHER 1601–1680

# Secret Listening Posts

1650

K IRCHER, A JESUIT PRIEST, was a professor of physics and mathematics at the Jesuit college in Rome. His studies in acoustics—a hitherto neglected science—were collected in his *Acoustics, Musurgia Universalis* (Acoustics, the Universal Expression of Music), in 1650. Kircher's diverse interests ranged from biology, optics, and microscopy to speculations about Earth's interior and experiments on the properties of air, the water cycle, and magnetism.

This illustration presents Kircher's method for the construction of secret listening posts. In the interior of an imaginary large building, three conch-shell horns in the walls collect and transmit the conversations taking place in the great hall at the left. The listening positions are concealed by statuary busts; at the right a gentleman stands at one of them (E) to eavesdrop on the conversation. In Fig. II, at the upper left, a similar arrangement is provided for listening (at busts) to a conversation in the room below (conch shell O). The small room at the middle (Fig. III) has an arched ceiling that provides sound focusing from the conch-shell horn that opens on the great hall.

In his book, Kircher illustrates aspects of the reflection and diffusion of sound, and ventures his support for the theory that sound waves cannot be transmitted in a vacuum. All of his works are notable for their technical ingenuity.

# Light-Wave Interference

WﾟHILE MAINTAINING AN ACTIVE medical practice in London, Young, a precocious polymath, also studied optics, concepts of work and energy, elastic properties of materials, tides, archaeology, and philosophy. He held the post of foreign secretary of the Royal Society from 1802 until his death in 1829. Sir Humphrey Davy, one of Young's colleagues at the Royal Society, said that "he knew so much that it was difficult to say what he did *not* know."

Young's report on his investigation of light-wave interference was delivered as a lecture to the Royal Society in 1803. He began by referring to the commonly observed effects of the production of two simultaneous waves in water: how, when they proceed from centers near each other, they can be "seen to destroy each other's effects at certain points, and at other points to redouble them."

To illustrate the analogy between the interference of light and the interference of two water waves, Young's diagram shows the light source coming from two slits at A and B, at the left. As the waves radiate toward the right, where a white card served as a viewing screen, brightly illuminated areas were seen between C and D and between E and F. The region between D and E appeared as a dark line. Young attributed the dark line to the meeting of a crest and a trough in the wave at the screen position: the two wave states would "interfere," and so cancel each other's energy to produce darkness.

The importance of Young's work was not quickly recognized by his contemporaries. But approximately fourteen years later, it was rediscovered by Augustin Fresnel (1788–1827). Fresnel confirmed and refined Young's theory that light waves are transverse waves, oscillating at right angles to the direction of their propagation.

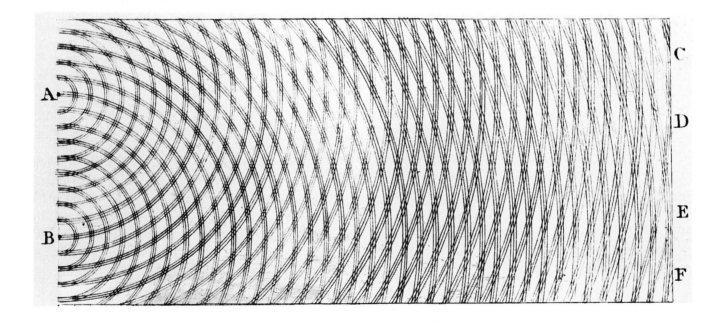

# The Spiral Tendency of Plant Forms

1831

BIOLOGICAL PROCESSES ARE OFTEN too subtle to be observed discretely by the investigator, although modern time-lapse photography and microphotography are effective tools for "freezing" stages in the development of an organism. Before photography became a scientific tool, investigators were compelled to develop mental images to explain the natural processes of growth and decay. Those imaginings—put on paper, crudely or elegantly, by the investigators—led to the development of theories of formative principles which attempted to explain essential aspects of the "life force."

While Goethe was studying law (a profession he never engaged in) at the University of Strasbourg, he developed a friendship with a biologist, J. G. Herder, whose influence moved Goethe to study biology throughout his career as an eminent poet, dramatist, and novelist. Goethe was especially drawn to that mystic feeling for nature expressed in the writings of Rousseau and Spinoza. This poetic bent may account for the confidence and assurance that color Goethe's intuitive (and sometimes incorrect) perceptions about natural phenomena.

The study of form in living organisms is called "morphology," a word coined by Goethe and introduced into biology in one of his papers, in 1831. He regarded all plants as variants of an original archetypal form: an axial structure, the stem, which supports lateral appendages, and the leaves. He proposed that plant growth was the result of replications of successive parts. Modifications of the fundamental, replicated units could be regarded as metamorphoses as, for example, a leaf culminating in a flower; and flowers, indeed, could be regarded as modified leaf structures.

Goethe abstracted these ideas into a diagram, reproduced here. Reading from right to left, the diagram begins with a simple spiral, which gets larger and then metamorphoses into a flower.

The spiral tendency in living organisms has been frequently noted by biologists, most recently in the double-helix structure of DNA discovered by James Watson and Francis Crick.

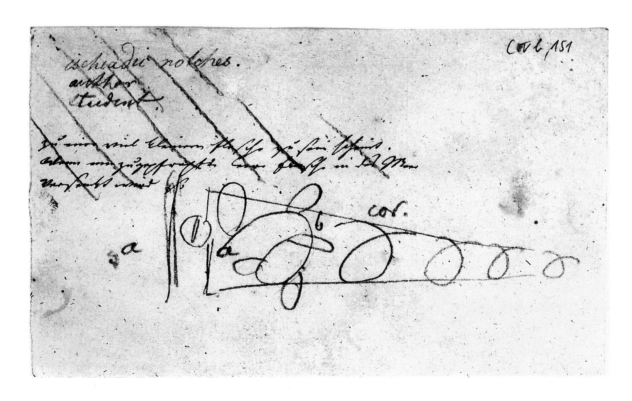

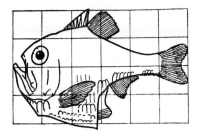

Fig. 146. *Argyropelecus olfersi.*

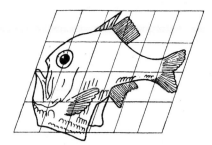

Fig. 147. *Sternoptyx diaphana.*

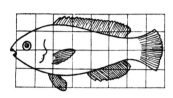

Fig. 148. *Scarus* sp.

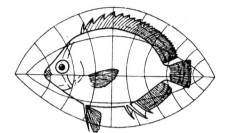

Fig. 149. *Pomacanthus.*

# Morphology of a Fish

1917

Thompson was a professor of natural history at the University of Saint Andrews, in Scotland, for sixty years. He translated Aristotle's *Historia Animalium* (The History of Animals) and was the author of a book on animal morphology, *On Growth and Form* (1917), which stands as a classic in the field of biology for both its text and its remarkable illustrations. Although the book does not promote any new or unique discoveries, it furthers Thompson's contention that organic forms could be analyzed quantitatively to reveal the orderliness of nature and the "harmony of the world." Profoundly fascinated by the question "Why is everything on Earth shaped the way it is?" Thompson probed for the answer by using the tools of geometry and physics. He accounts for size, the relationship of the surface areas of animals to their weights and volumes, rates of growth, and molecular forces in the animals' environment.

These illustrations from *On Growth and Form* demonstrate Thompson's imagined metamorphosis of one species of fish into another species. The *Argyropelecus olfersi*, an ocean fish (fig. 146) could be metamorphosed into a *Sternoptyx diaphana*, another ocean fish (fig. 147), by a shearing force. The grid lines superimposed on the first fish, when tilted ("sheared") by approximately 70°, produce the shape of the second fish. Thompson comments that such a deformation would be analogous to what might have occurred to some fossils as a result of the shearing forces exerted by the cooling of the molten rocks in which the organism had been caught.

Fig. 148 outlines a *Scarus*, over which Thompson has drawn a rectangular grid. When that grid is deformed into a system of coaxial ovals, and the new coordinates are filled "space by space and point by point with our former diagrams of *Scarus*, we obtain a very good outline of an allied fish, belonging to a neighboring family, of the genus *Pomacanthus* (fig. 149). This case is all the more interesting because on the body of our *Pomacanthus* are striking color bands, which correspond very closely to the lines of our new curved coordinates."

Thompson's position in the history of biology is considered unique because he was not an experimenter but a theoretician. Nevertheless, his speculations provoked others to new experimental approaches. The presently accepted idea that forms and their changes are related to biochemical reactions within the organism and in its environment is an indirect consequence of Thompson's influence.

ALFRED WEGENER
1880–1930

## The Origin of Continents and Oceans

1915

WEGENER RECEIVED HIS PH.D. in astronomy from the University of Berlin in 1905, and was a professor of meteorology, but he had a lifelong interest in geophysics. In 1910 Wegener noted the impression (as had some others before him) of the jigsaw puzzle congruence of the coastlines on either side of the Atlantic Ocean. The mapped contours of the east coast of South America and the west coast of Africa, especially, suggest that they may have been joined to each other in the distant past.

Initially, Wegener dismissed the idea as improbable. But a year later, in 1911, he accidentally came upon a brief report of paleontological evidence that a land bridge had existed at one time between Brazil and Africa: fossils of similar plants and animals had been unearthed on both coasts. Wegener began to read research papers on paleontology and geology, and became convinced that all the continents were at one time joined to each other in a single land mass, which he named "Pangea." He demonstrated his contention by making quite precise juxtapositions of the mapped coastlines of Africa and Asia and other continents (see illustration above).

Wegener presented this idea in 1912, first to the Geological Association in Frankfurt, and then to the Society for the Advancement of Natural Science in Marburg. While recovering from a severe bullet wound he received during World War I, Wegener completed a detailed account of his ideas, published in his book *Die Entstehung der Kontinent und Ozeane* (The Origin of Continents and Oceans) in 1915. The three maps shown here, from that book, are remarkable examples of the importance of illustration in scientific investigation.

(Top) The contiguous continental land masses joined into one great land mass, as they would have appeared during the Upper Carboniferous period, about 300 million years ago.

(Middle) The shaping of the continents, in the Eocene period, approximately 60 million years ago, after their fragmentation into land masses that "floated" on the ocean's basalt floor.

(Bottom) In the Older Quaternary period, about 2 million years ago, the continents assumed their presently mapped contours and positions on the Earth's surface.

The publication of Wegener's book generated vigorous controversy. After his tragic death in the course of an expedition to Greenland in 1930, the continental drift debate subsided and was virtually dismissed by geologists as a charming idea, but of little consequence.

In the 1950s a group of British geophysicists revived the controversy by suggesting that some of their problems in studying Earth's magnetism might be resolved by the application of the idea of continental drift. The eventual verification of Wegener's idea was accomplished through the collaboration of oceanographers, paleontologists, geophysicists, and biologists. The theory of continental drift, and its continuing influence in these fields, stands as one of the major achievements of the world scientific community in the twentieth century.

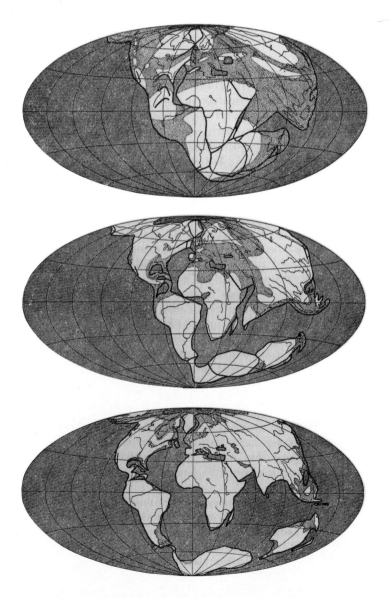

ABBÉ RENÉ JUST
HAÜY
1743–1822

# Speculation on Crystal Structure

1801

HAÜY ENTERED THE PRIESTHOOD at the age of twenty-seven, in 1770. An older priest whose hobby was botany urged Haüy toward the study of natural history; he soon became fascinated with mineralogy, and spent much of his free time visiting private collections of crystals in Paris.

While examining a piece of calcite in a friend's collection, Haüy accidentally dropped it, and it splintered into many small fragments. On close examination Haüy found that each fragment was in the form of a slanted cube, a rhombohedron, identical in form with the larger piece he had dropped. Subsequent studies convinced Haüy that the variations of the forms of crystals of the same substance could be explained by geometry, and he began to develop his concept of the growth of large crystals.

In this drawing, Haüy shows how the accumulation of minuscule calcite crystals could form a larger crystal having an identical rhombohedral form. He also theorized, correctly, that the forms of crystals of different substances indicate differences in their chemical constituents. (The idea of molecular structures, which involve the combination of atoms, was developed about a decade later by Amadeo Avogadro [1776–1856] and was published in 1811.)

Haüy's treatise marks the beginning of the science of crystallography, which has contributed significantly to the understanding of the structure of inorganic and organic matter.

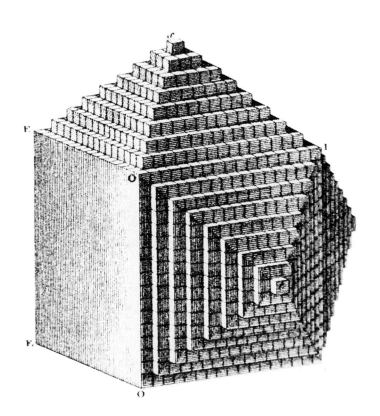

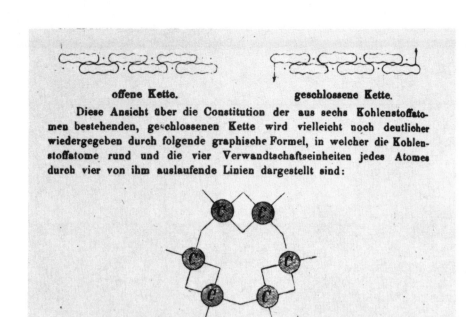

*offene Kette.*       *geschlossene Kette.*

Diese Ansicht über die Constitution der aus sechs Kohlenstoffato-
men bestehenden, geschlossenen Kette wird vielleicht noch deutlicher
wiedergegeben durch folgende graphische Formel, in welcher die Kohlen-
stoffatome rund und die vier Verwandtschaftseinheiten jedes Atomes
durch vier von ihm auslaufende Linien dargestellt sind:

# The Benzene Ring

1865

Benzene is a hydrocarbon compound, perhaps the most important of the organic compounds, obtained from coal tar and petroleum. It is the parent substance in the manufacture of thousands of substances, including dyes, drugs, and plastics. Although the compound was discovered by Michael Faraday in 1825, it was named by the German chemist Eilhardt Mitscherlich in 1834.

Benzene's atomic structure had eluded chemists until an astonishing experience enabled Kekulé, an eminent German chemist, to visualize the pattern of its atomic bonds. In 1865 Kekulé reported that while riding in a bus in a half-dozing state he had a sudden vision of chains of atoms whirling about in a dance; suddenly the tail of one chain attached itself to its head and formed a spinning ring. (Another version of this incident locates Kekulé in front of his fireplace.)

Until then, the customary expression for benzene had been $H_6C_6$, that is, six atoms of hydrogen connected in some fashion to six atoms of carbon, which does not, however, indicate the manner of the bonding of the two elements, a matter of primary importance to the chemist who intends to use benzene in a specific compound. Kekulé's vision suggested that the carbon and the hydrogen were bonded to each other in the form of a ring. The illustration is from Kekulé's paper on "aromatic" compounds, so called because benzene has a pleasant aroma, and the words benzene and aromatic had become synonymous in the chemical industry.

The top diagram emphasizes the ring arrangement of the six carbon atoms and the arms extending to the six hydrogen atoms that form the compound. Advances in chemical analysis resulted in a more specific indication of the number of bonds between the carbon atoms, so the modern form of the benzene ring is represented by this diagram:

Kekulé's vision was responsible for countless new chemical and biochemical discoveries, because it provided chemists with an effective basis for the construction of atomic linkages previously unimaginable.

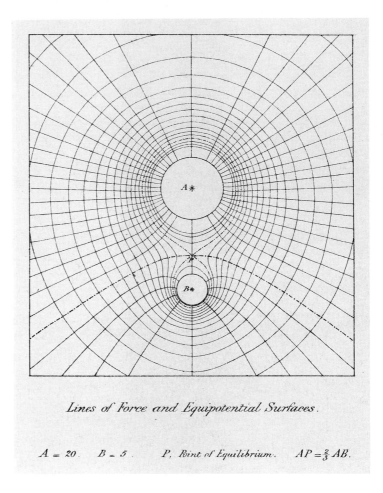

*Lines of Force and Equipotential Surfaces.*

$A = 20$.    $B = 5$.    $P$, *Point of Equilibrium*.    $AP = \frac{2}{3} AB$.

JAMES CLERK
MAXWELL
1831–1879

# Electromagnetic Fields

1871

M AXWELL'S *Treatise on Electricity and Magnetism*, published in 1873, sums up his theoretical work on the subject during the years 1865–71. Working in relative seclusion on his estate in Scotland, between his professorships in London and Cambridge, Maxwell produced one of the "greatest and most wonderful achievements of the human mind," according to Max Planck (1858–1947), the originator of the quantum theory. By mathematical analysis, without experimentation, Maxwell had arrived at the realization that light and electromagnetism are propagated with equal velocities and that light itself is an electromagnetic radiation phenomenon.

Because mathematical equations are intrinsically abstract, Maxwell made a series of drawings he called "experimental lines on paper" to visualize the "reality" of his equations. The example shown here is from his *Treatise*.

Two electrodes of unequal size, A* and B*, are assumed to be charged with positive electrical energy. Around each electrode "lines" of equipotential electromagnetic energy radiate into the "ether," the substance then believed to be filling space. The unequal sizes of the two electrodes produce unequal energy fields; so the greater electrical force radiating from the larger electrode repels the force from the smaller electrode. The mutual repulsion of the electric fields is indicated in the region immediately adjacent to the two electrodes. Maxwell represents this repulsion by drawing opposing, curving lines— "force fields"—that progress out and away from the electrodes.

Maxwell's electromagnetic field theory was verified eight years after his death by experiments conducted by Heinrich Hertz in 1887. Virtually every subsequent theoretical and technological advance in the understanding of light and electromagnetism can be traced to Maxwell's seminal *Treatise*.

# Propagation of Electric Waves

H ERTZ HAD ORIGINALLY INTENDED to become an engineer. He entered the University of Berlin at the time when two great experimental physicists, Helmholtz and Kirchhoff, were on the faculty. Hertz studied physics mainly with Helmholtz, received his Ph.D. in 1880 at the age of twenty-three, and continued working at the university as an assistant to Helmholtz for two more years.

When the Berlin Academy of Science announced the offer of a prize for original research in electromagnetism, Helmholtz persuaded Hertz, then on the faculty of the University of Kiel, to enter the competition. Hertz had been studying Maxwell's papers on electromagnetic theory; by 1887 he had developed a new electrical device, an oscillator, which could generate and radiate electromagnetic waves.

This illustration is from Hertz's *Untersuchungen über der Ausbreiung der elektrischen Kraft* (Investigations into the Propagation of Electric Force; 1892). The two small circles at the center of the drawing represent two metal balls, separated by an air gap. A high-frequency electric current was directed alternately to each ball; Hertz observed a shower of sparks crossing the air gap between the two balls.

At the other end of his laboratory Hertz had constructed a detector, or receiver: a single loop of wire with a gap, forming an incomplete circle. When the oscillator generated sparks across the air gap between the two balls, Hertz observed sparks leaping across the gap in the wire loop detector at the opposite end of his laboratory.

The only possible explanation for the sparks was that electromagnetic energy radiated in the space between the oscillator and the detector. The radiations were invisible, but Hertz then proceeded to map the progress of the waves from the oscillator to the detector. He constructed the pattern of isobars in the illustration from his precise recording of the intensities of the sparks in the detector, as he moved it to various positions in the room. In the illustration, arrows indicate the polarities of the radiating electromagnetic waves.

Hertz's experimental verification of Maxwell's theoretical analyses marked another fundamental advance in the understanding of electromagnetic phenomena. Hertz's experiments demonstrated that electromagnetic waves do indeed behave like light waves, that they follow the laws of refraction, that they are polarized, and that they travel at approximately the speed of light. The waves were later renamed "radio" waves, when Marconi adapted Hertz's technology for wireless communication in the late 1890s.

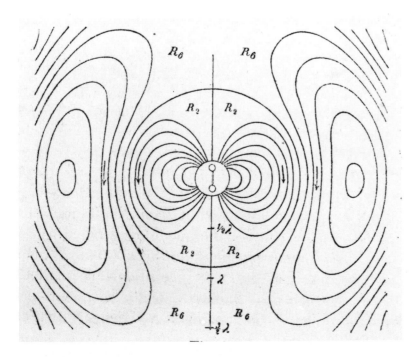

# A Theory of Immunity

1900

EHRLICH'S DOMINANT INTERESTS were biology and chemistry, and his extraordinary devotion to these sciences was responsible for prodigious, pioneering contributions to both fields; in essence, he merged cellular pathology and intracellular chemistry.

The first achievement that brought Ehrlich world renown was his work on the development in 1892 of an antitoxin for the treatment of diphtheria, the dreaded disease of childhood. His collaborator, the bacteriologist Emil Adolf von Behring (1854–1917), was awarded the first Nobel Prize in medicine in 1901, but it was Ehrlich who was responsible for the refinement of the antitoxin and for the dosage regimen. His reward was a professorship at the University of Berlin. Four years later, in 1896, the government appointed him to the directorship of a new institute for serum research.

Ehrlich developed a theory of the mechanisms by which invading organisms are rejected by the host's bloodstream. His paper was published by the British Royal Society in 1900, and these drawings were made to illustrate his concept:

1, 2: A bacterial organism, having invaded the bloodstream, attaches itself to an "antibody" (a defense substance) on the surface of a blood cell.

3, 4: The blood cell recognizes the presence of the bacterium and swiftly produces a larger than normal number of antibodies on its surface.

5, 6: The antibodies detach themselves from the cell body and swim into the bloodstream, where they neutralize the flow of invasive bacteria that may attach to the cells and cause disease.

Ehrlich further elaborated his concept by maintaining that all the antibody molecules necessary to combat any invader are present in the infant at birth, as inherited factors. This concept fell into disfavor in the 1920s, when biochemists demonstrated that blood cells were capable of producing antibodies to combat an enormous number of different substances—including some that were synthesized for the first time and had never before appeared in nature.

By 1957 molecular biologists had discovered a specific type of cell in the bloodstream named the "B lymphocyte," which is capable of producing a specialized antibody. Adult humans have many hundreds of millions of B lymphocytes to repel invasions by bio-organic foreign substances even though they may not be present in evolutionary development.

This concept was as difficult for biochemists to accept in 1957 as it was in Ehrlich's time. But increasingly sophisticated experimental analyses, available by the early 1960s, proved Ehrlich's original concept undeniable, and the antibody concept is now a basic concept in immunology.

Immunologists regard Ehrlich as the founder of their specialty, and medical historians agree that the treatment known as "chemotherapy" (Ehrlich's term) can be attributed to his lifelong search for substances that can destroy harmful organisms without causing harm to normal, healthy cells. The most famous of Ehrlich's many discoveries was the arsenic compound "salvarsan" in 1910, the first antibiotic capable of destroying the syphilis spirochete.

In 1908, Ehrlich finally won a Nobel Prize. He and Ilya Mechnikov (1845–1916) shared the award for their work in immunology.

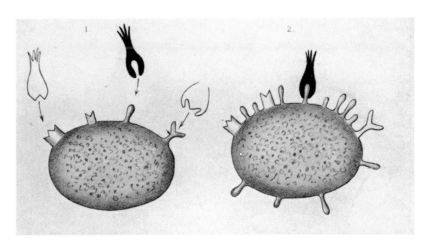

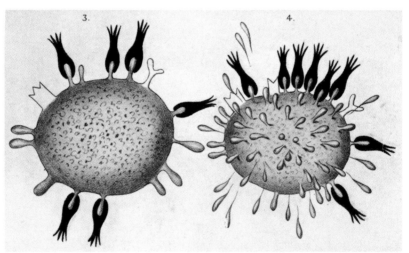

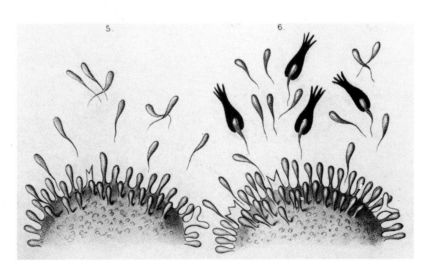

# Inkblot Test (No. 1)

1921

RORSCHACH, A SWISS PHYSICIAN and psychiatrist, was impressed by Carl Jung's interpretations of the pictures ("mandalas") drawn by his patients. The Inkblot Test was designed by Rorschach to assist in the diagnosis of the patient's psychological status without requiring the patient to make a drawing. These constructed images are not intended to provoke visual illusions but rather to act as probes into the symbolic content of the patient's memory and emotional state.

Ten bisymmetrical inkblot shapes, five in black and white and five in color, are presented sequentially to the patient, who is asked to respond with an oral interpretation of each pattern. The responses are then studied by the psychologist in three categories: location (how much of the blot area has the patient used); determinants (forms, shapes, colors, shading, and "movement"); and content (objects seen—human, animal, anatomical).

From the patient's responses the psychologist can derive a reliable, although partial, diagnosis of the patient's psychic state. The Rorschach test has been in use ever since its introduction in 1921.

toxic symbols (in visions) endless variation without improvement in significance is characteristic, the same with fever visions. Another important pathological symptom is the admixture of elements, which destroy or upset the intended significance, particularly so in schizophrenia. You mention Mrs. McCormick in your letter. She was such a case of latent Sch. and was very much on the edge, when I treated her. She dreamt right in the beginning of her analysis of a tree struck by lightning and split in half. ("Bruchlinie"!) This is, what one calls, a "bad" symbol. Another case, that suffers now from hallucinations and ideas of persecution, formerly produced pictures with Bruchlinien, breaking lines, thus f.i.

*Synthetic picture / strange admixture* or as

A great and puzzling problem is the "intended meaning or significance" of a symbol. It hangs together with the much bigger problem, whether the unconscious symbolisation has a meaning or aim at all or whether it is merely reactivated stuff i.e. relics of the past. I must say, I am inclined to assume, that the archaic material is merely a means to an end. It is, as far as I

I N THIS LETTER TO A COLLEAGUE, Jung describes the plight of a patient, diagnosed as schizophrenic, who is suffering from hallucinations and ideas of persecution. Jung draws three quick sketches to illustrate how the patient drew pictures which contained "break lines":

Left: A diagram showing a "synthetic picture" that is interrupted by a "strange admixture of elements; such an intrusion into the drawing serves to destroy or upset the intended significance" of the drawing.

Middle: The "quotation" by Jung of a schizophrenic's drawing. The head of the figure is overlaid with a pattern of waving lines. Jung's comment points to the uncertainty of the meaning of the admixture (of the real with the overlaid pattern): does the overlay signify some aspect of the patient's state while the drawing was being made, or does the overlay represent "merely reactivated stuff, i.e., relics of the past"?

Right: The patient's drawing shows both the present image of a countenance and its hesitant, retreating image.

Jung became increasingly aware of the importance of "lines of fracture," fragmentation, or "faults" (in the geological sense) that he found in the drawings made by his schizophrenic patients. His interpretation of such pictures led him to the recognition of the patients' alienation from feeling and emotion.

CARL JUNG
1875–1961

# A Note on Schizophrenia

1932

*Conceptualization*

219

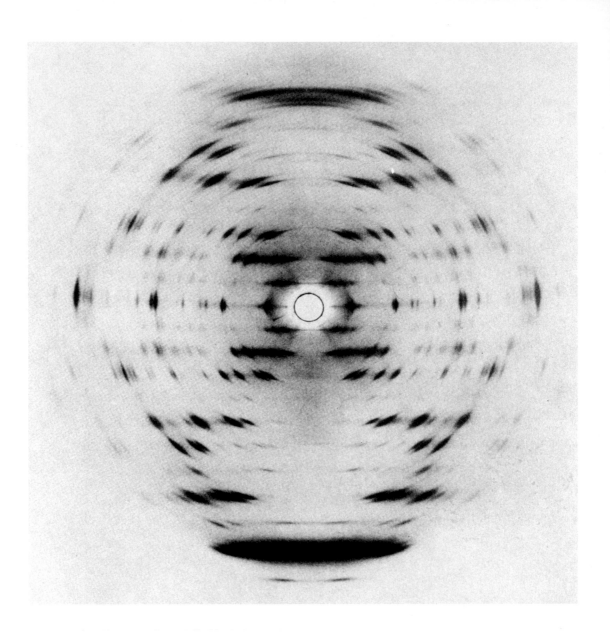

# X-Ray Photograph of a DNA Crystal

1952

FRANKLIN WAS A PHYSICAL CHEMIST, expert in chromatography and X-ray crystallography, who began to work in Maurice Wilkins's laboratory at Kings College in the University of London in 1951. Wilkins (b. 1916), a biophysicist, prepared samples of DNA which Franklin purified and then processed to form crystals. Such organic crystals have many of the structural properties of inorganic crystals and they can be subjected to X-ray photographic analysis.

This X-ray crystallograph provided the triggering clue for the recognition of the double-helix structure of DNA by James D. Watson (b. 1928) and Francis Crick (b. 1916). Watson and Crick, who were studying the DNA structure at Cambridge University, were dependent upon Wilkins's preparations of samples. Franklin's meticulous series of crystallographs included this one, whose manifest symmetry— right-to-left and top-to-bottom—was interpreted as a double helix, like a spiral staircase with two handrails, as seen from the ceiling above the center of the spiral staircase.

JAMES D. WATSON

B. 1928

# Symmetrical Bonds in the DNA Molecule

1953

THE WORLD SCIENTIFIC COMMUNITY considers the 1953 discovery by James Watson and Francis Crick of the molecular structure of deoxyribonucleic acid—DNA—to be the most important event in the history of biology since the publication of Darwin's *Origin of Species* in 1859. The efforts of a few biologists, chemists, and physicists, working in small groups, depended to a considerable extent on the faculty of visualization and the construction of molecular structural models. Such models, like Tinkertoy structures, enable the researchers to develop hypotheses describing the chemical bonds within the very complex DNA molecule.

These scribbled diagrams appear in Watson's letter to Max Delbrück (1906–1981), a nuclear physicist and geneticist on the faculty of the California Institute of Technology. Delbrück had encouraged Watson to study the DNA molecule, and Watson esteemed Delbrück as a brilliant critic and a supportive mentor.

The diagram shows how Watson and Crick visualized the bondings of the two essential nitrogen compounds—thymine (T) with adenine (A), at the left, and cytosine (C) with guanine (G), at the right—as symmetrically equivalent. The short line with the word "sugar" points to the connections of the T-A and C-G pairings (the "rungs") with the supports (sugar and phosphate units) that form the ladder-like, spiraling structure.

Watson noted that "our model, a joint project of Francis Crick and myself, bears no resemblance to either the original or to the revised Pauling-Corey-Shoemaker models. It is a strange model and embodies several unusual features. However, since DNA is an unusual substance, we are not hesitant in being bold." (Linus Pauling and his colleagues were engaged in DNA research at the California Institute of Technology at the same time.)

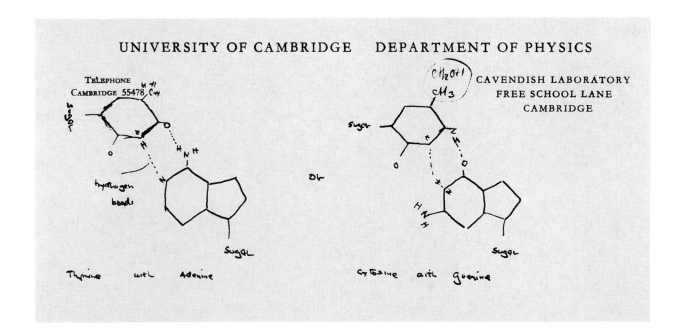

*Conceptualization*

221

JAMES D. WATSON
B. 1928
AND
FRANCIS CRICK
B. 1916

# Model of the DNA Helix

1953

THIS IS A PHOTOGRAPH of the model of the DNA molecular structure as constructed by Watson and Crick. The wire elements represent the spiraling, twin "outer rails" of sugar and phosphates and "rungs" of thymine-adenine and cytosine-guanine pairings. In constructing this model, a dimensional scaling had to be observed because of the critical distances between the connecting molecular substances. The scale at the bottom of the photograph describes those distances in Angstroms, that is, in tenths of a billionth of a meter. From this we cannot fail to get a notion of the complexity of Watson and Crick's "thought experiments."

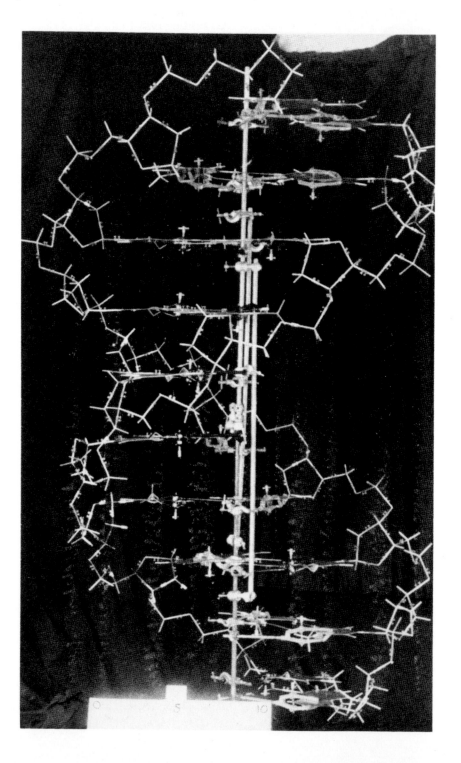

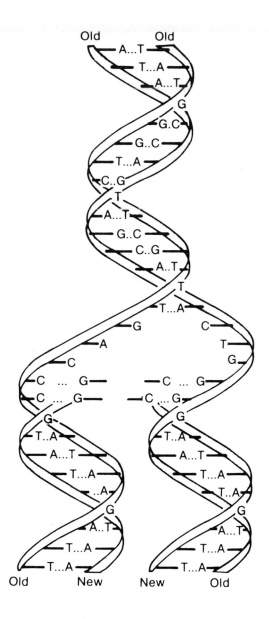

Old     Old

Old    New    New    Old

Wᴵᴛʜɪɴ ᴀ ꜰᴇᴡ ʏᴇᴀʀꜱ after the DNA (deoxyribonucleic acid) structure had been verified, several laboratories began earnest work in a new biotechnology, genetic engineering. Because DNA was known to carry the heredity code in the genes, "gene-splicing" could be used to alter the inherited traits of successive generations of living organisms. This activity generated concern about the unrestricted employment of the new technique.

In 1988 the U.S. Office of Technology Assessment prepared a booklet entitled *Biology, Medicine and the Bill of Rights* for distribution to members of the Senate and the House of Representatives, who were about to conduct hearings on the social and economic consequences of genetic engineering.

In this illustration the DNA molecule is shown in the act of replication. The original strands (marked "Old and Old" at the top) spiral down to split at the center, where a unit of thymine (T) stands alone. After separation of the thymine-adenine and cytosine-guanine bonds, "daughter" strands develop as copies of the parent strand, each now containing one of the parent strands ("Old-New" and "Old-New").

# The Structure of DNA

1988

*Conceptualization*

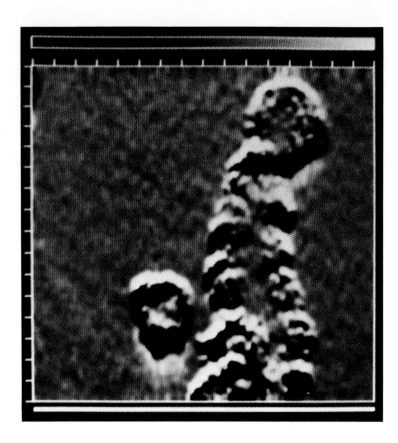

# Photograph of DNA

1989

I N JANUARY 1989 the Lawrence Berkeley Laboratory of the University of California at Berkeley published the first photograph of a strand of DNA. DNA had been photographed by electron microscopes before, but the DNA sample had to be coated with a fine layer of metal—usually a gold alloy—which was then subjected to the shower of electrons required to reflect an image of the sample.

This photograph is the first to reveal unaltered, uncoated DNA, in this case taken from cells in the thymus gland of a calf. The microscope was a scanning tunnel microscope, an improved version of an original that had been designed at the IBM Research Laboratory in Switzerland several years before.

This type of microscope employs a very fine, sharp-pointed needle to scan the surface of the sample without touching it. The needle's extreme proximity to the sample enables a current of electrons to cross the gap between the needle tip and the sample. The variations in the flow of electrons are recorded by a computer, and the stored data is then translated into a graphic image that displays the spatial characteristics of the sample. The resulting image on the computer graphic screen is photographed, and is precisely analogous to what an ideal, optical camera would show if its lens had magnification and resolving powers several million times greater than previously available microphotographic systems. The invention of the scanning tunnel microscope—the consequence of "thought experiments" in quantum electronics and computer graphics—makes it possible to study the details of a single atom.

In this picture of the DNA strand, the DNA makes a loop (at the top of the picture) and crosses over on itself. The double-helix structure is evident, and the researchers were able to measure the distances between the coils. Such images are already providing information about the nitrogen compounds that form the "rungs" of the DNA ladder-like structure; in addition, they enable geneticists to manipulate and slice the DNA.

THIS STUDY OF A PILOT's left arm motion was made by William Fetter, a researcher working in the Boeing Company's YC-14 program. Fetter devised a computer program instructing the graphic plotting device to draw the many gestures that a pilot's arm would be expected to make within the spatial constraints of the cockpit of a fighter airplane. Fetter coined the term "computer graphics," which became the generic name for such drawings.

The research objective was to establish the positions of the numerous flight controls to provide optimum operational efficiency. Economy of effort with maximum comfort and sustained high productivity have been the goals of scientific management for almost a century. Developed theoretically and practically by Frederick Taylor early in the twentieth century, scientific management now enjoys the benefits of the sophisticated evolution of computer graphics technology.

This technology has also become important in the advancement of several branches of medicine, especially in diagnosis, as in the CAT (computerized axial tomography) scan, PET (positron emission tomography) scan, and MRI (magnetic resonance imaging).

WILLIAM FETTER

"Computer
Graphics"
Study of an
Aircraft Pilot's
Arm Motion

1960

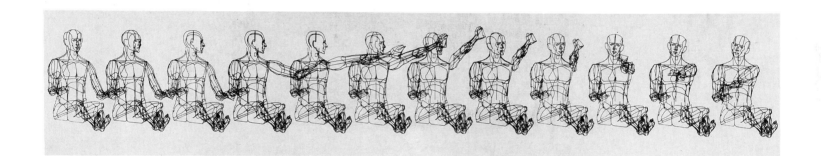

BENOIT B.
MANDELBROT

B. 1924

# Self-squared
# Fractal Dragon

1982

Т**HE SHAPES STUDIED** and manipulated in traditional Euclidean geometry are two- and three-dimensional: lines, squares, triangles, circles, cones, spheres, and other polygons and polyhedrons. But areas and solids in the natural world do not manifest themselves with the precise regularity that can be analyzed by Euclidean geometry.

In 1975, the mathematician Benoit B. Mandelbrot announced the development of a novel, effective mathematical procedure to express degrees of irregularity, or roughness, that are found in natural forms. Mandelbrot coined the word "fractal" to name his geometry. The word is from the Latin "frangere" (to break), and fractal geometry deals with figures that are characterized by their "formless" or "fragmented" dimensions, such as the wiggle in the contour of a coastline, the shape of a cloud, or the topography of mountains and valleys.

Fractal geometry procedures require computers and computer graphics for their expression. The display on the computer screen is the consequence of a series of sets of mathematical operations; in effect, the computer screen display is a visualization of the mathematician's thought experiment. No matter how irregular or chaotic the appearance of the figure, it can be traced back to specific mathematical procedures; indeed, fractal geometry has been called "the geometry of chaos."

Mandelbrot's *Self-Squared Fractal Dragon* is an especially vivid example of how fractal geometry can treat the factors of chance (irregularity), scaling (dimensional relationships), and self-similarity (details that imitate an overall shape on a smaller scale, or details that are deformed as they diminish in size). These characteristics can be appreciated by examining the dragon under a magnifying glass.

Fractal geometry is being applied to aerodynamics, astronomy, biology, physiology, particle physics, and linguistics. For each of these fields computer-generated graphics can create three-dimensional visualizations of the mathematical procedures.

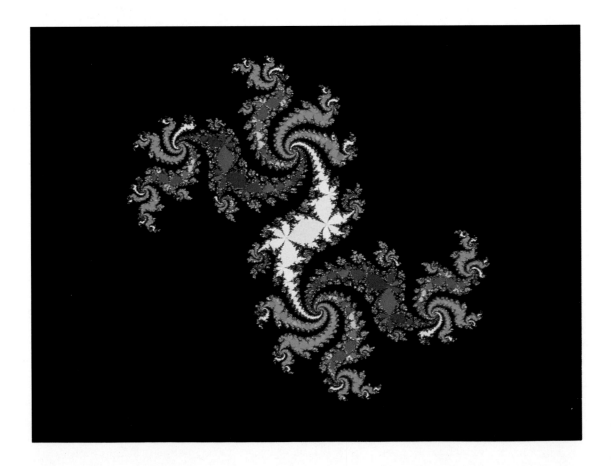

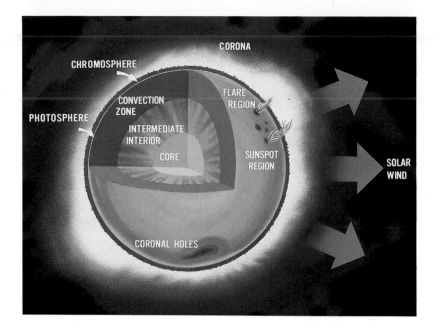

DAZZLING LIGHTS; the sensation of heat; daylight; the ominous, terrifying eclipses; flarings; and dark spots—all these aspects of the giant star of our galaxy, the Sun, were experienced by primal man at least a hundred thousand years ago. But it was not until the middle of the nineteenth century that the matter and structure of the Sun could be studied scientifically. In 1861, using an improved Fraunhofer spectroscope (see page 88), the German physicist Gustav Kirchhoff was able to identify sodium as one of the chemical elements in the Sun. By 1930, subsequent investigators had discovered the presence of hydrogen, helium, oxygen, nitrogen, and neon as well.

At present it is thought that the Sun was formed about four and a half billion years ago from the center of a huge cloud of gases and that the concentrated pressure of those gases generated a nuclear reaction in which hydrogen atoms fused to form helium and produced the giant sphere of the Sun. In 1959 the National Aeronautics and Space Administration sent Pioneer 4, the first of a series of space probes, to study the Sun's composition. The probes have also studied the solar atmosphere, solar flares, magnetic fields, and X-ray radiation. Germany's Helios 1 and 2 studied the Sun's surface at close range. Nevertheless, we must resort to the conjectures (thought experiments) of astrophysicists and astrochemists for an image of the Sun's interior.

At the center of this structural diagram is the Sun's hot core, with a temperature of approximately 27 million° Fahrenheit.

Hot loops of gases rise out of the core into the convection zone, the inner rind, reddish in color. The outer surface is the photosphere, from which the sunlight that fills our galaxy emanates. The flaring outer ring is the chromosphere, about 6,000 miles thick.

The prominences are enormous, amorphous plumes of luminous gases that jet out of the photosphere beyond the chromosphere, to altitudes of almost 100,000 miles. The corona is a field of hydrogen particles that extends millions of miles into space; it is visible only during a total solar eclipse, when the Moon blots out the photosphere.

A constant stream of hot plasma (ionized subatomic particles) flows out of the Sun. It is known as the solar wind, and moves—at speeds ranging from 450,000 miles per hour to 2 million miles per hour—into the farthest reaches of our galaxy. The solar wind affects Earth's magnetic fields, the paths of comets, and the surface of the Moon.

## Introduction

1. Albert Einstein, *What I Believe*, ed. Mark Booth (New York: Crossroad Publishing Co., 1984).

## I Observation

1. Thomas Huxley, *Nature*, vol. 1, no. 1 (November 4, 1869): 10. Huxley (1825–1895) was a cofounder of this British journal.

PAGE 22. Collection Biblioteca Nazionale Centrale, Florence.

PAGE 23. Johannes Hevelius, *Selenographia* (1647). Library of Congress, Washington, D.C., QB 29.H44, Rosenwald Collection (1321).

PAGE 24. Apuleius Barbarus, *Herbarium* (1484). Library of Congress, Washington, D.C., Incunabula X.A7, Rosenwald Collection (237).

PAGE 25. Erasmus Darwin, *The Loves of the Plants* (1789), Canto I, Part II of *The Botanic Garden* (London: J. Johnson, 1791). Library of Congress, Washington, D.C.

PAGE 26. Pedanius Dioscorides, *Materia Medica* (ninth-century manuscript): 148. Arabic manuscript 4947, folio 66. Bibliothèque Nationale, Paris.

PAGE 27. Mark Catesby, *The Natural History of Carolina* (1731–43). Library of Congress, Washington, D.C., Q44LC25 Rare Book Collection.

PAGE 28. Pierre Belon, *Histoire de la Nature et des Oiseaux*, Book IV (Paris: G. Cauellat, 1555). Library of Congress, Washington, D.C., QL 673.B45, Rare Book Collection.

PAGE 29. Carlo Ruini, *Dell'Anatomia et dell'Infirmita del Cavallo*, vol. 5, pl. 5. Library of Congress, Washington, D.C., SF765.R8 1598, Rosenwald Collection.

PAGE 30. Maria Sibylla Merian, *Metamorphosis Insectorum Surinamensium* (1705). Courtesy History and Special Collections Division, Louise M. Darling Biomedical Library, University of California, Los Angeles.

PAGE 31. Spanish Institute of Entomology, Consejo Superior de Investigaciones Científicas, Madrid. By permission of the artist.

PAGE 32. Charles Darwin, *The Voyage of the Beagle* (1840). Courtesy Louise M. Darling Biomedical Library, University of California, Los Angeles. Photograph: Martin Lovell.

PAGE 33. William Holmes, *On Fossil Forests of Yellowstone Park*, no. 12, miscellaneous, U.S. Geological Survey, Photo Library, Denver, Colo.

PAGE 34. © Elaine R. S. Hodges, 1988.

PAGE 35. Charles Darwin, *The Voyage of the Beagle* (1840). Courtesy Louise M. Darling Biomedical Library, University of California, Los Angeles. Photograph: Martin Lovell.

PAGE 37. The Royal Library, Windsor Castle. By permission of Her Majesty Queen Elizabeth II.

PAGE 38. Johann Dryander, *Anatomiae* (1537). Courtesy Louise M. Darling Biomedical Library, University of California, Los Angeles. Photograph: Martin Lovell.

PAGE 39. Charles Bell, *The Anatomy and Philosophy of Expression* (1865). Courtesy Louise M. Darling Biomedical Library, University of California, Los Angeles. Photograph: Martin Lovell.

PAGE 41. Andreas Vesalius, *De Humani Corporis Fabrica* (1543). The Burndy Library, Norwalk, Conn. Photograph: Joseph Szasfai, New Haven.

PAGE 42. Robert Hooke, *Micrographia* (The Royal Society, 1665). The Royal Society, London.

PAGE 43. Marcello Malpighi, *Anatome Plantarum* (1675–79). Library of Congress, Washington, D.C.

PAGE 44. Santiago Ramón y Cajal, *Recollections of My Life* (1937). By permission of the American Philosophical Society. Courtesy Louise M. Darling Biomedical Library, University of California, Los Angeles. Photograph: Martin Lovell.

PAGE 45. Antony van Leeuwenhoek, *Ontledingen et ontdekkingen* (1696–1718). Library of Congress, Washington, D.C., QH9.L4, Rare Book Collection.

PAGE 46. Biocosmos/Science Photo Library.

PAGE 47. CNRI Science Source/Photo Researchers, Inc.

PAGE 48. Hermann Fol, *Recherches sur la Fécondation*, pl. III (Paris: 1879). Zentralbibliothek, Zurich.

PAGE 49. Eduard Strasburger, *Uber den Bau und das Wachstum der Zellhäute* (Jena: Fischer, 1882). Courtesy Louise M. Darling Biomedical Library, University of California, Los Angeles. Photograph: Martin Lovell.

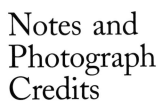

# Notes and Photograph Credits

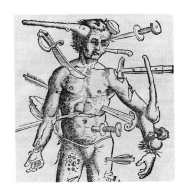

## II Induction

1. *The Language of Drawing* (New York: Prentice Hall, 1966).

PAGE 52. J. Needham and C. A. Ronan, *Shorter Science and Civilization in China*, vol. 2 (Cambridge, England: Cambridge University Press, 1978), 206. Inscription translated by Dr. Hung-hsiang Chou of the Department of East Asian Languages and Cultures at the University of California, Los Angeles.

PAGE 53. Left: Alexander Marshack, *The Roots of Civilization* (New York: McGraw Hill, 1972). Right: Musée des Antiquités, Saint-Germain-en-Laye, France. © Alexander Marshack 1972.

PAGE 54. Museo Arqueológico, Valencia, Spain. Photograph: MAS, Barcelona, Spain.

PAGE 55. Photograph Joseph Muench, Santa Barbara.

PAGE 56. René Descartes, *Discours sur la Méthode* (1637). Courtesy Special Collections Division, University Research Library, University of California, Los Angeles.

PAGE 57. Stephen Switzer, *An Introduction to the General System of Hydrostatistics and Hydraulics*, vol. I (London, 1729). Science Museum, London.

PAGE 58. Ms. 130E31, 211, fol. 20. Biblioteca Universitaria, Pavia, Italy.

PAGE 59. Albert Bettex, *The Discovery of Nature* (New York: Simon & Schuster, 1965).

PAGE 60. Louis Claude Richard, *Mémoires sur les Conifères et les Cyadées* (Stuttgart: 1826), p. 3, 1. Hälfte. Zentralbibliothek, Zurich.

PAGE 61. Charles Darwin, *The Different Forms of Flowers* (New York: D. Appleton & Co., 1896).

PAGE 62. Richard Owen, *Memoir on the Pearly Nautilus* (London: Royal Society, 1838). Library of Congress, Washington, D.C.

PAGE 63. Ibid.

PAGE 64. A. H. Church, *On the Interpretation of Phenomena of Phyllotaxis*, Botanical Memoirs, no. 6 (Oxford: Oxford University Press, 1920). Library of Congress, Washington, D.C.

PAGE 65. Asa Schaeffer, *Amoeboid Movement* (1920). Library of Congress, Washington, D.C.

PAGE 66. National Aeronautics and Space Administration.

PAGE 67. Sir D'Arcy Wentworth Thompson, *On Growth and Form*, abridged ed. (Cambridge, England: Cambridge University Press, 1961). © Cambridge University Press.

PAGE 68. Otto Lilienthal, *The Science of Flight* (1889).

PAGE 69. Germanisches National Museum, Nuremberg, Germany.

PAGE 70. René Descartes, *L'Homme* (1664). Courtesy Louise M. Darling Biomedical Library, University of California, Los Angeles. Photographs: Martin Lovell.

PAGE 71. Ibid.

PAGE 73. Giovanni Alfonso Borelli, *De Motu Animalium* (1680). Courtesy Louise M. Darling Biomedical Library, University of California, Los Angeles. Photograph: Martin Lovell.

PAGE 74. P. Gaspar Schott, *Physica Curiosae, Pars II* (1699). Courtesy William and Victoria Dailey, Ltd., Los Angeles.

PAGE 75. *Kunstformen der Natur* (Leipzig and Vienna: Verlag des Bibliographischen Instituts, 1904), plate 30, folio 518. Courtesy University Library, Karl-Marx University, Leipzig, Germany.

PAGES 76 AND 77. Left: Adrian Spigelius, *De Formatu Foetu*. Right: *The Compleat Midwife*. Library of Congress, Washington, D.C.

## III Methodology

1. On the occasion of his appointment as Curator of the Experiments of the British Royal Society, in 1663.

PAGE 81. Jan Blaen, *Atlas Major*, V. I. (1663). Library of Congress, Washington, D.C., Rare Book Collection.

PAGE 82. Christoph Scheiner, *Rosa Ursina*, Book III. Science Museum, London.

PAGE 83. Bonaventura Cavalieri, *Lo Specchio Ustorio; Overo, Trattato delle Settioni Coniche, et Alcuni Loro Mirabili Effeti Intorno al Lume* (Bologna: Presso Clemente Ferroni, 1632). Courtesy The History of Science Collections, Cornell University Library, Ithaca.

PAGES 84 AND 85. Newton. Ms., N.C. 361, Vol. 2, fol. 45 "Chronology." By permission of the Warden and Fellows of New College, Oxford. Bodleian Library, Oxford.

PAGE 87. Newton's correspondence. Collection The Royal Society, London.

PAGE 88. Deutsches Museum, Munich.

PAGE 89. Robert Boyle, *A Continuation of New Experiments, Physico-Mechanical, Touching the Spring and Weight of the Air, and Their Effects* (1669–82). Library of Congress, Washington, D.C., QC161.B793, Rare Book Collection.

PAGES 90 AND 91. Left: Robert Routledge, *A Popular History of Science* (London: 1881). Ann Ronan Picture Library, Taunton, Somerset, England. Right: Amédée Guillemin, *The Forces of Nature* (London: 1873). Ann Ronan Picture Library, Taunton, Somerset, England.

PAGE 92. Otto von Guericke, *Magdeburg Experiments* (1672). Library of Congress, Washington, D.C., Q155.G93, Rare Book Collection.

PAGE 93. Ibid.

PAGE 95. Stephen Hales, *Vegetable Staticks* (London: 1727). QK711.H2 1727 RB NMAH, Special Collections Branch, National Museum of American History, Smithsonian Institution Libraries.

PAGE 96. Marcelin Berthelot, *Les Origines de l'Alchemie* (1885). Courtesy Bibliothèque Nationale, Paris.

PAGE 97. Lazarus Ercker, *Berschreibung aller furnemisten mineralischen Ertz und Bergwerks Arten* (Frankfurt a. M.: J. Feyerabendt, 1598). Library of Congress, Washington, D.C., TN664.E7, 1598, Rare Book Collection.

PAGE 99. Georgius Agricola, *On Metals (De Re Metallica)*. The Burndy Library, Norwalk, Conn.

PAGE 100. William Gilbert, *De Magnete* (1600). The Burndy Library, Norwalk, Conn.

PAGE 101. Guido Guidi, *Chirurgia e greco in latinum conversa* (Paris: 1544). Courtesy Louise M. Darling Biomedical Library, University of California, Los Angeles. Photograph: Martin Lovell.

PAGES 102 AND 103. Left: Louise M. Darling Biomedical Library, University of California, Los Angeles. Photograph: Martin Lovell. Right: Hans von Gersdorff, *Feldtbuch der Wundartzney* (1540). Philadelphia Museum of Art, Smith, Kline, and French Laboratories Collection.

PAGE 104. Jacob Reuff, *De Generatione Hominis* (Frankfurt: 1580). Philadelphia Museum of Art, Smith, Kline, and French Laboratories Collection.

PAGE 105. Georg Bartisch, *Opthalmodouleia* (1583). Courtesy World Health Organization, Geneva.

PAGE 106. Sanctorius, *Commentarium in Primam Fen Primam Libri Canonis Avicenna* (1625). Collection New York Academy of Medicine.

PAGE 107. *A Brief Account of Mr. Valentine Greatrak's and Divers of the Strange Cures by Him Lately Performed* (London: 1666). By permission of the Houghton Library, Harvard University, Cambridge, Mass.

PAGE 108. René Descartes, Appendix to *Discours sur la Méthode* (1637). Courtesy of Special Collections Division, University Research Library, University of California, Los Angeles.

PAGE 109. Edward Jenner, *An Inquiry into the Causes and Effects of the Variolae Vaccinae* (London: 1798). The Burndy Library, Norwalk, Conn. Photographs: Joseph Szasfai, New Haven.

PAGE 111. William Harvey, *De Motu Cordis et Sanguinus in Animalibus* (1628). Courtesy Louise M. Darling Biomedical Library, University of California, Los Angeles. Photographs: Martin Lovell.

PAGE 112. Otto von Guericke. *Experimenta Nova* (1672). The Burndy Library, Norwalk, Conn.

PAGE 113. F. H. Winckler, *Essais sur l'Electricité* (1748). The Burndy Library, Norwalk, Conn.

PAGES 114 AND 115. Left: *A History of Electricity* (1752). Center: Benjamin Franklin, *Experiments and Observations on Electricity*, fifth edition (London: 1774). The Burndy Library, Norwalk, Conn. Photograph: Joseph Szasfai, New Haven. Right: *A History of Electricity* (1752). Deutsches Museum, Munich.

PAGE 116. L. Figuier, *L'Elettricità e le sue Applicazioni* (1884): 153. The Burndy Library, Norwalk, Conn.

PAGE 117. Wellcome Institute Library, London.

PAGE 118. Luigi Galvani, *De Viribus Electricitatis in Motu Musculari Commentarium* (1791). The Burndy Library, Norwalk, Conn. Photograph: Joseph Szasfai, New Haven.

PAGE 119. *Philosophic Transactions of the Royal Society* (London: 1800). The Burndy Library, Norwalk, Conn. Photograph: Joseph Szasfai, New Haven.

PAGE 120. Bern Dibner, *Oersted and the Discovery of Electromagnetism* (1961). The Burndy Library, Norwalk, Conn. Photograph: Joseph Szasfai, New Haven.

PAGE 121. By courtesy of the Director of The Royal Institution, London.

PAGE 123. Edison National Historic Site, Orange, N.J., U.S. Department of the Interior, National Park Service.

PAGE 124. Left: *Proceedings of the Royal Bavarian Academy of Science* (Munich: 1912). Courtesy Deutsches Museum, Munich. Right: Max von Laue, *Röntgenstrahl Interferenzen* (Leipzig: Akademische Verlagsgesellschaft, 1941). By permission.

PAGE 125. Courtesy Professor Hans Dehmelt, Physics Department, University of Washington. Photograph taken in collaboration with Professor Warren Nagourney and Mr. John Sandberg.

# IV Self-Illustrating Phenomena

PAGE 128. Courtesy the California Institute of Technology, Pasadena, Calif. © 1962.

PAGE 129. National Aeronautics and Space Administration.

PAGE 130. American Museum of Natural History, New York. 56.74, 13, 69, 11.

PAGE 131. Photograph: Terence Moore, Tucson.

PAGE 132. National Aeronautics and Space Administration.

PAGE 133. Courtesy Dr. William Bickel, Physics Department, University of Arizona, Tucson.

PAGE 134. Ernst Chladni, *Entdeckungen im Reich des Klanges* (Leipzig: 1787). Musikbibliothek der Stadt Leipzig.

PAGE 135. Ernst Heinrich and Wilhelm Weber, *Wellenlehre* (Leipzig: 1825). Tab. VII, fig. 53. Zentralbibliothek, Zurich.

PAGE 136. Sir James Jeans, *Science and Music* (New York: Macmillan, 1938). Pl. VII.

PAGE 137. Collection Carleen Hutchins, Catgut Acoustical Society, Montclair, N.J.

PAGE 138. Sir Francis Galton, *Finger Prints* (London: Macmillan, 1892). Courtesy the Library of Congress.

PAGE 139. Deutsches Museum, Munich.

PAGE 140. Courtesy Harold E. Edgerton.

PAGE 141. Lockheed Aeronautical Systems Co., Burbank, Calif. Photographs: Eric Schulzinger, chief photographer.

PAGE 142. Julius T. Fraser and Nathaniel M. Lawrence, eds., *The Study of Time: Proceedings of the First/Second Conference of the International Society for the Study of Time*, 2 vols. (Heidelberg: Springer Verlag). Courtesy Science Museum, London.

PAGE 143. CERN Laboratory (European Laboratory for Particle Physics), Geneva.

PAGE 144. Courtesy Dr. Allan E. Kreiger, The Jules Styne Eye Institute, University of California, Los Angeles.

PAGE 145. Courtesy Drs. Michael Posner et al., Washington University School of Medicine, Saint Louis, Mo.

# V Classification

1. Wolfgang Pauli, "The Influence of Archetypal Ideas on Kepler's Theories," in Carl Jung and Wolfgang Pauli, *The Interpretation of Nature and the Psyche* (New York: Pantheon Books, 1955), 152.

PAGE 148. Egyptian Museum, Cairo.

PAGE 149. Courtesy Aberdeen University Library, Scotland.

PAGE 150. Musée de l'Homme, Paris.

PAGE 151. Johannes Ketham, *Fasciculus Medicie* (Venice: 1522). Biblioteca Casanatense, Rome. Photograph courtesy Fototeca Unione, Rome.

PAGE 152. Victoria and Albert Museum, London.

PAGE 153. Euclid, *Elementia Geometriae*. Library of Congress, Washington, D.C., Incunabula 1482.E8616, Rare Book Collection.

PAGE 155. Erich Lessing, *The Discovery of Space* (Freiburg, Germany: Herder, 1969).

PAGE 156. National Aeronautics and Space Administration.

PAGE 157. Carolus Linnaeus, *Genera Plantarum* (Leiden: 1737). Zentralbibliothek, Zurich.

PAGE 158. Pierre André Latreille, *Histoire Naturelle des Fourmis* (Paris: 1802). Courtesy Bibliothèque Nationale, Paris.

PAGE 159. Vinson Brown, *The Amateur Naturalist's Handbook* (Boston: Little, Brown, 1948). © Vinson Brown 1948.

PAGE 160. By permission of the Syndics of Cambridge University Library, Cambridge, England.

PAGE 161. Ernst Haeckel, *Natural History of Man*, as reprinted in Francis Hitching, *The Neck of the Giraffe* (New York: Ticknor & Fields, 1982). © 1982 Francis Hitching.

PAGE 162. Sir Gavin de Beer, *Atlas of Evolution*, as reprinted in Francis Hitching, *The Neck of the Giraffe* (New York: Ticknor & Fields, 1982). © 1982 Francis Hitching.

PAGE 163. By permission of the British Museum of Natural History, London.

PAGE 164. W. E. Le Gros Clarke, *History of the Primates* (London: Macmillan, 1970). By permission of the British Museum of Natural History, London.

PAGE 165. Pien Ch'iao, *Wang Shu-ho t'u-chieh Nan-Ching mo-chueh* (Secrets of the Pulse). Courtesy The Wellcome Trustees, London.

PAGE 166. *Chi ch'eng ma i fang, niu i fang* (Collected Works of Veterinary Medicine for Horses and Cows). Library of the Chinese University of Hong Kong.

PAGE 167. Ms. Chinese 5341, folio 8. Bibliothèque Nationale, Paris.

PAGE 168. Charles Singer, *Short History of Anatomy and Physiology, from the Greeks to Harvey* (New York: Dover, 1957).

PAGE 169. Ms. Ethé 2296 (f. 3a). British Library, London.

PAGE 170. Andreas Cleyer, *Specimen Medicinae Sinicae* (1682). Courtesy Louise M. Darling Biomedical Library, University of California, Los Angeles. Photograph: Martin Lovell.

PAGE 171. Louise M. Darling Biomedical Library, University of California, Los Angeles. Photograph: Martin Lovell.

PAGE 172. Johannes ab Indagine. *Chiromantia* (1531).

PAGE 173. Courtesy New York Academy of Medicine.

PAGE 174. Vinson Brown, *The Amateur Naturalist's Handbook* (Boston: Little, Brown, 1948). © Vinson Brown 1948.

PAGE 175. John Dalton. *A New System of Chemical Philosophy*, Part I (1808). Library of Congress, Washington, D.C., QD28.D15, Rare Book Collection.

PAGES 176 AND 177. Courtesy Edward R. Tufte, *The Visual Display of Quantitative Information* (Cheshire, Conn.: Graphics Press, 1983).

PAGE 178. Vinson Brown, *The Amateur Naturalist's Handbook* (Boston: Little, Brown, 1948). © Vinson Brown 1948.

PAGE 179. National Aeronautics and Space Administration.

## VI Conceptualization

1. Albert Einstein, *Geometry and Experience*, an expanded version of an address to the Prussian Academy of Sciences in Berlin, January 27, 1921. Reprinted in Albert Einstein, *Sidelights on Relativity* (New York: Dover, 1983).

PAGE 182. Carl Jung et al., *Man and His Symbols* (London: Aldus Books Ltd., 1964). © 1964 Aldus Books Ltd., London. Courtesy Miss Ariane Rump.

PAGE 183. Courtesy Ciba-Geigy Ltd. Archives, Switzerland.

PAGES 184 AND 185 . John Holywood, *Sphaera Mundi* (1488). Zentralbibliothek, Zurich.

PAGE 186. Ann Ronan Picture Library, Taunton, Somerset, England.

PAGE 187. Nicholas Copernicus, *De Revolutionibus Orbium Coelestium* (1543). Library of Congress, Washington, D.C., QB 41.C76 1543 Rare Book Collection.

PAGE 189. Universitätsbibliothek, Basel.

PAGE 190. Leonard C. Bruno, *The Traditions of Science* (Washington, D.C.: Library of Congress, 1987).

PAGE 191. Above: Library of Congress, Washington, D.C., QB41.K42 Rare Book Collection.

PAGE 192. Library of Congress, Washington, D.C.

PAGE 193. Harold C. Urey, "The Origin of the Earth," *Scientific American*, Oct. 1952. Courtesy *Scientific American*.

PAGE 194. Courtesy The Huntington Library, San Marino, Calif.

PAGE 196. *Le Livre Croquis de Villard de Honnecourt.* Bibliothèque Nationale, Paris.

PAGE 197. René Descartes, *Principia Philosophiae* (1644). Courtesy Special Collections Division, University Research Library, University of California, Los Angeles.

PAGE 198. The Royal Library, Windsor Castle. By permission of Her Majesty Queen Elizabeth II.

PAGE 199. Daniel Santbech, *Problematum Astronomicorum* (Basel: 1561).

PAGE 200. Above: Codex Madrid I, ms. c, folio 7r. Below: Biblioteca Ambrosiana, Milan, Codex Atlantico, folio 9, verso A.

PAGE 201. Ms. B, Folio 74 R. Bibliothèque de l'Institut de France, Paris. Photograph: Photographie Bulloz, Paris.

PAGE 202. *Demonstration of Perspective* (1525).

PAGE 203. *Perspective* (Amsterdam: 1604). New York Public Library.

PAGE 205. Domenico Fontana, *Della Trasportazione dell'Obelisco Vaticano* (Rome: 1590). Leaf 15 FDT62.02F6 1590X RB NMAH. Special Collections Library, National Museum of American History, Smithsonian Institution Libraries.

PAGE 206. Athanasius Kircher, *Acoustics, Musurgia Universalis* (1650). Courtesy Beinecke Rare Book and Manuscript Library, Yale University, New Haven.

PAGE 207. *The Interference of Light.* By courtesy of the Director of The Royal Institution, London.

PAGE 208. Nationale Forschungs und Gedenkstatten. National Archives of Classical German Literature, Weimar.

PAGE 209. Sir D'Arcy Wentworth Thompson, *On Growth and Form* (Cambridge, England: Cambridge University Press, 1917). Courtesy University of Saint Andrews Library, Scotland.

PAGES 210 AND 211. Library of Congress, Washington, D.C., GB60.W4.1922.

PAGE 212. René Just Haüy, *Essai d'une Théorie sur la Structure des Crystaux* (1785). Library of Congress, Washington, D.C.

PAGE 213. Friedrich August Kekulé, *Organic Chemistry* (1860).

PAGE 214. James Clerk Maxwell, *Treatise on Electricity and Magnetism* (Oxford, England: Clarendon Press, 1873). Library of Congress, Washington, D.C., QC518.M46.

PAGE 215. Library of Congress, Washington, D.C.

PAGE 217. "On Immunity with Special Reference to Cell Life," *Proceedings of the Royal Society*, vol. 66 (1900), 424, plate 6. Courtesy the Royal Society, London.

PAGE 218. Hermann Rorschach, *Ten Ink-blot Tests* (Bern, Switzerland: Hans Huber, 1921). Rorschach H., Psychodiagnostik. © Hans Huber, Bern, 1921, 1949.

PAGE 219. The Smith Ely Jelliffe papers, ms. division, Library of Congress, Washington, D.C.

PAGE 220. James D. Watson, *The Double Helix* (New York: Atheneum Press, 1968).

PAGE 221. Letter reproduced from the original in Max Delbrück Papers, file 23-22. California Institute of Technology Archives, Pasadena.

PAGE 222. James D. Watson, *The Double Helix* (New York: Atheneum Press, 1968).

PAGE 223. U.S. Office of Technology Assessment, *Biology, Medicine and the Bill of Rights* (Washington, D.C.: U.S. Government Printing Office, 1988).

PAGE 224. Courtesy Lawrence Berkeley Laboratory, Berkeley.

PAGE 225. Boeing Aircraft Company, YC-14 Program, 1960. Collection the author.

PAGE 226. Benoit B. Mandelbrot, *The Fractal Geometry of Nature* (New York: W. H. Freeman, 1982). © 1982 by B. B. Mandelbrot.

PAGE 227. National Aeronautics and Space Administration.

# Bibliography

The author has found helpful publications of the National Aeronautics and Space Administration, as well as the monthly magazines *Discovery*, *Natural History*, *Scientific American*, and *Smithsonian*.

Azimov, Isaac. *Biographical Encyclopedia of Science and Technology.* New York: Doubleday, 1982.

Bettex, Albert. *The Discovery of Nature.* New York: Simon & Schuster, 1965.

Brown, Vinson. *The Amateur Naturalist's Handbook.* Boston: Little, Brown, 1948.

Bruno, Leonard C. *The Traditions of Science.* Washington, D.C.: Library of Congress, 1987.

Burke, James. *The Day the Universe Changed.* London: British Broadcasting Corporation, 1985.

Calder, Nigel. *The Key to the Universe.* New York: Penguin Books, 1977.

Capra, Fritjof. *The Tao of Physics.* Berkeley, Calif.: Shambhala Publications, 1975.

Cohen, I. Bernard. *Albums of Science.* New York: Charles Scribner's Sons, 1980.

Cook, Theodore Andrea. *The Curves of Life.* New York: Dover Publications, 1979.

Darius, John. *Beyond Vision.* Oxford, Eng.: Oxford University Press, 1984.

da Vinci, Leonardo. *On the Human Body.* New York: Dover Publications, 1983.

Descartes, René. *Geometry.* Translated by D. E. Smith and M. L. Latham. New York: Dover Publications, 1954.

Einstein, Albert. *Ideas and Opinions.* New York: Crown Publishers, 1982.

Garrison, Fielding H. *An Introduction to the History of Medicine.* Philadelphia: W.B. Saunders & Co., 1929.

Gregory, Richard L. *Eye and Brain.* New York: McGraw-Hill, World University Library, 1966.

————. *The Oxford Companion to the Mind.* Oxford, Eng.: Oxford University Press, 1987.

Harrison, Edward. *Masks of the Universe.* New York: Macmillan Publishing Co., 1985.

Hellemans, Alexander, and Bryan Bunch. *The Timetables of Science.* New York: Simon & Schuster, 1988.

Herdeg, Walter, ed. *The Artist in the Service of Science.* Zurich: Graphis Press Corp., 1973.

Hodges, Elaine R. S., ed. *The Guild Handbook of Scientific Illustration.* New York: Van Nostrand Reinhold, 1982.

Hogben, Lancelot. *Science for the Citizen.* New York: Alfred A. Knopf, 1938.

Hoyle, Fred. *Astronomy.* London: Rathbone Books, 1962.

Hulton, Paul. *America 1585: The Complete Drawings of John White.* Chapel Hill: The University of North Carolina Press, 1984.

Jaffem, Bernard. *Crucibles: The Story of Chemistry.* New York: Dover Publications, 1976.

Jastrzebski, Zbigniew. *Scientific Illustration: A Guide for the Beginning Artist.* Englewood Cliffs, N.J.: Prentice-Hall, 1985.

Jung, Carl G., et al. *Man and His Symbols.* New York: Doubleday & Co., 1964.

Krupp, E. C. *Echoes of the Ancient Skies.* New York: Harper & Row, 1983.

Lessing, Erich. *Discoverers of Space.* Freiburg, Germany: Herder & Herder, 1969.

Lyons, Albert S., and R. Joseph Petrucelli. *Medicine: An Illustrated History.* New York: Harry N. Abrams, Inc., 1978.

Menninger, Karl. *Number Words and Number Symbols.* Cambridge, Mass.: MIT Press, 1969.

Morrison, Philip and Phylis. *The Ring of Truth.* New York: Random House, 1987.

Nasr, Seyyed H. *Science and Civilization in Islam.* Cambridge, Mass.: Harvard University Press, 1976.

Needham, Joseph. *Science and Civilization in China.* Cambridge, Eng.: Cambridge University Press, 1954.

Panofsky, Erwin. *Studies in Iconography.* New York: Harper & Row, 1939.

Restak, Richard M. *The Mind.* New York: Bantam Books, 1988.

Ritterbush, Philip C. *The Art of Organic Forms.* Washington, D.C.: Smithsonian Institution, 1968.

Ronan, Colin A. *Science: Its History and Development Among the World's Cultures.* New York: Facts on File Publications, 1982.

Sarton, George. *A History of Science.* Cambridge, Mass.: Harvard University Press, 1952–59.

————. *Six Wings.* Bloomington: Indiana University Press, 1957.

Thompson, D'Arcy Wentworth. *On Growth and Form.* Cambridge, Eng.: Cambridge University Press, 1961.

Von Franz, Marie-Louise. *Time: Rhythm and Repose.* London: Thames & Hudson, 1978.

Wechsler, Judith, ed. *On Aesthetics in Science.* Cambridge, Mass.: MIT Press, 1987.

Whyte, Lancelot Law, ed. *Aspects of Form.* New York: Farrar, Straus, Cudahy, 1961.

Wolf, Edwin, II. *Legacies of Genius: A Celebration of Philadelphia Libraries.* Philadelphia: The Philadelphia Area Consortium of Special Collections Libraries, 1988.

Yenne, Bill. *The Atlas of the Solar System.* New York: Bison Books Corp., 1987.

# Index

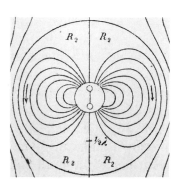

Galvani, Luigi, 15, 118, 119

*Genera Plantarum*, 157

genetics: chromosomes, 18, 173; finger prints, 138. *See also* deoxyribonucleic acid

geology: Amethyst Mountain, 16, 33; global temperature profile, 179; layered structure of Earth, 197; origin of oceans and continents, 18, 210–11; rock avalanche, 198; water turbulence, 198

geometry: Euclid, 153; fractal, 19, 226; perspective drawing, 202, 203; of solar mirrors, 83. *See also* spiral(s)

George II, king, 172

Gersdorff, Hans von, 12, 102–3, 171

Gesner, Konrad von, 74

Gilbert, William, 100, 112, 116

Goethe, Johann, 208

gold: alchemy, 96, 183; ore, 97

Golgi, Camillo, 44

Gould, John, 16, 32, 35

Gourdelle, Pierre, 28

graphing: Napoleon's Russian campaign, 176–77

Grassius, Bartholmeus, 204

Greatrakes, Valentine, 107

Guericke, Otto von, 92–93, 112

Guerra, Giovanni, 204

Guidi, Guido, 101

Haeckel, Ernst, 16, 75

Hale, George, 132, 195

Hales, Stephen, 94–95

Halley, Edmond, 129; comet, 129

hand: prints, 138; X ray of blood vessels in, 139

*Harmonice Mundi*. See *Harmonies of the World, The*

*Harmonies of the World, The*, 191

Harvey, William, 14, 110–11

Haüy, René Just, 174, 212–13

Helgald, 107

Helmholtz, Hermann von, 215

Henslow, John, 61

*Herbal*, 59

*Herbarium*, 24

herbs: medicine from, 59

Herder, Johann Gottfried von, 208

heredity. *See* genetics

Hertz, Heinrich, 15, 214, 215

Hevelius, Johannes, 23

Hill, Edward, 50

Hippocrates, 168

*Histoire Naturelle des Fourmis*, 158

*History of the Primates*, 164

Hodges, Elaine R. S., 34

Holmes, William H., 16, 33

Holywood, John of, 11–12, 184–85

Honnecourt, Villard de, 196

Hooke, Robert, 42, 78, 92

Hoover, Herbert, 98

Hoover, Lou Henry, 98

*Hortus Sanitatis*, 24

Hubble, Edwin, 128

Hunter, William, 36

Hutchins, Carleen, 137

Huxley, Thomas, 20

Huygens, Christian, 74, 199

immunology, 18, 216–17

Indagine, Johannes ab, 172

insects: ant, 16, 158; beetle, 34; butterfly, 30, 31; gall caused by, 43

*Integrative Action of the Nervous System, The*, 46

Isidore of Seville, 149

James I, king, 100, 110

Jenner, Edward, 109

Jesus, 107

John of Holywood. *See* Holywood, John of

Jung, Carl, 218, 219

Kekulé, Friedrich August, 15–16, 213

Kelley, Don Greame, 159, 174

Kepler, Johannes, 13, 80, 154, 187, 188–89, 190, 191

Ketham, Johannes, 151

Kircher, Athanasius, 12, 74, 139, 206

Kirchhoff, Gustav, 88, 215, 227

Kreiger, Allan E., 144

Latreille, Pierre-André, 16, 158

Laue, Max von, 124, 174

Lawrence, Nathaniel M., 142

Leeuwenhoek, Antony van, 45, 48

Legrand, 120

Leo X, pope, 69

LeRoy, Francis, 46

Leucippus, 175

Levan, Albert, 173

light: deflection of, 17, 194–95; prism, 14, 84–85; velocity of, 90–91; waves, 15, 207; white, 14, 84–85. *See also* colors

lightning, 15; artificial, 117; electrocution by, 116; spectrum of, 133

Lilienthal, Otto, 18, 68

*Ling-Hsu*, 166

Linnaeus, Carolus, 59, 157

Lippershey, Hans, 22

Lonicerus, Adam, 59

Lucian, 83

Lyell, Charles, 16